DATE DUE

DATE DUE

TO THE
TOP
OF THE
WORLD

THE STORY OF
PEARY AND HENSON

TO THE
TOP
OF THE
WORLD

THE STORY OF
PEARY AND HENSON

by PAULINE K. ANGELL

illustrated with Photographs and Maps

RAND McNALLY & COMPANY

Chicago • New York • San Francisco

J B
P

Dedicated to my grandchildren
Judy and Paul Cohen

10/65

CONTENTS

I.	Lone Wolf	9
II.	Hungry for Fame	16
III.	Cabin Boy	28
IV.	"Meet Lieutenant Peary"	39
V.	Heading North	54
VI.	Eskimos to the Rescue	72
VII.	Across the Frozen Desert	86
VIII.	Tempting the Devil	107
IX.	The Devil Takes His Due	128
X.	Small Victory at Great Price	144
XI.	Limping Ahead	168
XII.	One Last Hope	190
XIII.	A Race with Death	205
XIV.	Down But Not Out	223
XV.	On Top of the World	234
XVI.	Crown of Thorns	255
XVII.	Afterglow	270
	Men Who Tried to Reach the Pole	277
	Acknowledgments	279
	Index	281

ILLUSTRATIONS

Statue of Peary near his birthplace   11

Owls mounted by Peary   19

Peary at 22, in 1878   23

Peary's mother   41

Josephine Peary in 1891   63

Red Cliff House and Eskimo homes   68

Building of domed igloo and
cross-section of interior   82

Swinging the whip to drive a dog team   84

Eskimo woman chewing sealskin for a boot   87

Musk oxen   100

Eskimo village designed by Peary   110

Hugh Johnson Lee   124

Henson at about 30   152

Peary at about 40   154

Three meteorites discovered by Peary   158

Silk flag made by Josephine Peary
in 1898   181

Captain Bartlett in crows'-nest
of Roosevelt   199

Roosevelt in winter quarters
at Cape Sheridan   201

Crossing a pressure ridge   210

Shattered ice that seemed endless   224

Four Eskimos, Henson, and flags
at North Pole   252

Peary and dogs on deck of Roosevelt   256

Captain Bartlett, Mrs. Peary,
and Peary's daughter   273

President Eisenhower and
Mr. and Mrs. Henson   275

Governor Tawes of Maryland
and Mrs. Henson   276

MAPS

Red Cliff House, Anniversary Lodge,
and icecap route   112

Nansen's route in 1888; Peary's routes
in 1886, 1891–2, and 1893–5   134

Peary's route from 1898–1906; part
of Nansen's route; Sverdrup's
route; Abruzzi's route   186

Peary's route in 1906   230

Peary's successful journey to North Pole 250

I

LONE WOLF

Robert E. Peary, who discovered the North Pole, started life as a mama's boy and his schoolmates wrote him off as a sissy. This is the story of how, in spite of such a handicap, he succeeded in overcoming the "Devil of the North"—who had destroyed or driven back all previous invaders of his territory —and stood at last on top of the world.

He was born May 6, 1856, on the western slope of the Allegheny Mountains in Pennsylvania, where his father was in the lumber business. They named him Robert, after his mother's oldest brother, Dr. Robert G. Wiley, of Bethel, Maine, but everyone called him Bertie.

His father, Charles Peary, had had a good commercial education and expected to make a fortune. He also was adventurous, and looked forward to the time when he could leave the business to his son, and travel with Mary, his wife, all over the world.

But Fate decreed otherwise. Shortly before Bertie was three, his father died, and his mother took him back to the home in Maine that Charles had built for her when they were married. So Bertie grew up on Cape Elizabeth, just south of Portland.

He had red hair and blue eyes like his father's, and his mother found comfort in trying to make him into a living image of her husband. Charles had made a hobby of nature study and, as she walked with Bertie along the shore, she told him what his father had told her about the animals that had made their homes in the shells they found there. In the woods, she would point out a bird or a flower, giving it the name her husband had taught her. She showed him how to press the flowers, and by the time he was six he had a scrapbook half full, and a row of shells on the window sill in his bedroom.

She told him stories about men who, like his father, were adventurous, and wanted to explore the world. If she wanted these tales to stimulate his ambition, she succeeded, for one of them had much to do with shaping Bertie's later career. It was about Elisha Kane, who had gone farther north than any American ever had been, and had spent two winters among the Eskimos. Bertie asked for the story again and again and, when he was old enough, he read Kane's two volumes that described what men must do in order to survive in the Arctic, and how important it was to make friends with the Eskimos.

Hunting for shells on the beach, and for birds' eggs and nests among the low-growing shrubs in the woods, kept the boy busy and happy. It was not until he was seven and began to go to school that he learned how cruel life could be. The other boys on Cape Elizabeth had a poor opinion of a boy that always went around with his mother, and turned a cold shoulder to all his efforts to make friends.

Like a snail that withdraws into its shell when its tender feelers have been hit, Bertie took refuge in pastimes he could enjoy without companionship. He added to his scrapbook of pressed flowers, built up his collections of shells, birds' eggs, and nests, labeling and arranging them on the shelves his mother had put up for him.

Fortunately, he had a chance to play with other boys during his vacations in Fryeburg, where his mother's family, the Wileys, owned large and prosperous farms along the Saco River. Here he had many gay and lively cousins, with whom

Life-size statue of Peary by Joseph P. Pollia, erected at his birthplace near Cresson, Pa.

he played marbles, flew kites, and went fishing. As time went on, he learned to swim and dive, ride horseback, and use a shotgun. During the Christmas holidays, he mastered the art of skating and gliding over the fields on snowshoes.

When he was ten, a display of mounted birds attracted his attention, and inspired him with an ambition to become a taxidermist. His mother, always ready to further his interest in nature, bought him a book on the subject. It took many hours of trial and error before he could produce a specimen that satisfied him, but he stuck to it, and by the time he was twelve, several mounted birds adorned the mantelpiece and the center table in the parlor.

He had been so absorbed in his taxidermy and his collections, and so thoroughly delighted with the opportunity for sports of all kinds during his vacations in Fryeburg, that it was only now that his mother realized that, aside from his cousins, he had no friends. There was a small boarding school not far away, and she decided to send him there, hoping he'd find more suitable companions than the neighborhood boys.

Bertie didn't want to leave the fascinating occupations that filled his spare time at home, and went away only because his mother wished it. To his dismay, he was given a very sociable roommate who was always bringing in a group of boys when Bertie wanted to study. Before long, Bertie was given a room to himself and he was pleased, for by now he didn't care whether he had friends or not.

The discovery that her son preferred solitude to companionship alarmed Mrs. Peary. The successful career she'd predicted for him depended, she thought, on his ability to be a good mixer. Therefore, when he was ready to enter high school, she bought a house in Portland, and did everything she could to make him a social success.

She gave him a large room where other boys could come and go as they wished, kept cookies and gingerbread on hand,

and greeted warmly any who came. Sometimes Bertie was glad to see them; more often he didn't want to be interrupted when he was studying or skinning a bird, and a would-be friend would find a "Busy" sign on the door. Naturally, after a while, the boys stopped coming.

Worse yet, during his sophomore year he showed signs of changing from a loving son into a boy his mother no longer understood. He lost interest in his hobbies, and her suggestions that they go to concerts or lectures together were met with indifference or distaste. She was worried, and consulted her brother, Robert.

Doctor Wiley told her that all this was natural. Her son was growing up and had reached the age when he needed to get out from under her wing and go off on his own for a while. When Mary objected that this would mean taking him out of school, Doctor Wiley answered that at this point a chance to prove his independence was more important.

Since it was winter, they decided he should go south, and with a money belt around his waist, and plenty of advice as to what he should eat and where he should stay, he started off in high spirits. But when he found himself among people whose customs and manner of speaking were quite different from his own, he began to feel lonely and a little apprehensive as to how a Northerner would be received.

He took the edge off his loneliness by writing long letters to his mother, and she noticed with interest that he signed them "Bert," instead of "Bertie." His fears proved groundless. In Raleigh, where he spent hours in the State Library examining the life-size pictures in Audubon's *Birds of America*, every courtesy was extended to him. In Augusta, a man who sold minerals handed him forty specimens without charging him a cent. In Aiken, everyone was so friendly that he spent the rest of his time there, hiring a gun and mounting the birds he shot. He was persuaded to display some of them in a store window, where they were greatly admired. The rest he shipped back to Portland.

These three months in the South, where he stood on his own feet and won recognition in the midst of strangers, made a man of him. He came back ready to face the future with confidence, but without bravado. "Resolved not to exaggerate," was the last entry in the diary he'd kept while he was away.

In spite of his long absence from school, he passed the final examinations, and after the two months of hard study necessary to do so, he was glad to leave books behind and stretch his muscles in Fryeburg.

He returned to Portland refreshed and eager for work, advertised his mounted birds in a city newspaper, and added that he would stuff any birds or animals that were brought to him. The response was encouraging. Women wanted bright-colored birds for their parlors, sportsmen were eager to display game birds they'd shot, milliners bought them to trim hats, and museums ordered his specimens because he mounted the birds in lifelike positions—a hawk with a bluejay in its claws, a partridge with wings spread ready to spring into the air—and other taxidermists did not. Within a few weeks he had all the work he could handle.

His classmates decided that a boy who had the get-up-and-go to travel around the South by himself and, on top of that, come home and set himself up in business, must be worth knowing. They began asking him to go places and to do things with them, and whenever he had an hour or two to spare, he accepted an invitation to go swimming or skating, or to do whatever was suggested. Soon they discovered he had skills that no one outside of Fryeburg knew anything about. Challenged to dive from the highest springboard, he responded with a double jackknife. On skates he was a whirlwind—circling, leaping, speeding ahead in the races.

His indifference to cold was especially marked. A school-mate with whom he went skating tells how Bert crashed through the ice and scrambled out wet to the hips. Long before they reached home, Peary's pants were frozen stiff, and clanked like stovepipes as he jogged along. Another report tells how, on a cold November day, Peary broke the ice with a fence rail, swam out, and brought back two ducks for a hunter who had no dog to retrieve them.

Such incidents as these young Peary took as a matter of course, and it never occurred to him to brag about achievements that other boys considered remarkable.

He had other accomplishments that won the admiration of his classmates. Once when it was his turn to deliver an original oration, they listened in something like awe as he recited a heroic poem. Later he wrote a skit about Adam and Eve, and bursts of laughter interrupted the teacher who was reading it aloud.

But the rejection he'd suffered, as a small boy looking for playmates, had left its mark, and he had no wish to break the habit he'd formed of devoting most of his time to diversions he could enjoy alone. He went hunting and fishing by himself and took long walks along the coast, stopping occasionally to chat with the seamen he met, now and then hiring a rowboat to explore the islands in Casco Bay. One of them, which seemed to him the most beautiful spot he'd ever seen, he bought when he was a freshman in college. He named it Eagle Island, and years later he built his summer home there.

When he felt like it, he asked one or two boys to go exploring with him, and they were flattered at being chosen. At the same time, his self-sufficiency discouraged intimacy, and even classmates who were boon companions regarded him, not as a friend, but rather as an older brother whom they respected and trusted.

II

HUNGRY FOR FAME

By the time he was seventeen, he was ready for college, and already his mother had chosen a career for him. The most distinguished men in her family, she said, had been surveyors. Therefore she hoped her son would go to Bowdoin College at Brunswick, Maine where there was a Civil Engineering course, and get his degree in that field.

Peary offered no objection, and won a scholarship that he held throughout his college course. But his mother had stiff opposition to contend with when she announced that she was going to take rooms in a boardinghouse near the college, make a home for him, and see that he made the right friends. Her family argued that her son was too old to be tied to his "mother's apron strings." She silenced them with the flat statement, "I am going to college!" And for two years Peary lived with his mother instead of living with his classmates on the campus.

By now he was six feet tall, and still growing, and his all-round physical development was outstanding. The gymnasium director decided he could use him to good advantage in public exhibitions.

"Send me that Peary lad," he said.

"But he lives in town," objected the boy to whom he'd spoken.

"All the better. It makes him walk."

Peary didn't disappoint him. In the public demonstration the director put on in Portland that winter, Peary's ability in tumbling and turning handsprings won applause. Later he won first place in throwing a baseball, and was not far behind in hammer throwing and the running broad jump.

Although the discipline of training appealed to him, he rebelled against the military drill that had survived from the days of the Civil War, and for that he was suspended. But before long the drill was dropped, and Peary went back to his classes.

In spite of the fact that he was off campus, he was tapped for the Delta Kappa Epsilon fraternity during his Freshman year. It was the first time in his life that he'd been asked to join a club, and years later he expressed his pride by raising the fraternity flag alongside the Stars and Stripes at the North Pole.

But never having been a member of any social group, he hadn't learned the art of getting along with people. A fraternity brother says that the only hard feeling that arose in the organization during the four years he was in college was due to Peary's angry protest against what he considered an unjust decision. He had his own idea of what was right and, even with a majority against him, he fought for it with "sledgehammer blows" wrote a classmate. However, if a strong counter-offensive convinced him that he was wrong, he was man enough to admit his mistake.

For this he was respected, but he was not popular. His classmates recognized his ability; above all, the talent he showed as an organizer. They made him chairman of the Junior Prom Committee, and of the Class Executive Committee in his Senior year, when he also was elected president of the Engineering Society. Twice he was chosen to represent his class in oratorical contests, was class poet, and editor of one of the college papers. But not one of his classmates was able to get behind the barricade he had erected against familiarity.

After his Sophomore year, his mother went back to Portland. As often as possible he walked the twenty-five miles down to the city to spend a weekend with her, and enjoyed swinging along the highway with long, rhythmic strides.

Although he had distinguished himself in various field events, he did not shine as an athlete except for one thrilling episode. Baseball and football were in their infancy, and the big events were the annual boat races, varsity and intramural. In his Junior year, the captain of the class crew asked him to take the place of the man who'd been pulling the No. 2 oar. Thoughtfully Peary twisted the end of his sandy mustache. Training would take more time than he wished to give to it, but the race was only two weeks off and the offer was tempting.

"I'll try it just for the fun of the thing," he said at last, "but you needn't count on my keeping it up."

The captain was stunned. Never before had he been up against a man who didn't have the least understanding of what it means to be a member of a team, who could say light-heartedly, "You needn't count on my keeping it up," when obviously at this late date there wouldn't be time to train a substitute if he decided to drop out. But Peary was the best man for the place, and the captain decided to risk it.

Luckily, Peary found that the training didn't interfere too much with his other work, and he resolved to give his mother the pleasure of seeing his name on a championship cup. So he rowed in the only boat race won by his class during the four years they were in college.

"I have read in books about the victors in college sports being carried home on the shoulders of their classmates," he wrote to his mother, "and now I know how it feels. It has all been so unexpected that I don't know what to make of it."

But the captain of the varsity crew knew what he'd make

Nine of the ten species of owls native to Maine, mounted by Peary. From left to right: Richardson's, Short-eared, Barred, Great Gray, Snowy, Great Horned, Long-eared, American Hawk, and Screech Owl

of it if he could. He asked Peary to join his crew and pull an oar in the intercollegiate races, which would be the big event of the next season. Any other man would have jumped at the chance, but such momentary glory failed to dazzle Peary, who realized that the months of practice preceding the event would mean neglect of work more essential to his future career.

He'd built up a big business in taxidermy and needed the money it brought in. In addition to the time he spent stuffing the specimens his customers brought him—sometimes as many as five in a single day—he was also spending time in the field doing practical work in engineering. Consequently, he often worked from five in the morning until eight at night.

Although he was a good student, he was by no means docile. His bold and inquiring mind prompted him to challenge the statements of professors and even of textbooks. More than once he discovered how to solve an engineering problem by a simpler method than the one shown, and later textbooks included his methods. His work in the field was equally brilliant; he took top honors in engineering and was elected to Phi Beta Kappa.

Like most young people about to take off on their own,

he began to speculate on his chance for success in the outside world. As he put it in a letter to his mother, "It seems almost an impossibility to me now how anyone, as some of our farmers do, can look forward to living their life out in the same place and doing the same things that their fathers and grandfathers did before them. Today as I think of what the world is and that I have my life before me, nothing seems impossible."

He came to the conclusion, however, that there were opportunities for surveying in Fryeburg on which he couldn't afford to turn his back. After the Civil War, the White Mountains had become popular as a summer resort, and the railroad through Fryeburg to the Crawford Notch was bringing not only tourists but unprecedented prosperity to owners of land along the route. Lumber and crops, hitherto transported by wagon, now found a ready and growing market on the East Coast, and farmers were increasing their acreage or selling it at a high price. Peary figured, therefore, that he could develop a good business running new lines and restoring old ones, especially as he was well known throughout the area. Immediately after his graduation in 1877, he rented an office in the village and put up a bold placard reading, "Robert E. Peary, Surveyor."

Alas for his rosy dreams! Few orders came in, and he was forced to face the fact that he had overestimated the situation. To keep himself busy, he made a map of the town and established a line running due north, indicating the direction by stone markers which for many years were used by local surveyors to correct their instruments.

All this was good experience, but otherwise seemed useless as far as his future was concerned. Should he go somewhere else? If so, where? Often despair overcame all hope of escape, and he discovered that he was the victim of an uneven temperament. "Ebbs and flows," he called it: on top of the wave one day, down in the depths the next.

It was here in Fryeburg that he'd spent his happiest days. Now he was lonely and sad. The cousins who had been his companions were busy with families of their own, or were spending the summer with relatives. At last he wrote to his mother and begged her to come and make a home for him. By September, they were living in a small cottage on Elm Street.

He fell back on taxidermy to take care of their immediate needs, and was gratified to find that his work was so well known that orders came not only from the vicinity, but from places as faraway as Boston, Philadelphia, and London. But this success failed to satisfy his ambition. He had counted on surveying to pave the way for outstanding achievements in the field of civil engineering, and the village offered no chance to take even the first step in that direction.

What it did offer was an opportunity to adapt himself to social life. Shut up as he was, in a closely knit community, he began to realize that he lacked something that might be important to him later on.

"I am testing my ability to make myself agreeable," he wrote in his diary. "I find no trouble at all with the little folks; they come to me at once. With the young folks I have to exert myself more, and with some of the old folks I can't as yet break the crust of their unsociability and old fogeyness. However, I mean to try as I should like to gain that attractive personality that when I was with a person they would have to like me whether they wanted to or not."

He made enough progress in overcoming his reserve to accept invitations to dances and to fancy-dress parties, with the result that the belles of the village and their matchmaking mothers began to compete for his attention, and to save embarrassment he never went out with the same girl twice, except for his cousin Ella, who had returned from a visit to Biddeford. They rode horseback, skated, and snowshoed together, and when he discovered she was taking painting lessons, he made sketches of the landscape for her to color. But since a cousin could not be considered a rival for his hand, efforts to capture him for a husband continued, and on Valentine's Day he received many lacy effusions. He himself sent three: one to Ella, one to his mother, and one to the little girl next door.

Only with children, and within the safety of his family circle, could he release the warmth and tenderness of which he was capable. Against outsiders his heart remained closed. When he went to church, he was aware only of unpleasant details: the unbecoming hats and ill-fitting coats he saw in the congregation; the fact that the leader of the choir started the hymns too high; the preacher's dirty cuffs. Such a cold and thoughtless appraisal is not the soil in which generosity and human understanding flourish, and his lack of these qualities eventually turned what should have been a triumph into a nightmare.

Fryeburg offered him the best it had to give in the way of honors. He was asked to run for Superintendent of Schools, declined with thanks, but was sufficiently elated to write, "Will someone put a brick on me to keep me down?" Soon afterward he was appointed Justice of the Peace, and relished the power it gave him to make out deeds and "even marry folks!!!!"

However, his longing for recognition was only briefly appeased. He had made a name for himself as a taxidermist, and locally was widely known for his daring and skill in breaking colts. Was this the best he could hope for? Must he be content to marry and settle down in the same place where his ancestors had lived and died? The prospect appalled him, and he was unable to conquer the low spirits that assailed him

Portrait of Peary in 1878, when he was twenty-two

as the months slipped by and he found himself getting nowhere.

The offer of a position as science instructor at the Massachusetts Institute of Technology lifted his spirits momentarily, but he rejected it because he couldn't endure the thought of a future shut up in laboratories and classrooms. He wanted to work in the open, using his mind and muscles to deal with nature in the raw.

At last, shortly before his twenty-third birthday, a notice, tacked up in the Post Office, showed him a way out of the blind alley into which he had stumbled. The Coast and Geodetic Survey in Washington wanted draftsmen. The salary would be ten dollars a week, and a specimen of the applicant's work was to be sent.

Peary was one of the four applicants chosen for a six-months' trial. In January, 1880, the appointment was made permanent, and while it was gratifying to know that he had made good, he was dismayed by the prospect of being confined in an office. By now there was no challenge in the tasks assigned, and he saw nothing ahead but working like a machine, his greatest achievement only a name on the payroll.

At that time, Washington was full of talk about an inter-ocean canal and, one morning, as he was brooding over his coffee, it occurred to him that there was a chance to make himself widely known by exploring the Isthmus of Panama. He might find a more practicable route for a canal than the one surveyed by the United States, or the one chosen by the French. Failing that, he might rescue his name from obscurity by becoming an authority on such little-known subjects as the mineral, agricultural, and industrial resources of the Isthmus.

These possibilities he outlined in a letter to his mother, saying, "I would like to acquire a name . . . which would make my mother proud and which would make me feel that I was the peer of anyone I might meet."

Knowing that his mother would be reluctant to accept a plan that would take him so far from home, he explained that work in the Tropics would be possible only in the dry season, and that he could be with her every summer and fall.

She thought it over for a long time before she answered. From the first she had known that office work would not suit her son, and had hoped he would find something in another field, but certainly not in another country. He was twenty-four, and she felt she had no right to veto his plan, but, as he had admitted in his letter, there was danger and a chance of death in the undertaking he proposed. At last she wrote that she didn't like the idea, and suggested that if he would postpone his decision, he might find something equally promising without going abroad.

Peary doubted it, but was forced to admit that her suggestion was reasonable, and agreed to wait a year. Then a second letter followed, telling him that she didn't want him to go a year later, or at any other time. "I bow to her wishes," he wrote in his diary, "although it may change my entire life." And so it did, though not for the worse as he had imagined.

For nine months he continued to endure the tedium of office work, relieving his boredom now and then by visiting the Corcoran Art Gallery or the museum at the Smithsonian Institution. At last a notice was called to his attention advertising competitive examinations for positions in the Civil Engineer Corps of the U.S. Navy.

Peary had always had "a feeling for the Navy," and, as an engineer, part of his work, at least, would be outdoors. He engaged a room where he could study nights and weekends without interruption, and went to work. He passed the technical and physical tests without difficulty. The main examination lasted ten days, and he was one of the few men able to stick it out.

Weeks passed with no announcement of the result. The shooting of President Garfield in July of 1881 caused further delay and when, by the first of October, no word had reached him, he was sure he had failed. He inferred that it was because he had told his examiners that there were some questions he could not answer without further study. This, however, happened to be in his favor, for they took it to show that he was a man who, if he didn't know a thing, didn't hesitate to admit it, but "would keep at it until he did, and so was the kind of man the Navy needed."

Ten days later, as he entered the office building, a fellow

draftsman slapped him on the shoulder and congratulated him on his appointment. Peary thanked him, bought a newspaper, found a seat on a bench, and considered the situation.

Only four of the two hundred men who had taken the final examination were accepted, and he was one of them. His feelings were a mixture of exultation and apprehension, apprehension predominating. His career as an explorer had been stymied. In spite of his triumph, he felt trapped.

On October 18, 1881, he was given the rank of Lieutenant, and only then did he tell his mother that he had tried for the position. She, of course, was filled with pride; she was also relieved, for now, she thought, his work would keep him in the United States. Later, she discovered she'd been mistaken.

The engineer in charge of the Navy's Department of Yards and Docks had been on the examining board, and was so impressed by Peary's ability that he made him his assistant and sent him to Key West to inspect a pier under construction there.

Although the contractor was a man with a national reputation, he was finding great difficulty in sinking the iron plates needed to support the superstructure. Peary's ability as a swimmer now served him well. He plunged into the harbor and, with the skill of a skin diver, minus the breathing apparatus, fins, and other accessories that have transformed this difficult art into a popular sport, he made a careful examination of the bottom. Instead of the bed of sand that the contractor supposed he could penetrate, he found a conglomeration of coral covered with sunken cargoes, telegraph cables, and other junk, among which was an ancient Spanish cannon, possibly a relic from the expedition of Ponce de Leon.

It was plain that some other method must be substituted for that adopted by the contractor, and the young lieutenant so reported. Thereupon the contractor entered a complaint against "a young upstart named Peary," and threw up the job.

In a brief report to the Department, Peary offered to finish the job himself, was given authority to do so, devised his own methods and tools, and then came down with yellow fever. As soon as he began to recover, he had himself carried to the harbor on a stretcher, supervised the work, and the pier was finished at a cost of $6,000 instead of the $60,000 which had been the contractor's estimate.

Now ace-high in the estimation of his superior officer, he was sent to Nicaragua in charge of Navy engineers who were to survey a route for a canal through the unbroken jungle. And so, four years after he had dreamed of winning fame on the Isthmus of Panama, he was on his way to a destination that offered a similar opportunity.

But during the voyage something occurred that drove from his mind all thought of making a name for himself in the Tropics. Late one afternoon, as he stood on deck admiring the sunset, he caught sight of the island of San Salvador off the starboard bow— "the land that first gladdened the eyes of Columbus," he wrote in his diary, and after paying due respect to the setting sun, he gave his thoughts full rein:

"Birthplace of the new world, purple against the yellow sunset, as it was almost four hundred years ago when it smiled a welcome to the man whose fame can be equaled only by him who shall one day stand with 360 degrees of longitude beneath his motionless feet and for whom East and West shall have vanished—the discoverer of the North Pole."

And so he was caught up in the dream that dominated his life, and in which many other men became involved. Even as he sat in his cabin musing on what at the moment seemed only a wild flight of fancy, a boy was growing up who would make it possible for Peary to reach the Pole and win the fame for which he hungered. His name was Matthew Henson, and he was a Negro.

III

CABIN BOY

Although Matthew Henson was a southern Negro, his parents never had been slaves, and his father owned the farm in Charles County, Maryland, where his son was born on August 8, 1866.

In Maryland, this was not unusual, for almost half the Negroes who lived there were free even before the Civil War began. They had established day and night schools that were well attended, and paid taxes on over a million dollars' worth of real estate.

Since Maryland had remained in the Union, it was not included among the states whose slaves were freed by the Emancipation Proclamation, but the next year it abolished slavery voluntarily. Slave owners, maddened by the loss of their valuable property, organized a political party to repeal the law, and when they were defeated, their opposition became violent.

To terrify the Negroes and keep them in their place, the Ku Klux Klan began riding through the state, leaving death and destruction behind them. Even before he saw the skull and crossbones painted on his barn, Mr. Henson had made preparations to leave. A white neighbor was ready to buy his farm, and while Matt was still a baby, the family moved to Washington, D.C.

They settled in Georgetown, which in those days was a slum. There, when Matt was seven, his mother died and he went to live with an uncle who had promised to see that the boy had a good education. He went to the Negro school on N Street until he was almost fourteen, and had completed the sixth grade.

Matt liked going to school, and never missed a day if he could help it, though holidays were always welcome, for then he had a chance to play ball or use his muscles mopping floors or running errands or doing other simple tasks that brought him a few pennies.

On April 14, 1876, came a holiday he didn't expect, which he enjoyed in a way he couldn't have foreseen. It was the eleventh anniversary of the day Abraham Lincoln was shot, and a monument, built by contributions from the Negroes of Washington, was to be presented to the city. Although his uncle hustled the family off right after breakfast, they found that already hundreds of people, white and black, were there before them. They managed to work their way forward to a spot where the platform was in full view, and were pressed nearer and nearer as the crowds continued to come.

At last, President Grant appeared on the platform, followed by the members of his cabinet, Justices of the Supreme Court, and members of Congress. Since it was now illegal to deny a man's right to vote because of his color or previous condition of servitude, there was one Negro among the Senators, and seven among the Representatives.

The speech of presentation was made by Frederick Douglass, a Negro who had risen from slavery and won such influence and respect that both President Lincoln and President Grant had consulted him in critical situations that concerned his people.

Some of the words he spoke on this occasion, Matt never forgot, nor the cheers that followed the oration. It made him proud to be a Negro, though he'd never felt inferior because of his color. The fact that he'd spent all his life among

Negroes had kept him from realizing the prejudice against them. When at last the awakening came, it was a blow that temporarily knocked him off balance.

In June, 1880, Matt had to leave school. His uncle couldn't afford to support him any longer, and his father, who had remarried, was dead, having left his widow with other children to raise. So this year it was not only the summer vacation that lay ahead of him; it was the beginning of his life as a man.

To look at him, no one would think he was anywhere near grown up. He was small for his age, and his face was still as round and untroubled as a child's. But his body was wiry, his muscles hard, and though not quite fourteen he could do a tough day's work and come up smiling.

The summer before, he'd had a job in a near-by restaurant. Now that he had to fend for himself, he applied for it again. The woman who owned the place was glad to hire him, and allowed him to eat leftover food and sleep on the kitchen floor. For two months he waited on tables, washed dishes, and scrubbed the floors, but always in his mind were the words of Frederick Douglass—"progress and enlightenment" are "before us"—and the problem of where and how he could find work that would lead to that goal haunted him day and night.

It was one of the steady customers who gave him the answer: Baltimore Jack, an old salt who had started life as a slave and was ending it spinning yarns about his adventures on the bounding main. And that is how it happened that when other boys were going back to school, Matt was hiking up the road to Baltimore and, he hoped, a life at sea.

Luck was with him. He reached the heights above Baltimore just before sunrise, and against the reddening sky he saw the tall masts of the *Katie Hines* swaying gently as she tugged at the hawsers that held her. Her skipper, Captain Childs, had been born in Maryland, where his father owned a large tobacco plantation. The cruelty with which the white foreman treated the slaves had outraged the captain when he was still a boy. He had so many rows with his father about it that at last they stopped speaking to each other and, when he was twenty, he ran away to sea. When Matt met him strolling on the wharf beside the *Katie Hines* and asked for a job on the ship, he saw a chance to do what his father had cursed him for believing was right: he could give the young Negro a start in life equal to the one he would have had as a white boy.

Captain Childs asked the usual questions: Matt's name, age, schooling, whether his folks approved of his going to sea, and when he learned that Matt had walked all the way from Washington, he felt that the boy had earned the job. But first he owed it to the lad to warn him that they were bound for China, and would be gone a year. At Matt's reply that it made no difference to him where the ship went as long as he went, too, the captain smiled down at him and, taking his arm, led him up the gangplank.

"Mr. Tracy," he said to the first mate, "meet my new cabin boy, Mr. Matthew Alexander Henson. Take him along to my cabin and let him get a few winks."

Late in the afternoon, the mate woke him and took him to the galley to get his orders from Billy Pincus, the cook. Matt set the captain's table, carried in the food, and washed up afterward. It was an easy job, but the cook watched him with a frown that left Matt uncertain as to whether the man was mean and ugly or just trying to hide a kind nature that he thought unfitting for a hard life at sea.

That evening the crew came aboard. Although Matt's bunk was in a small locker room opposite the captain's cabin, the commotion in the fo'c'sle kept him awake far into the night. In the morning the crew was piped aft and divided into watches, but since Matt's duties could not be parceled out into periods of four hours each, he discovered he was what is called an "idler," because although he worked all day, he could sleep all night.

As soon as the watches were assigned, the captain took him to the shipping office, signed him on officially as his cabin boy, and then sent him back to the ship to give Pincus a hand in the galley.

Toward the middle of the afternoon, Captain Childs, who was pacing the poop with an eye to windward, decided there was enough wind to give steerageway. The anchor at the stern was already up. Now he ordered the mooring chains released, and told the mate to make ready to sail.

"All hands, smartly," called the mate. "Take the chain to the capstan and rig."

Seamen ran forward, fastened the anchor chain to the capstan, unshipped long, heavy bars, thrust them like the spokes of a wheel into the sockets around the capstan head, and bolted them fast. As soon as a rope had been stretched through the notches in their outer ends, the mate sang out, "To the bars, my hearties!"

Back in the galley, old Pincus saw an imploring look in Matt's eyes. "Go ahead," he said, jerking his head toward the deck.

Already sailors were between the bars, four abreast, and others had seized the rope.

"Heave away!" cried the mate and, to Matt's amazement, Chips, the ship's carpenter, began to sing.

"Baltimore is no place for me," he chanted.

"Way, Rio," sang the crew, as they began to push on the bars or pull on the rope and march round and round, turning the capstan head and winding in the chain that held them to the anchor.

Mr. Tracy, leaning over the rail, watched as the *Katie Hines* was pulled slowly forward until the chain was straight up and down.

"Hove short, sir," he reported and, in response to a sign from the captain, he called out, "Heave and pawl."

The pawls dropped into place, holding the capstan so that it wouldn't spring back; the captain raised his arm in a gesture the mate understood, and he gave the order to lay aloft and loose the sails.

The crew raced for the ratlines, and presently sails began to fall in soft folds from yard after yard. The next orders, which had to do with turning the ship about, were given by Captain Childs, who'd come forward for the purpose.

"Back foreyards," he called. "Square away the main! Sheet home lower tops'ls! Upaloft there, overhaul bunt lines and spilling lines!"

"Aye, aye, sir. Hoist away."

As Matt watched and listened, he began to learn the language of the sea.

"Hoist foretops'ls!" the captain commanded.

"Stand by the foretops'ls halyards," ordered the mate.

Chips took his place by the block and pulley, and again began to sing: "Blow the man down, bullies, blow the man down."

"With a way hay, *blow* the man down," chanted the seamen, giving a long, strong pull on the halyard at *way* and *blow*, taking a short breather as Chip sang another line, then pulling again "with a way hay, *blow* the man down."

Matt's muscles tensed with the rhythm, and his fists clenched as if he, too, were pulling on the rope, while the heavy yard moved slowly up the mast until the sail was taut.

"Up anchor," said the captain.

"Hurrah for the last time," shouted the mate, and the crew responded with a rush of power that forced the anchor out of the mud and, to the tune of "Time for us to go," it was catted home.

Slowly the distance between the ship and the wharf

widened until she had room to turn and sail out of the harbor. One by one the other sails were set, and Matt waved triumphantly at the receding shore as the *Katie Hines*, like a sea bird released from captivity, winged her way toward the ocean.

Three bells went. This was the first day Matt had worked by the bells, and it took him a minute or two to figure out that it was five-thirty, and time to set the captain's table. He hurried aft to the cabin, picking his way carefully through the confusion of ropes that seamen were coiling and hanging on their proper belaying pins.

On a shelf against the forward bulkhead just inside the door, he noticed three clocks he'd never seen before, strange clocks mounted in boxes, and all of them more than five hours fast. He stood for a moment staring down at them, and Captain Childs, seeing that he was puzzled, told him that they were his chronometers, and the time they showed was Greenwich time; in other words, longitude zero. Realizing that this was far from enlightening, he went to to explain that because the sun appears to pass across fifteen degrees of longitude per hour, the difference in time between Greenwich time and the ship's time showed the longitude where they were.

So Matt had his first lesson in navigation, and there were more to follow, not only in navigation, but in other subjects too. The captain laid his hand on a pile of books he had just unwrapped—geography, history, mathematics, astronomy—and told Matt these were textbooks he'd bought for him so that he could continue to go to school even though he'd shipped on a windjammer.

After that, Matt spent every afternoon from two to four in the captain's cabin, lapping up learning as a thirsty animal laps up water. From the crowded bookshelves that lined the walls, he was invited to help himself when he wanted lighter or more exciting reading and, during the years he lived on the *Katie Hines*, he absorbed the works of Shakespeare and

Dickens, as shown by the ease with which he quoted from them in his later life.

With the other members of the crew he had little contact. His work was in the galley, his free time was spent in the captain's cabin, or in studying and reading. Sometimes he worked with Chips in his carpentry shop, or helped Sails mend torn canvas. All the seamen, in fact, took a friendly interest in his efforts to learn the ropes, except for a new hand called "Frenchy," who seemed disdainful. Perhaps, thought Matt, he was jealous because the captain spent so much time with a boy who was only the cook's helper. But soon he found out how wrong he was.

He was sitting in the doorway of the galley peeling potatoes when Frenchy stopped, peered into the galley and, seeing that it was empty, told Matt to get out of his way. It was against orders for a seaman to enter unless Pincus was there, and Matt didn't move.

"I ain't never liked you, you dirty nigger," said Frenchy, with such a look of contempt that for the first time in his life, Matt understood that a Negro was looked upon as inferior to a white man. Rage such as he had never known exploded in his heart. He jumped up to bar the way, but Frenchy knocked him down and swaggered into the galley. Matt got to his feet and lunged at the sneering face with the paring knife. Frenchy warded him off and, raising his fist, brought the sharp edge of his knuckles against Matt's mouth, sending him flat on his back.

When Pincus returned, Matt was on his hands and knees gathering up the potatoes. The cook took one look at a large cut in the leg of lamb on the table and the shreds of meat on the knife lying beside it, and understood what had happened. When Matt rose to put the pan of potatoes in the sink, the old fellow saw blood streaming from his mouth, and made no effort to stop the boy when he ran out of the galley.

Matt threw himself down on his bunk and sobbed like a child lost in the dark. What was the use of going on with his studies? They only encouraged false ideas of what he could expect.

He went to the captain's cabin as usual, but showed no interest in his lessons. For a couple of days, the captain appeared not to notice. Then he asked Matt what was wrong.

Matt stared at the table and said nothing.

"Bah!" said the captain with disgust. "What's the use? I see you don't give a hang, so why should I? Chuck your education overboard, and we'll call it quits."

"Why not?" said Matt. "What difference does it make? Isn't it better that I never get educated? I've learned what I am. I'm a 'nigger.'"

Now that he understood what had upset the boy, sympathy replaced the captain's anger.

"I hoped this wouldn't happen to you aboard my ship," he said with a sigh, "but I guess prejudice and hatred can reach a man no matter where he is. I'd set your course wrong, Matthew, if I told you this thing wouldn't hound you the rest of your life. It will. That's the way the minds of men have shaped the system, and what can you or I do about it?"

Matt knew what he would do. He set his jaw and clenched his fist. He'd fight, and never stop fighting.

Captain Childs covered the fist with his hand, and patted it gently. "That's one way, Matthew, but you can't beat intelligence into a man's head with your fists."

He opened one of the textbooks and laid it in front of Matt. "Your fight is with the ignorance in people," he said, "and your best weapons are knowledge and intelligence. These books are the beginning. Make them your fists, Matthew."

The boy's fist relaxed, and he looked at the calm face above him with a rueful smile of repentance.

In the days that followed he tackled his studies with renewed ambition, and had a few lessons in practical navigation. By the time they reached the Equator, he had learned how to use a sextant and take a noon observation of the sun, noting the moment when it paused on reaching its highest altitude for the day, and registering its degrees above the horizon by moving the vernier scale to the correct position.

But that was only half the problem of determining the ship's latitude. The other half meant figuring the angular distance from the sun to the zenith, which required a knowledge of higher mathematics. Tables in the captain's almanac of navigation supplied that information and, adding or subtracting the sun's altitude, according to whether or not the ship and sun were on the same side of the Equator, was all that was necessary to find the latitude.

For five years Matt sailed on the *Katie Hines*, four of them as an able seaman, on voyages that took him not only around Cape Horn to China, Japan, and the Philippines, but across the Atlantic to France, northern Africa, and southern Russia, and through the Arctic to the city of Murmansk. He took his turn at the wheel, sweated for days in heat so torrid that pitch boiled up in the seams of the deck, and reefed sails frozen as stiff as boards in the fierce winds below the Horn and, like most seamen, became a Jack-of-all-trades.

On his first homeward voyage out of Hong Kong, the captain, who also was the ship's doctor, had made him his assistant, or "loblolly boy." Members of the crew had returned from shore leave in a deplorable condition, and Matt dosed them with medicine or gave injections according to the captain's orders.

But when, on the homeward voyage in 1885, the captain himself became ill, neither Mr. Tracy nor Matt could find anything helpful in his medical handbook. Matt kept cold cloths on his hot forehead until at last he regained consciousness. He sat up, then fell back gasping for breath. Matt placed his hand on the heaving chest, and sobbed as the heart-beats grew weaker and finally stopped altogether.

They buried him at sea, and Matt, heartbroken by the death of the man who had been like a father to him, could not face the prospect of sailing on the *Katie Hines* under the command of another skipper.

He shipped on a two-masted fishing schooner bound for Newfoundland. But the captain was either drunk or cursing the crew, so Matt left at the first port and bought a ticket for Boston, where he found temporary work as a stevedore. He moved on to other cities, trying one course after another, but no favoring wind filled his sails. He had become a good carpenter and a master mechanic, but employment in these trades was controlled by labor unions that did not allow Negroes to join them.

In Buffalo, where he was a night watchman, he met several Negroes from the South who had come north, they said, to escape a life little better than slavery. For a few years after the war they'd had a chance to know how it felt to be citizens, because Federal troops had protected them when they went to the polls. But when the troops were withdrawn, Negroes who voted did so at the risk of their lives or their jobs. The plantation owners, with the cooperation of northern business men, were back in the saddle, and many who had played an active part in the rebellion were now sitting in Congress.

Where, Matt wondered, was the progress that Frederick Douglass had foreseen for his race? He went back to Washington where he got a job as stock boy in the store of B. H. Steinmetz and Sons, hatters and furriers.

It was not a menial job, but at the same time it was far beneath Matt's capabilities, and he found himself becalmed in the doldrums, seeing nothing ahead but years of drifting through sluggish water.

IV

"MEET LIEUTENANT PEARY"

Matt was not the only ambitious young man who was becalmed in the doldrums. Shortly before he had left the *Katie Hines* in the fall of 1885 and embarked on a fruitless search for work that would demand the best he had to offer, Lieutenant Peary had returned from Nicaragua. He turned in his report, together with a map showing the route surveyed and a design for lock-gates that was an improvement on previous designs and brought him special recognition.

The Canal Company had collapsed, so Peary was assigned to the Washington Navy Yard. Since the canal project seemed to be postponed indefinitely, he turned his thoughts from the Tropics to the Far North. The dream of discovering the North Pole that had occurred to him on the outward voyage still held him spellbound, and he believed the key to success lay on the unexplored icecap of Greenland.

Poking around in a bookstore one evening, he found a paper on the subject and, as he says, "a chord which as a boy had vibrated intensely at the reading of Kane's wonderful book, was touched again." He read accounts written by men who had made attempts to penetrate the Inland Ice of Greenland, noted their conflicting conclusions, and felt that he must discover for himself the truth about its mysterious interior.

His work for the Navy was mostly routine and did not

interfere with his study of the subject that fascinated him. The only obligation he resented was the necessity of attending receptions where, as a Naval officer, he was duty-bound to show himself.

It was on one such occasion that he met Josephine Die-bitsch, the daughter of a professor at the Smithsonian Institution and a popular debutante admired for her beauty and social charm. But what attracted Peary was her tact, which showed itself in her close attention to what he said, and an intelligent interest in his point of view.

He was bursting with ideas he wanted to talk about, and before long he told her about his plan to explore the Greenland icecap. If he found traveling conditions good, he said he would go again in order to discover whether, as some believed, a chain of islands extended from the northern coast over which people in ages past had migrated from Siberia and over the Pole to the western hemisphere.

Josephine was thrilled by the possibility, and wished him all the luck in the world. But she had a keen sense of humor, and when he asked if she would marry him when he returned from his first trip, she smiled and shook her head, saying that a man who was about to expose himself to unknown dangers might better wait until he was safely home before proposing.

There was no immediate prospect that work on the canal would be resumed and, since Peary had done so well, the Navy granted him the six-months' leave he asked for. His pay, less than a hundred a month, was not enough to finance the trip, so on his way north he stopped in Portland and asked his mother if she could lend him $500. To his surprise she could and did, which was lucky, for without her generosity his expedition would have ended in failure.

The only ships going as far north as Disko Bay, which was his objective, were whalers, and at Sydney on Cape Breton he

Portrait of Peary's mother

learned that whaling captains would not take passengers. But in return for the payment of a larger sum than he had expected to pay, he was accepted as supercargo on a vessel that landed him at Godhavn on June 6, 1886 and then steamed north to the whaling grounds.

Godhavn was a Danish trading station, surrounded by a small settlement of Eskimos. Here Peary found that everything he needed also cost more than he'd counted on. He managed to make the Danish inspector understand what he wanted: provisions, and boats with Eskimo crews to take him across the bay to the head of the fjord he'd selected as the starting point for his climb to the icecap. Though this took a big chunk out of his funds, he still had enough in reserve to carry him through.

As soon as the bay was clear of ice, he sailed away in a round, tublike boat with kayaks alongside carrying food and equipment. Luck was with him again when the boats landed at an Eskimo village on the mainland. This was the headquarters of the assistant governor of the district, Christian Maigaard, a young Dane who agreed to go with him. Neither could understand what the other said, but each was eager to do his share of the hard work ahead of them; each was quick to see when the other needed a helping hand, and a smile was enough to indicate their mutual friendship.

On June 25, Peary, as leader of the expedition, climbed the glacier alone to find the best way to the top. Three days later, after several trips with sledges, skis, provisions, and other equipment on their backs, all their gear was on the edge of the icecap, nearly two-thousand feet above the coast. Just in time, too, for the next night a violent storm swept down on them and for twenty-four hours they lay huddled against their sledges completely buried in snow.

Being romantic young men, they named the sledges in honor of the most attractive girls they knew. Maigaard's was the "Princess Thyra," the youngest Danish princess; Peary's, the "Sweetheart," for Josephine. The "Princess" and the "Sweetheart" were not subjected to the indignity of being harnessed to dogs, for no dogs had been brought along, but before the adventure was over both had endured hardships that would have appalled the tenderly raised young women whom the two explorers had in mind.

They waited until July 2 for the weather to clear, because just ahead lay the most perilous part of the journey. The icecap, in reality a great glacier constantly moving and gathering speeds as it descends, breaks apart as it nears the fjords which give it an outlet to the sea, forming deep cracks called "crevasses."

Peary, hauling his "Sweetheart" across a network of these crevasses, whose open mouths were hidden under bridges of snow and ice, suddenly felt the surface give beneath him. Throwing out his arms, he stopped his fall and, while chunks of frozen snow went hurtling down to the depths beneath, managed to lift himself out and escort the "Sweetheart" to safety.

Farther along the way, Maigaard, following Peary across a thinly frozen pond, heard a crash behind him, and there was "Princess Thyra" in five feet of water. The two men hauled her ashore, and lost a day thawing her out, and themselves as well.

It was only when their clothes were wet that they minded the cold. The temperature was well above zero, ten degrees being the lowest mark their thermometer registered. But after two weeks of dragging their sledges up the slopes in the teeth of the wind and facing the glare of the sun on glittering fields of snow, their eyes were bloodshot and their faces cracked and blistered.

On July 19, Peary's altimeter showed that they were more than a mile and a half above sea level. No one except a small party of Lapps ever had been so far out on the icecap. No one at all had reached such an altitude there. (See map, page 134.)

But this achievement was far from satisfying to Peary. Through narrowed eyes he looked at the smooth expanse toward the north, wondering how far it extended, and whether or not it would prove to be an "imperial highway" to the Pole.

Maigaard spoke, but Peary didn't hear him. "He was like a man in a dream," said Maigaard afterward.

At last Peary wrenched his thoughts away from the future, and decided that this time they could go no farther. Their food would last only six days more, and it had taken seventeen to reach this point. Speed was essential, and changes for the worse in the route they had followed might delay them. In their favor was the fact that they would be going downhill with the wind behind them, and Peary was quick to take advantage of the chance it offered, not only for speed but for fun too. He placed the "Sweetheart" and the "Princess" side by side and began to lash them together. Maigaard got the idea and helped. Together they put up one of the nine-foot alpenstocks for a mast and Peary fastened a flag to the top of it; the other alpenstock served as a yard, and a rubber blanket was the sail.

They started off in high spirits, walking rapidly behind the little catamaran they'd made with the sledges, guiding it or checking its speed when necessary. By the time they stopped to make camp, Peary had figured out how they could ride. Fastening the hatchet to the end of a ski, he made a rudder, and the next day they coasted until they were stopped by the sight of crevasses ahead. They were visible because the frozen snow that would have concealed them had fallen in. Many of them proved to be fifty feet wide.

They walked cautiously ahead, pushing the catamaran across every furrow until the ends projected far enough on both sides to support it in case the snow beneath masked a chasm. Then Peary grasped the yard, swung himself over, and pulled, while Maigaard gave the sledges a push before following.

After half a mile of this slow and perilous procedure, they were relieved to find themselves at the top of another steep descent, and for an hour they coasted again at a speed that left them breathless. Then the changes that had occurred during their absence put an end to the rapid progress they'd made so far. Pools of water filled every depression, and they lowered the sail and walked until a morass of slush extending right and left as far as they could see barred any further advance. They waited until midnight for it to freeze, only to find that fifty yards from camp they sank to their knees. Plowing ahead, dragging the catamaran, they reached a solid surface at last, and, having cleared the wet snow from the sledges, started off on a run to get the blood circulating in their numb feet.

After several hours, they came to another area criss-crossed by crevasses. They used the same method they had used before, but in spite of this precaution, they nearly lost their lives. Halfway across, with the catamaran placed as planned, Peary pulled and Maigaard pushed, but as he started to spring over, he tripped. The snow on which he landed gave way and down he went, still clinging to the rear of the sledges. Peary's end shot up with a jerk that almost tore it from his hands, and he was dragged toward the abyss. For a moment the catamaran teetered on the edge, but Peary was heavy enough to get his end down and, pulling with all his might, he moved the sledges toward him until the leverage was in his favor. When Maigaard's head appeared, Peary threw the full weight of his body across the front, thus raising the rear until his friend was able to swing himself across to solid ice.

A few days later, Peary had another close call. He'd waded up to his hips in a glacial stream in order to carry the "Sweetheart" and the "Princess" across, but midway the current swept his feet from under him and rushed him toward its outlet into the fjord below. Fortunately, he was wearing spiked shoes, and a stretch of shallow water gave him enough purchase to spring against the bank, scramble up, and run to Maigaard to help rescue the sledges.

Thanks to the speed they'd made by coasting, the return trip, despite its delays and mishaps, had been made in a week. Even in that short time, as they discovered going down the face of the glacier, thousands of flowers had bloomed among the rocks, and the heat became so oppressive that by the time Peary reached the tent by the shore he was carrying most of his clothes.

Here Maigaard left him, both men regretting that his official duties made it impossible for him to go on another exploring trip Peary was about to undertake.

It was late in July, and since the whaler wouldn't call for him until September, he hired a few Eskimos and their kayaks to take him northward along the coast to another fjord from which he planned to reach the icecap. When they entered the narrow inlet, they found that an active glacier was discharging icebergs into it, which broke off with sharp reports like heavy artillery and raised such waves when they fell that the little fleet was in danger of being swamped.

They managed to reach the head of the fjord, however, and since this was as far as the Eskimos had agreed to go, Peary worked his way up alongside the glacier, pitched his tent on the edge of the Inland Ice, and traveled over it twenty-five miles and back.

Rejoining the Eskimos, he continued to explore the peaks along the coast. Last of all he examined the famous fossil beds high up on a mighty cliff overlooking Disko Bay, where he gathered slabs of stone on which leaves from trees growing long ages before had left their imprint.

With these trophies, he returned to Godhavn, and sailed home on September 6. Since his leave wouldn't expire until late in November, he expected to have plenty of time to stop in Portland to visit his mother. But in harbor after harbor the ship anchored among other whalers, sending out boats to cruise for whales, and arranging to sell at the trading stations the cargo already on board. Altogether forty-five days were devoted to these activities; two more were lost when a hurricane forced them to take shelter in a bay above Hudson Strait; and by the time they reached port it was November 17.

Long before that Peary had realized that a visit to his mother was out of the question. Instead, he used the days when the whaler lay at anchor to write her a long letter. He started another to Josephine describing his adventures, but never finished it and decided to send her a telegram instead. The few paragraphs he'd written had suggested the possibility that such an account, with scientific observations added, would be welcomed by some geographical journal and would supplement the preliminary outline of the project that he'd submitted to the National Academy of Sciences before leaving Washington.

Within two months of his return, the article was published in the *Bulletin of the American Geographical Society*, accompanied by a chart showing three possible routes across Greenland. This report created a stir among influential men whose support Peary needed for the more ambitious plan he had in mind.

Josephine was proud of his achievement, and listened with sympathy to his plans for another expedition; but when once more he asked her to marry him, she laughed and said she could see no point in having an absentee husband.

His hope for another trip to the Arctic was blasted, however, by orders to return to Nicaragua, where a reorganized company was ready to resume work on the canal. Peary was to command the locating expedition, for which thirty-five engineers had been engaged. Work would not begin until the opening of the dry season in January, 1888, but in the meantime Peary had to take charge of outfitting the party, and compare the various routes proposed to make sure that the one selected was the most advantageous.

It took all his will power to keep his thoughts from straying to the more congenial plans for a northern expedition, and it was a gloomy young man who entered the store of Steinmetz & Sons one morning in August and asked for a tropical helmet, size seven and three-eighths.

"Matt," Mr. Steinmetz called, "bring in a size seven and three-eighths sun helmet. They're on the shelf above the Panamas."

While they waited, Peary asked Steinmetz if he could recommend a young man to go to Nicaragua as his body servant, and Steinmetz recommended Henson.

"This is the boy I was telling you about, Lieutenant," he said, as Matt set the hatbox on the counter.

The tall stranger looked Matt up and down with a cool, analytical glance, then turned to the mirror.

"My name is Peary," he said as he adjusted the sun helmet. "I need a boy to go with me to Central America as a valet. Keep my clothes and quarters clean. Must be honest with regular habits. Mr. Steinmetz recommends you."

Sam Steinmetz leaned over the counter and spoke apologetically. "Now, Matt, it isn't that we want to lose you. Why I just told Lieutenant Peary that in the eighteen months you've been with us, you proved to be the best boy we've ever had, but I was only thinking of you, Matt. It sounds good to me—yes, a most interesting proposition."

Peary turned away from the mirror. "I'll take the hat," he said, then leaned against the counter and faced Matt. "Well, do you want the job?"

Henson's athletic build already had convinced Peary that this was the man he wanted. Henson, although he was favorably impressed by Peary's quiet but resolute manner, didn't like the idea of taking a position as valet. He'd had enough of that when he'd been valet to a millionaire in New York.

"What are you going to do in Central America, sir?"

"Finish a survey job for a proposed canal in Nicaragua."

Matt's heart gave a bound. A canal across the isthmus, an end to the long and dangerous journey around the Horn. A part in it, however small, would be worthwhile.

"Sir," he said, "I'd like the job very much."

They sailed from New York in November, 1887, in order to reach Nicaragua while there was still enough water in the San Juan River to carry them over its sand banks to the island where they were to build their headquarters. It was the same island Peary had used for a camp on the previous expedition, because it lay near the mouth of a river on which he could travel by canoe to and from the jungle where he was working then, and where the main part of the present job was to be done.

Already four parties of surveyors were in the field with instructions to follow the course of the canal already charted, and to lay out the route for a railroad alongside to transport men and material when construction began. Peary had started them off from Greytown, accompanied by a crew of borers to probe for firm foundations for locks and embankmènts, and hydrographers to measure the flow of streams.

Gangs of natives went ahead of them, Indians of mixed blood who were familiar with the jungle. There the undergrowth was so thick that it was impossible to see more than ten feet ahead until the natives, armed with machetes, had cleared a path. Negroes Peary had taken aboard at Jamaica brought up the rear, carrying provisions, camping equipment, dugouts, and baggage.

Now, from his base on the island, Peary, followed by a fleet of canoes, led the rest of his party into a continuation of the tangled wilderness. He himself did no surveying, but went from camp to camp to see how the work was progressing, and to find ways to overcome the difficulties encountered. Knowing from experience how hard it was to run a survey through jungles and swamps, he was not impatient because progress was slow. He appreciated the fact that his men were well seasoned and good-natured, tackling the job with unflagging energy, and he was proud of them.

In addition to making these tours of inspection, he had to explore large areas on each side of the route to discover, if possible, where it might be shortened. Because of the thick undergrowth, this was a tedious process. You could be at the foot of a hill before you knew it was there, or on the bank of a stream and learn of it only when you stepped over the edge. He had to feel out the lay of the land much as a blind man becomes familiar with his surroundings.

It was necessary also to investigate the watershed, in order to know the amount of water that could be counted on to fill the canal. Accompanied by rubber hunters who knew the area, he paddled up streams to their sources, and climbed tall trees to locate the highest hills from which other streams might flow.

Meantime, Henson, with the help of natives, built more commodious headquarters according to the plan Peary had drawn up. On his own initiative he added shelves for Peary's books and a long table, made by laying planks across boxes of canned goods, on one end of which he placed Peary's case of drawing instruments.

Soon Peary was bending over it, sketching in the courses of the streams and watersheds he'd located, the sites where locks could be built, and so on. But before long he was off again, and Henson had little to do.

Peary really didn't need a servant. The company, realizing that he had undertaken the job with reluctance, thought it was due to the discomforts of jungle life, and had presented him with a valet in an effort to appease him. Whenever he returned from reconnoitering or inspecting trips, Henson cooked his meals, washed his clothes, and cleaned shoes and puttees caked with mud from the swamps and rivers through which he'd waded.

It was the swamps that ended Henson's career as a body servant. They had been in Nicaragua three months. Peary had left headquarters the day before, and Matt was hanging freshly washed shirts on the line when Peary unexpectedly returned with a bedraggled man at his heels.

Turning to Henson, Peary explained that the man was wading through a swamp, stepped in a bed of quicksand, and sank to his waist before the gang pulled him out. He'd quit the job then and there, which left the transit crew short a chainman. Filling that vacancy, he said, was more important than having his shirts washed, and he wanted Henson to bundle up some clothes and go back with him.

Henson, of course, jumped at the chance to take part in the actual work of surveying the route for a canal that would be a godsend to seamen, and within ten minutes they were on their way. They found the surveying crew eating lunch. Peary introduced Matt to the section engineer and suggested that the instrument man show him what was expected of the rear chainman.

The instrument man swallowed the last of his coffee and set up his tripod, which supported a small telescope, a compass, levelers, and vernier scales to measure angles to small fractions of degrees. Carefully he placed it above a small stake, in the center of which a tack had been driven, let down the plumb bob, moved the tripod until the bob was directly above the tack, and pressed each leg firmly into the ground. Then, having made sure that the transit was level, he told Matt that his job was to hold the end of the chain directly under the plumb bob, and not to allow it to move a hairsbreadth until the other end was in place.

Peary stopped long enough to eat a couple of sandwiches and drink some cocoa, then got into his canoe and paddled off toward the camps below.

Matt proved from the first that he could hold the chain with the patience and accuracy required. What made the job tough was the swarm of gnats driven from the underbrush, cut by the natives to open a path. As he squatted below the transit, they settled on his face and hands, crawled inside his shirt, and even found their way into his nose and ears. With only a wriggle or a cautious left-handed counterattack, he had to endure their stinging and itching assault while the head chainman moved his stake to the right or left until the instrument man signaled that it was in line, after which the chain was drawn tight, the distance marked, and Matt was free to release his end and deal with the pests.

When Peary returned, the section chief had nothing but praise for Henson. His work with the chain was careful and accurate, he was always good-natured, and he was popular with everyone, including the natives and the Negroes from Jamaica. From then on, Henson worked as a member of the surveying crew.

He was shorter than the others and, as he made his way through the swamps, holding an axe and extra stakes above his head, the muck often reached to his shoulders. His eyes, nose, and throat smarted from its acrid odor. His clothes were always wet, for there was no sun in the jungle to dry them, and always in the swamps there was the danger of quicksand. But, like everyone else, he accepted discomfort and hardship as part of the game.

Every few days, native and Negro helpers moved baggage and equipment to the newly established station, and in fifteen or twenty minutes had set up another collection of little huts, thatched with palm leaves and open at the sides so that hammocks could be slung to get the benefit of the trade winds.

As they worked their way slowly forward, Henson picked up information as avidly as the parakeets picked up crumbs around the breakfast table. He learned how the transit worked, why side lines and flowage lines had to be run, altitudes taken and borings made, so that before long he realized the scope of the problems Peary must solve before the construction of the canal could begin.

After three months of contending with difficulties and obstacles which, as Peary reported, no one could imagine who hadn't endured them, they reached the spot where the eastern section of the canal would join the upper San Juan River, and the toughest part of the job was behind them. A dam across the river would raise its level to that of Lake Nicaragua, providing over a hundred miles of still water; the lake itself would take care of another seventy, and bring the canal within seventeen miles of the Pacific. There the land was open, and there were no swamps. By the first of June, 1888, the survey was finished, and about a month later they were back in New York where Peary was to stay and prepare his report in the office of the canal company.

Already he had made up his mind that Henson, on account of his strength, endurance, and adaptability, would be valuable in the Arctic, and in order not to lose track of him, asked where a letter would reach him. Henson told him Mr. Steinmetz expected him back, and mail could be sent to the store. Peary handed him his card, telling him to let him know if he went elsewhere, for he was going to try to find a job for him in connection with his next naval assignment, a promise that made it easier for Henson to endure the months of tedious routine that followed.

V

HEADING NORTH

All during the homeward voyage, Peary had been trying to figure out how to finance another expedition to Greenland. He would have to find backers willing to contribute thousands of dollars. What could he offer in return? Not the discovery of the Pole. Men with years of Arctic experience had failed. No one would believe that he, with only three months to his credit, could succeed. Reluctantly he faced the fact that even exploration of the northeast corner of Greenland would seem a goal too ambitious for a novice. The only practical proposal would be to cross at the southern end by the short route shown on the chart he'd published in 1887. It offered little in the way of discovery, but there would be a dramatic and sporting appeal in the prospect of financing the first man to cross Greenland.

Unfortunately, Fridtjof Nansen, a young explorer in Norway, had long had the same ambition, and reports of Peary's preliminary trip had convinced him that he had no time to lose if he wanted that honor for himself.

Peary, cooped up in a New York office and happily unaware that he had a rival, raced against time in order to finish his report and go ahead with his project of winning fame in Greenland.

At the same time there was something else he was determined to win, and that was Josephine. He wasted no time in that matter either. Less than six weeks after his return, he wrote her that she had put him off long enough, and he wanted to marry her at once. Her reply that their Washington House was closed for the summer, rugs rolled up, furniture wrapped in dust covers, and that it would be best to wait for a proper wedding in the fall, had no effect. They were married a week later, on August 11.

When she came down to breakfast on the morning of her wedding day, Josephine was surprised to find Peary's mother sitting calmly in the parlor. The two women looked enough alike to be mother and daughter. They had the same square jaw, firm mouth, and steady eyes that gazed without flinching into the face opposite. It was a tense moment, for Mrs. Peary had not been invited to the wedding. Her son had said that the heat—it was now 101 degrees in the shade—might kill her. What he knew for certain was that giving up her son to another woman would cut her to the quick.

"But," Josephine had said, "we'll have to wire at least. And I think the fair thing is to let her know the day before. Then she won't feel you forgot her in the midst of your affairs."

The telegram was sent, his mother came, and she stayed with them for a year. It was a hard year for all of them, and Josephine's capacity for patience and sympathetic understanding was taxed to the utmost.

Josephine knew she was marrying a man too poor to give her the luxuries to which she was accustomed; yet when he suggested that they try to get along on fifty dollars a month she was somewhat taken aback. But after he explained that the other fifty dollars would make it possible to repay the money his mother had loaned him, she gladly agreed.

She knew, too, that she had married a man who was determined to explore the Arctic. "I am going to be the first man to cross Greenland," were words she heard nearly as often as "I love you." Presumably they were to share expenses equally, but Peary often had to borrow from her in order to meet the cost of the voluminous correspondence with societies and individuals whose financial backing he was seeking.

When favorable responses began to come in, she was happy because he was happy, although she flinched a little when she read the last words in a letter he received from Professor Heilprin of the Academy of Natural Sciences of Philadelphia. "I really believe you can cross Greenland," he wrote. "And if you do it first, you shall have made a name for yourself. Future help will come easily after that."

A few days later, Peary came home from the office looking, she thought, "as if he had just seen someone die." He sat down heavily on the edge of the bed, and seeing by her face that she was frightened, said abruptly, "Jo, Nansen has crossed Greenland." (See map, page 134.)

His main argument, that he would make a record by crossing first, had been swept away. Those who had promised money were betting on a winner. They'd have no interest in an also-ran, and would withdraw their support.

Most of them did, and Peary's spirits hit bottom. But, like the giant who gained new strength whenever he hit the ground, he rose at last from the depths of despair, ready to go on fighting.

If men with money wanted to contribute only to an enterprise that promised to establish a record, he would give them that opportunity. He'd ask them to finance an expedition that would cross the icecap far to the north of Nansen's route, not just for the sake of crossing it, but in order to reach the northeast coast, which no man ever had seen.

By now his work for the canal company was finished, and he was sent to supervise the building of a dry dock in the Brooklyn Navy Yard.

As soon as they were settled and work on the dry dock was under way, he sent out a new series of letters, pointing out that while Nansen's crossing deserved the highest praise for its daring, it had been made close to the southern tip of the island and had revealed nothing not already known. In order to fill the blank space on the maps where northeast Greenland should be, another crossing must be made near the 80th parallel. This he proposed to do. A detailed plan would be sent on request.

Like a general about to go into battle, he mapped out his campaign. The distance to the coast and back was about twelve hundred miles. In 1886, he'd covered two hundred miles in three weeks. At that rate the present trip would take two and a half months. A small party would be sufficient. He would contribute their services, as well as his own. The food for the journey must be light in weight, but nourishing. He'd chosen pemmican, which Indians and pioneers had used on the trail and which he had found satisfactory on the icecap. It would be made of beef, dried and chopped fine, mixed with suet, currants, and sugar. Also he'd take tea, condensed milk, hardtack, and dehydrated soup. To transport it, he would follow the Eskimo custom and use sledges pulled by dogs.

The best months for traveling on the icecap were May, June, and July, when there would be twenty-four hours of daylight and the sun had not yet softened the snow in the Far North sufficiently to make traveling slow. Since ice made navigation above Hudson Strait impossible in the spring, he would sail in the summer of 1891, build winter quarters, and start from there as soon as conditions were favorable in 1892.

He hired a stenographer to type copies of the plan, and embarked on a series of lectures in Brooklyn, hoping they would bring in enough money to cover the expense of the appeal.

To add to Peary's worries, his mother had become increasingly fretful and complained of poor health. She had been unable to adjust to the necessity of sharing him with another woman, and made little effort to conceal her bitterness. At last he persuaded her to go back to Portland where she would be close to her family and friends. Before she left, he returned the money she had loaned him, and raised her spirits by saying that whatever success he won as an explorer would be due to her generosity in supporting his first expedition.

As soon as the dry dock in Brooklyn was completed, the Navy informed Peary that his services were needed in Philadelphia to superintend the building of a timber dry dock in the League Island Navy Yard.

Again he made arrangements for a series of lectures. His reputation spread, and when his colleagues at the Navy Yard got wind of his efforts to organize another exploring expedition, their general attitude was that he was a fanatic, and the Navy was no place for him. But his ability as an engineer was too great, his devotion to duty too constant, for his superiors to consider any idea of dismissing him.

Before the end of his first year at League Island, the American Geographical Society had endorsed his plan for crossing Greenland; the Brooklyn Institute of Arts and Sciences, the Academy of Natural Sciences of Philadelphia, and Professor F. W. Putnam of the American Association for the Advancement of Science added their endorsement. Prominent men had promised financial support, and in January, 1891, when success seemed assured, Peary sent for young Henson, and had him put on the Navy payroll as his messenger boy.

In February, Peary applied to the Navy for an eighteen-months' leave, enclosing an outline of his plan, mentioning the approval it had received from scientists, and saying he trusted his request would be granted, since he proposed to contribute the time and service of himself and other members of the party, as well as his leave pay. The rest of the money

needed would come from various scientific societies. Therefore he asked no assistance from the government beyond the
granting of his leave.

Such an application would have been dismissed out of
hand in ordinary circumstances, but it received serious con-
sideration because Peary's purpose, if accomplished, would be
a valuable contribution to the Navy's coastal surveys.

As soon as word came that the leave had been granted beginning May 1, Peary sent a news item to papers throughout
the country announcing that he was fitting out an expedition
to sledge across the snow-covered interior of Greenland to try
to discover how far north it extended, adding that his companions were not yet decided upon.

Henson saw the paragraph in a Philadelphia paper, and
was pleased, though not surprised, when Peary asked him if he
would be willing to go along. He was not only willing, he
considered it a privilege, and said so. When Peary confessed
that all of his money had gone into the preliminary preparations, that he had only eight dollars in the bank, and wouldn't
be able to pay him or any other assistants, Henson assured him
it made no difference. It was something that ought to be done,
and he wanted to help do it.

Eivand Astrup, a young Norwegian who recently had
come to this country, also had seen the notice in a Philadelphia paper. He had won several prizes in ski-running contests
and, having been thrilled by accounts of Nansen's record-
breaking trip across the icecap, was eager to try his skill on the
Inland Ice of Greenland. Like Henson, he was willing to vol-
unteer his services, and two days after Astrup had called on
him, he received word that Peary had chosen him as an
assistant.

Now that a leave of absence had been granted, the
promised contributions began to come in. The American Geographical Society sent $1,000; Professor F. W. Putnam paid

$1,000 for photographs of Eskimos to be exhibited in his department of ethnology at the World's Fair; the *New York Sun* offered another $1,000 for letters; and smaller amounts were received from many other sources, including Peary's mother and the Portland Society of Natural History.

At the same time, the newspapers, to add suspense to their stories about the expedition, were featuring tragedies that recently had befallen other American explorers in the Far North. They reminded their readers of the fate of Lieutenant George W. DeLong, whose ship, in 1881, had been crushed in the ice pack, with only two men surviving to tell the tale. They played up the story of Major Adolphus W. Greely, who in the same year that DeLong and his men perished, had sailed north with twenty-three companions, of whom seventeen starved to death. They stressed the fact that both Greely and DeLong had government backing, while Peary had only private support. The Navy had sent ships to rescue DeLong's party; the Army had sent ships to Greely's aid, but their efforts had ended in failure. Could private backers succeed in doing what the Army and Navy had been unable to do? Those other explorers had experienced men with them. Peary had only a handful of greenhorns. Another tragedy was inevitable.

In spite of these gloomy predictions, Peary received hundreds of letters from young men, offering their services. In addition to Henson and Astrup, he chose three, all of whom were in their twenties and, in addition to physical fitness, had the background necessary for the scientific work he planned.

Dr. Frederick A. Cook, an ethnologist as well as a physician and surgeon, was selected for his ability to prepare the exhibit ordered for the World's Fair. He was a pleasant young man, just out of medical school and, since he had no practice to speak of, took this opportunity to satisfy the craving for adventure that marked his later career.

The others were Langdon Gibson, a member of the American Ornithologists' Union, and John M. Verhoeff, son of a wealthy Southern family, a mineralogist and meteorologist, who wanted to add to his collection of specimens, and was able to assist in making a study of weather conditions in the Arctic.

Peary had planned to sail on June 1, but in May he struck a snag which made it look as if he couldn't get started then, if at all. The Dundee whaling companies and the director of the Greenland trade flatly refused to transport his party in any of their ships. The only alternative was to charter a vessel, which would double the expense of the voyage, and Peary hadn't an extra cent.

Again Professor Heilprin came to the rescue. He organized a group of scientists interested in making explorations of their own along the western coast of Greenland, and willing to embark on a summer cruise. Their passage money, plus a couple of thousand contributed by young Verhoeff, made it possible to charter the *Kite*, a sealer with auxiliary steam, so small that she was barely able to accommodate passengers and cargo.

A brief notice in a Philadelphia paper, that Peary's ship was being fitted out in the harbor, brought a few curious citizens down to look at her.

"The wormy old sealer will never reach Greenland," was their verdict, which the newspapers duly reported, with the result that those who didn't ridicule Peary's ambitious undertaking, pitied the men who were going with him. They didn't know yet that his wife was going too. With a firmness equal to that of his mother's when she announced she was going with him to college, Josephine had stated that she was going with him to Greenland.

"Now we know he's crazy!" one paper asserted on learning that Mrs. Peary had sailed on the *Kite*.

From Sydney, on Cape Breton Island, where they stopped

for coal, Peary sent a telegram to his mother, telling her all were well, and they were having a pleasant voyage. But the next day as they steamed across the entrance to the Gulf of St. Lawrence, they ran into heavy weather, and the passengers, except Peary and Henson, were miserably seasick. The wind freshened to a gale and the ship was plunging violently when Captain Pike, seeing Henson walking the deck with an easy roll, spotted him for a sailor, and said the men on the mizzen could use another hand.

Henson ran for the ratlines, and the next minute was helping to reef the billowing sails. Throughout the voyage he was among the first to answer the call for "All hands!"

The Atlantic Ocean gave them a boisterous welcome. The little *Kite* pitched and tossed until by the third day she was filled with water forward and in her waist. Peary and Henson took their turn at the pumps, but the other passengers kept to their bunks until the cry of "Land ahead!" brought them on deck to catch their first sight of Greenland.

As they gazed at the grandeur of that rock-bound coast, their misery gave way to awe at this exhibition of the powerful forces that had shaped the mighty dam that holds back the ice and snow under which the mountains of the interior are buried.

But there are breaks in the dam, and south of Disko Bay they met a squadron of icebergs, dropped into the sea from glaciers flowing through gaps between the cliffs. Their first stop was at Godhavn, Peary's headquarters five years before. With his wife and Professor Heilprin, he called on the Inspector who gave the party freedom to go wherever they wished.

It was a delightful week end. Most of them started at once for the icecap in the center of Disko Island, Josephine, with an alpenstock, climbing the cliffs as sturdily as the men. It took them four hours to make the climb, and when they got there they were glad to take a rest and admire the view 2,400

Josephine Peary, from a photograph taken in 1891

feet below. Before leaving, Henson and Astrup gathered
enough stones to make a cairn, in which Peary placed a tin
box with the date, their names, and a few American coins inside, as a memorial to their visit.

They steamed away through a calm sea that gave Peary a
chance to start work on the prefabrication of the building that

was to be their Arctic home. Knowing that it was impossible
to get lumber in Greenland, which is bare of trees, he had
brought along all he was likely to need. Calling Henson to his
cabin, he showed him the plan of the house, with precise
measurements indicated. Henson got his carpenter's kit, and
they went to work.

By the time they reached Upernavik, most northern of
the Danish trading stations, rafters and floor boards were
ready. Here Peary had hoped to find Frederick, the Eskimo
half-breed who had been his interpreter in 1886. But the
Governor said that although Frederick stopped there from
time to time, he hadn't seen him lately, and knew no other
Eskimo who could speak English. This was a great disappointment, for now it would be difficult to communicate with the
natives whose help he would need in the Far North.

They stayed only long enough to return the Governor's
official call, and the next morning anchored at the Duck
Islands. From a bold summit on the outer island, whalers
coming north in the early spring look out over Melville Bay,
hoping to see leads between the ice pans through which their
ships can pass. Many had died while waiting for these lanes
of open water to appear and, as Peary climbed the bluff to
see what chance the Kite might have of crossing the bay, he
stopped to look at their crudely marked graves.

As far as he could see, there was plenty of open water,
and happily he joined the boys in a hunt for eider ducks,
which breed by the thousands on these islands and give them
their name. Within a few hours they had a good supply, and
since by now it was always light, they steamed away at once.

But sixteen miles to the northwest, the Kite stuck her
nose into the dreaded pack. She managed to keep moving by
fits and starts, but by July 4 she was drifting helplessly in the
grip of the ice. In spite of his anxiety, for this was the date

when he'd hoped to land at his base some 200 miles further north, Peary organized a Fourth of July celebration. He ordered the *Kite's* cannon fired and her flags run up, and all on board drank a toast to the Stars and Stripes. Dinner consisted of roast eider duck, followed by plum duff and a "Melville Bay" punch made of snow, milk, rum, and a little lime juice and sugar.

The "Melville Bay" punch was a treat, but spending a winter in the Melville Bay ice was a prospect they did not relish. One or another of the men was always up in the crow's nest scanning the pack for some sign of opening. None appeared, and by the end of a week they were asking how much food and fuel was on board.

Peary, remembering the graves below the lookout on Duck Island, where men trapped by the ice had perished for lack of shelter, took advantage of the ship's stability to work with Henson on the prefabrication of the house, so it could be put up as soon as possible, whenever they had a chance to land.

Suddenly, without warning, on July 11 the ice slackened, and the *Kite* began to ram her way ahead. Peary stepped to the stern rail to watch her performance and, as he did so, a cake of ice struck the rudder and jammed it hard over so that the wheel was torn from the hands of the two men on duty. The next instant the iron tiller smashed Peary's leg against the wheelhouse, snapping both bones just above the ankle.

He was carried below, where Dr. Cook, and the surgeon attached to the scientific party, set the shattered bones as carefully as they could with the ship careening from side to side when the floes pressed against her.

Meanwhile, Professor Heilprin and his colleagues decided that since Peary obviously was incapable of carrying out the expedition he had planned, the wisest course was to turn back immediately. But when they went to Captain Pike with their

proposal, he said, "I take orders only from Lieutenant Peary."
The professor replied that the lieutenant was in no state of
mind to judge what was best.

"If Mrs. Peary says turn back, I'll do it," said the captain.

Certain that she would see the wisdom of taking her husband home, Professor Heilprin asked her to issue the order.

"If he wants to be taken home, all right," she said. "I will
talk it over with my husband."

But Peary, who had been in such a delirium of pain that
once he had begged Josephine to pack his leg in ice and have
someone shoot it, refused to give up. When Fate got really
tough, he could get tough too.

They did not turn back. The *Kite* continued to hammer
her way through the pack, every jolt giving Peary a stab of
intense pain, until at last she reached open water off Cape
York, and began the voyage up Smith Sound on an even keel.
This gave Henson a chance to continue cutting and fitting the
lumber according to the plan Peary had drawn up. The uprights, siding, and roofing were finished by the time they
rounded Cape Parry and steamed toward the inlet where
Peary expected to land. But the ice had not moved out and
they were forced to go on into McCormick Bay, 200 miles
north of Cape York. Here the *Kite* was able to steer a course
between icebergs to a ribbon of open water along the coast.

Josephine and the boys, as Peary called his assistants, went
ashore in one of the whaleboats Peary had brought, and spent
the morning hunting for a good location for the house. It was
Josephine who found it, a grassy knoll bright with flowers, far
enough from the cliffs so that no falling rocks could crush the
house, high enough so that torrents from the melting snow of
early summer couldn't sweep it away, and near enough to the
beach so that lumber, coal, and boxes of provisions could be
brought to it without difficulty.

Early the next morning the boys went ashore with pickaxes and shovels and began to dig the cellar. The earth was soft, which made it easy to level it off, and before the end of the day, the excavation was finished. Meantime the crew had landed the pre-cut lumber and, on the following day Peary, strapped to a board, was carried from the ship to a tent pitched behind the house, from which he could supervise the building operations.

All day the lively tattoo of hammers brought resounding echoes from the cliffs, and the crew continued to land the cargo, a slow process because the floating ice made it impossible for the *Kite* to anchor, and as she steamed back and forth, everything, including a hundred tons of coal, was transferred to the whaleboats and rowed ashore. That done, she left on her homeward voyage, taking with her the scientists and letters from Peary, Josephine, and the boys to parents who would be anxious to hear from them.

During the four days when the crew was unloading the *Kite*, it had been sunny, and so warm that the boys worked in their shirt sleeves. But a few hours after the ship left, it began to rain, and the wind blew with such fury that they couldn't keep a foothold on the rafters. Leaving the roof half finished, they crowded into the little tent, ate the dinner Josephine had prepared, and then, since she refused to leave her husband or allow anyone else to take her place, they tightened the guy ropes, placed stones on the lower edge of the walls to keep the wind from getting under, and then ran for shelter to the end of the house that was roofed over.

All night Josephine sat beside her husband, expecting every minute that the tent would be wrenched from its fastenings and planning how, if that happened, she could raise it enough to shelter him. After a few hours, water began to stream in from the slope above, and she rolled up her long skirts and sat cross-legged on a box.

When, just before morning, the water rushed in with

Red Cliff House, with Eskimo homes beside it (from a drawing by F. W. Stokes). This type of Eskimo house was called a "tupik." It was an all-year-round igloo, covered in summer with sealskin, over which snow was piled in winter

enough violence to sweep the oilstove before it, Josephine waded in and rescued it in time to make breakfast for the party.

By the next afternoon, the storm had blown itself out, work on the house went ahead, and the following day the roof was on. When the oilstove had warmed the room, Peary was carried inside and placed on a row of boxes covered with blankets. Doors and windows were put in place, thick boards were nailed to the inside of the frame, and heavy brown paper was pasted over the seams. Bunks built for the boys, and a small room partitioned off for Peary and his wife, gave them a building which, though not yet winter-tight, was adequate for the present. Peary named it Red Cliff House from the massive wall of dark red rock that rose behind it. (See map, page 112.)

To keep everyone in good spirits, Peary had planned to celebrate all holidays and every anniversary of interest to members of his party. Henson's birthday on August 8 was the first. Josephine asked him to choose the menu for dinner, and he came back from a hunting trip early enough to make plum duff for dessert. On the eleventh, Peary and Josephine celebrated their wedding anniversary with a luxurious feast served in tin plates on a bare board table.

After this brief vacation, all energy was directed toward accomplishing what must be done before the Great Night enveloped them. The first and most pressing need was to find Eskimos and make friends with them. Without their dogs to pull sledges carrying the thousand pounds of food required for men and dogs during the three-month journey on the Inland Ice, and without their women to prepare the skins and make the windproof clothing necessary for survival, the trip to the northeast coast would be impossible. Failure to attain his goal would end all prospects of raising money for another expedition. In short, Peary's success as an explorer depended on winning the cooperation of the Eskimos, a fact he had recognized and prepared to meet while he was working in Brooklyn.

His first effort was made on August 12, when he sent Gibson, Cook, Verhoeff, and Astrup, under the command of Gibson, to cruise in a whaleboat along the coast in search of Eskimo settlements. Having failed to get an interpreter, they would have to show the Eskimos by signs that anyone who would bring his family and live nearby could have the use of a rifle.

But Peary warned them always to leave a man to guard the boat and its contents whenever they were in the neighborhood of natives. While they were gone, he and Josephine took turns keeping watch at night. The day watch was assigned to

Henson, who was building a wall of stone and turf around the house.

For two days the scouting party looked in vain for Eskimo houses that were inhabited. At noon on the third day they caught sight of three igloos made of stone, and were about to land when they heard a shout and saw an Eskimo coming toward them. He showed no sign of fear, but came down, helped with their boat, smiled, talked to them, and they gathered that his name was Ikwa. Soon he was followed by his wife and two children, one a baby carried in his mother's hood.

The boys shared their lunch with the family, who liked the coffee and crackers but, after one taste, refused the baked beans and tomatoes. By signs they tried to make Ikwa understand that they wanted to take them to a big house and let him use a rifle, but they weren't sure whether or not he was willing to go.

They waited the rest of the day, hoping Ikwa would give some indication of his decision. They slept on the shore beside their boat and were preparing to leave when Ikwa came down again, and they made another attempt to persuade him. This time they succeeded. He brought down his dog, his kayak, his harpoon, and a sledge. His wife and the children followed and got into the whaleboat. Stopping just long enough to fasten the kayak astern, they rowed rapidly away, giving Ikwa an oar to pull so that he'd be too busy to regret his decision.

Near the end of the journey, they passed a belt of ice where walrus were sleeping. Ikwa grabbed his harpoon and plunged it into one of them, but a shot from Astrup's rifle sent it to the bottom. With some difficulty, they pulled it up and towed it triumphantly behind them.

When they landed in front of Red Cliff, the first person Ikwa saw was Henson, who had stopped work on the foundation to watch the approaching boat. Seeing that he was not white, but brown like himself, Ikwa ran toward him with out-stretched hands.

"Innuit!" he cried, "Innuit!"—which is the name by which the Eskimos call themselves.

He was a wild-looking man with tangled black hair hanging about his shoulders and half covering his face, but his white teeth gleamed in a broad smile.

Henson took his hands, smiled back at him, and shook his head.

But Ikwa insisted that Henson was a member of the tribe, believing, as Henson discovered later, that he had wandered far away and forgotten the language and the ways of his brothers. At the moment, Henson couldn't understand a word. He knew only that the man was arguing.

"Matthew," he said, pointing to himself. "Not Innuit. Negro."

"Marri," repeated Ikwa, which was as close as he could come to saying "Matthew."

Then, ignoring whatever else Henson had said, he slapped his own chest and said, "Ikwa."

Like Ikwa, all the Eskimos who joined Peary in the months and years to come, accepted Henson as a brother. The name they gave Peary was *Pearyaksoah*, "the big Peary," while Henson was *Marri Palook*, "dear little Matthew."

VI

ESKIMOS TO THE RESCUE

As soon as Ikwa saw Josephine standing in the doorway beside her husband, he indicated by gestures that he wanted to trade wives. Peary, aware that this was an Eskimo custom and that Eskimos have been known to murder a man in order to get his wife, was careful to show no displeasure, and smiled as he shook his head. Ikwa, however, continued to press his demand, and while he argued, Josephine hurried into the house and came back with gifts laid out in preparation for native visitors.

To Ikwa's wife she gave a package of needles, and a small mirror to his three-year-old daughter, Annadore, who took one look at the strange face peering up at her and began to cry. Her mother, bending down to see what had frightened the child, saw the reflection of her daughter's face, lifted the looking glass, and for the first time in her life saw her own face. Grinning from ear to ear, she held the mirror in front of Ikwa, and both of them burst into peals of laughter.

Then Peary struck a match from the box Josephine handed him, and Ikwa's laughter stopped abruptly. He'd never seen a man make fire except by striking stones together, and he drew back in alarm, thinking that Peary was an *Angakok*, a magician whom it was dangerous to oppose. There was no more talk, then or thereafter, about trading wives.

Peary handed him the box of matches, took a small knife

from his pocket, and gave that also. This Ikwa took for a sign that the white man was a friendly *Angakok* who had wonderful gifts to bestow and, taking courage from the fact that a brother Eskimo was living with him, he went down to the shore for his kayak, his harpoon, and his dog.

Peary and Josephine saw to it that the couple had plenty of food, Henson pitched the tent near the house, blankets were provided, and the family spent a comfortable night. In the morning, Ikwa began to collect stones for an igloo. His wife helped, and late in the afternoon as she stopped to rest before moving a heavy boulder, suddenly shouted "Awick! Awick!" and pointed down the bay where the walrus were lying on a cake of ice.

Ikwa ran for his harpoon; Gibson and Cook got their rifles, and rowed rapidly toward their prey. Peary, who was able to get about on crutches, went out to see what was going on, and watched until they came back with a half-ton walrus.

Using his new knife, Ikwa skillfully removed the hide and saved it to cover the stones of his igloo so that it would be airtight. Josephine broiled some of the meat, but no one liked it.

The long summer days were coming to an end, and on August 29 they used artificial light for the first time. Before the months of darkness began, Peary wanted depots of food established on the icecap in preparation for the crossing next spring. Therefore, on August 31, he sent Astrup off on his skis to find the best way to get up there.

He was gone sixteen hours and came back to report that the best route would be from the northeast angle of McCormick Bay. Climbing the moraine had been difficult because of the shattered rocks deposited alongside the Sun Glacier, but above he'd gone ahead easily, except for a few hours when clouds hid the sun. Then it was impossible to tell where the snow ended and the sky began, and it was hard to keep going in that unbroken whitness. Except for the pressure of his skis against the snow, it was if he were walking on air. That was the only part of the trip he hadn't enjoyed.

The approach Astrup had found was a four-mile route up the bluffs at the end of a valley that Ikwa called "*Tooktoo*," the Eskimo word for reindeer. Peary had the large whaleboat loaded with supplies, left Henson to guard the house, and with his four other assistants, Josephine at the tiller, and Ikwa to guide them, they went up the bay to the valley. There they left Astrup, Gibson, and Verhoeff to deposit the boxes of food above the bluffs, and returned to Red Cliff, bringing back a deer Astrup had shot and another Ikwa had killed with the rifle Peary loaned him.

The valley was well named. Two days later they went up again after the rest of the reindeer herd they had seen there. Since Henson was to go with them, doors and windows were nailed shut, and Ikwa's wife, Mane, was told to explain to visitors that they had gone hunting. Ikwa tied his kayak to the whaleboat, Dr. Cook helped Peary into the stern beside Josephine, and off they sailed. When they landed, they saw footprints, but no other sign of the boys.

Peary decided they'd run into trouble, but was relieved to see no evidence of injury.

A tarpaulin was rigged up to make a tent and, while Josephine stayed to keep her husband company, Cook, Henson, and Ikwa went after deer. Cook had no luck, but Henson and Ikwa got nine in the two days they were there.

They removed the hides, cut off the meat and stowed it in the boat, laid the hides on top of it, and sailed back to Red Cliff. There Ikwa scraped off the fat and laid the skins fur side down to dry.

It was a good beginning for their winter suits, but they needed Eskimo women to make them. Peary began to fear he had relied too confidently on help from the natives. Perhaps he should have ordered fur clothes sent over from Copenhagen.

To add to his worry, the icecap party returned and reported that fierce wind and heavy snow had made it impossible to establish even one depot. Verhoeff's face had been frozen, Gibson's feet were blistered, and they wanted to know whether they should make another attempt.

Peary gave them a few days to recover, then sent them back to look for another ascent where dogs could be used to pull the supplies up on sledges.

Ikwa hitched his dog and one of Peary's Newfoundlands to his sledge, but the Newfoundland didn't like this new job. Verhoeff tied a rope to the dog's collar, Astrup ran beside him with a switch, and Gibson pushed the sledge forward until it hit the dog's legs and shoved him ahead.

Peary frowned. Ikwa laughed, and pointing southward said, "Mikkies amusuah!"

Henson, who had picked up a few Eskimo words from Ikwa and his wife, explained that, down in that direction, Ikwa claimed there were plenty of Eskimo dogs.

Peary had his largest whaleboat, named "Mary Peary" for his mother, stocked with food for a week. Again, Josephine, Dr. Cook, and Henson went along, with Ikwa to guide them to the most likely locations and explain their errand. The men took their Winchesters and Ikwa his harpoon, hoping they might see walrus. As it turned out, that was about all they did see.

Entering Inglefield Gulf, fifteen miles from McCormick Bay, they found icebergs drifting about, and between them large floes on which hundreds of the enormous animals were sunning themselves.

Peary took up his camera, and was so absorbed in snapping pictures that he forgot to cry "Stop!" until the boat was so near the ice that she ran up on it until he prow was high in the air. The startled walrus slid off with a splash that tipped the boat so far to port that she shipped water, and Henson was thrown flat on his back. Ikwa managed to get to his feet and stand long enough to throw out the line of his harpoon and sink the barb on the end of it into one of the beasts. In its effort to escape, it gave the line a jerk that righted the boat; but the barb held and the wounded walrus towed them this way and that, while Dr. Cook stood in the prow, ready to cut the line if the animal dived under an iceberg, and Peary and Henson tried to stop it by putting a bullet through its head.

The sound of the shots and the sight of their bleeding comrade infuriated the rest of the herd and, barking out their battle cry of "Ook! Ook!" they came up around the boat in bunches, bellowing and snorting as they tried to hook their great tusks over the side. Well-placed shots from Henson and Peary sent them plunging below, but immediately fifty to a hundred others rose to the attack. Dr. Cook picked up his Winchester, and the three men blazed away at the new bunch of monsters, while Ikwa pounded on the bottom of the boat with his harpoon to discourage any walrus from coming up underneath and capsizing it.

Josephine, thinking it an even chance whether she'd be shot or drowned, and so close to the gleaming tusks that she could have touched them with her hand, protected her husband's leg from the excited hunters and steadily reloaded the magazines of their repeaters until the herd retreated under the incessant fire, and the harpooned walrus had given up the ghost.

Not stopping to remove the ivory tusks, Henson and Ikwa rowed rapidly out of the dangerous area with the walrus in tow.

Opposite a cape near the outlet of the gulf, Ikwa raised his oar and, holding it so that it pointed toward the land, said that Eskimos lived there.

Peary looked eagerly, saw no one, and impatiently ordered the men to keep rowing.

But Ikwa insisted, waving his hand toward a wide area.

So they landed, and while Ikwa stayed with Peary to talk with any native who might happen by, Dr. Cook and Henson walked up the coast to look for igloos.

Twenty miles beyond the cape they found four igloos, but only one showed signs that anybody lived there, and it was empty. For a long time they waited, hoping its owner would come home, then gave up and walked back to the boat. No Eskimo had appeared there either, and new ice, rapidly forming on the surface of the water, defeated any further attempt to find native helpers.

They rowed on up the sound, where they found it necessary now and then to force their way through the thickening ice by breaking it with the boat hooks. When at last they reached Red Cliff, Peary learned that the icecap party also had met with defeat. No depots of food had been established. All the work of getting supplies up the cliffs must be done in the spring, and unless the boys could accomplish it with more speed than they'd shown to date, he couldn't start his three-month trip to the northeast coast early enough to get back before the *Kite* arrived to take them home.

But he managed to conceal the anxiety he felt because of their failure and his own. They'd all done the best they could. Now they must pitch in and finish the house, for in two weeks the sun would be halfway below the horizon and there wouldn't be light enough to work outdoors.

Soon the steady ring of hammers split the frosty air as the pre-cut boards were nailed to the outside of the uprights. Two layers of heavy tar paper nailed over them made an airtight outer shell for their winter home, leaving an airspace between outer and inner walls to retain the heat in their living quarters. They left a similar space between ceiling and roof, and covered the ceiling and walls with thick red blankets which made the room look as cozy and warm as it proved to be.

Windows were doubled, ventilators installed, and a section of flooring was removed between the two rooms to make a pit for the stove so that its heat would reach both, and air near the floor, usually the coldest part of a room, would be comfortably warm.

As soon as the stovepipe was connected so that it passed out through metal plates set in one of the windows, Peary lighted a fire. Ikwa, who had never seen such a big blaze, went into a war dance and kept touching the stove to feel how warm it was, until it burned his fingers and he gave a yelp of pain and surprise.

Their canned goods had been packed in wooden boxes which, with his usual foresight, Peary had ordered made exactly the same size. These were now piled row on row on top of the foundation of stone and turf Henson had built four feet from the house. When a canvas was stretched from the roof to the top of the pile, the building was surrounded on three sides by a corridor that looked like a grocery store. Later it would be banked with snow and reached by a tunnel such as Eskimos use to go in and out of their igloos.

From morning to night, Peary had limped around supervising the erection of their Arctic home. It was no palace— only twenty-one feet long, twelve feet wide, and eight feet from floor to ceiling—but it was a triumphant example of his engineering know-how. Even when the thermometer registered fifty degrees below zero, used air rose through the ventilating shafts in clouds of steam, and the cries heard were not "Shut the door!" but "Open the door!"

By October 13, the sun was less than halfway above the horizon, and Gibson, Astrup, and Cook used the swiftly diminishing light to go after deer. The evening before, Henson had caught sight of a flickering light far out on the bay. It looked like an Arctic will-o-the-wisp, but Ikwa said it was an Eskimo lantern. In the morning he started across the ice toward the place where the light had been. Five miles out he heard the "Huk! Huk!" of a dog driver and saw a sledge approaching. When it halted beside him, he gave a glad cry, for the man was the Eskimo who lived in the empty igloo Henson and Cook had found on the cape right after the walrus hunt. He had been told that Ikwa had gone off with white men (*Kabloonas*), and wanted to find out how they were treating him.

Ikwa gave a glowing account, saying that one of their Eskimo brothers had come north with the white men and was now living with them in peace and plenty.

By the time they reached the house, Peary was standing in the door, ready to greet the native who, he hoped, would be the first of several more. He led him into the house, pulled out a chair beside the table, placed a leg of venison before him, and entertained him over night.

Ikwa had introduced him as Now-ding-yah, and since he was the largest Eskimo Peary had ever seen, he always spoke of him as "Jumbo," a name easier to remember than Now-ding-yah. In the morning, Peary offered him a knife in exchange for one of his dogs, but the dog Peary wanted was the leader of the team, and Jumbo shook his head. Then Ikwa spoke to him. Jumbo nodded and held up three fingers, indicating that he would come again and bring three dogs.

When their visitor left, Ikwa went with him, and they spread the news that not only were Eskimos welcome at the white man's igloo, but that another Eskimo had been living with him a long time, and wanted to make friends with more members of the tribe.

In a couple of days Ikwa came back, saying that other natives where Now-ding-yah lived would soon visit Red Cliff. The next day they arrived—Now-dingh-yah and two other

Eskimos, Kyutah and Arro-tok-shua, with their sledges and six dogs. Arro-tok-shua was an old man, whose friendly face, above a collar of white fur that suggested a beard, gave him the nick-name of "Horace Greeley."

They sold Peary a sledge and two dogs for a couple of hunting knives, then left to get their families, and before the end of the week had built their igloos beside Ikwa's. Kyutah's wife was a quiet, industrious woman, but Mrs. Horace Greeley was a lively creature. When she saw Josephine, she burst into gales of laughter, shouting "Chimo Koonah! Chimo Koonah!" (Welcome woman), until finally Josephine said "Chimo! Chimo!" Then Mrs. Greeley seated herself beside the stove and talked on and on until Henson said she reminded him of Sairy Gamp in *Martin Chuzzlewit* and that is what she was called forever after.

The hunting party brought back ten deerskins. While Ikwa and Kyutah were scraping the hides, their wives chewed those previously scraped and dried, in order to remove the fat lodged between the sinews. This they did by folding each skin with the hair inside and chewing and sucking along the edge until the sinews were soft. They repeated the process until the entire skin had been chewed. Then Ikwa and Kyutah scraped them again with a dull tool to break the fibers and make the hides pliable enough to be cut and sewed.

It took two days to finish a buckskin. Then the women had to wait a day to give their jaws a rest before starting an-other pair of skins. It was a slow job. More Eskimo women were needed.

The sun had left, not to return until the middle of February, but in the few hours of twilight that remained, visitors began to arrive. Unfortunately there was only one woman among them. She and her husband, Ahnalka, who lived farther north than anyone else in Greenland, had driven two days to get there because they'd heard that their friend Kyutah was at Red Cliff and they wanted to see him.

Kyutah persuaded Ahnalka to stay by telling him that Peary would give food and whatever else he needed in return for his wife's help on the skins. She went to work with a will, and while she chewed Ahnalka started to build their igloo. Kyutah helped by sawing out blocks of frozen snow which Ahnalka laid in a large circle he had tramped out beside Kyutah's igloo. Henson, seeing that Kyutah was cutting blocks faster than Ahnalka could use them, carried them up the slope so that Ahnalka could build without stopping.

It was slow work, for each block had to be shaped so that it fitted tight against the blocks on each side and below, and each tier laid so that the wall curved inward. When he reached the critical spot where the key block must be inserted to complete the dome, Ahnalka went inside, shaped a block to fit the space and inserted it from below. (See next page.)

When the igloo was finished, Henson gave him a rubber overcoat to line the walls with; Gibson contributed a blanket and pieces of tarred roofing paper; Peary shaped the side of a cracker tin to make a lamp, and provided bits of blubber to burn in it. A small soapstone cooking pot, that an Eskimo had given Peary in return for a pair of smoked glasses, completed their furnishings and would answer all purposes until they could bring their household goods down from the North.

The supply of blubber was small, and when the full moon began to circle the horizon, Ahnalka borrowed a harpoon and started for the bay. Ikwa, who wanted sealskins for his stone igloo, his kayak, and new boots for his family, joined him. As they stood on the ice waiting for a seal to rise in the air hole beside them, loud barking diverted their attention. Looking toward shore, they saw Gibson trying to control the Newfoundland dog. A bucket of ice chipped from the stranded

Left: Eskimo cutting blocks from hard-packed snow to make a domed igloo; Below: At top, a domed igloo being built; at bottom, the cross-section shows the interior—the snow platform used for a bed; two frames above soapstone saucers hold seal oil and a wick, used as stoves for cooking the food hanging above them, and to warm the igloo. Skin lining keeps the heat from melting the walls

berg that supplied fresh water for cooking and drinking was on Gibson's sledge, and he was trying to make the dog pull it to the house.

A splash and a grunt brought the eyes of the hunters back to the air hole, and a quick throw of Ahnalka's harpoon gave them their first seal. They pulled it out, and while waiting hopefully for another, turned again to see what progress Gibson was making. He was making some, but only because he had the dog by the collar and was pulling both dog and sledge.

Ikwa explained that the white men didn't know how to drive dogs, and neither did Marri Palook.

Vigorous splashing sent them running to a large pool farther on, where two more seals were harpooned. Since this was all they needed, they went back to their igloos, where the blubber and meat were divided, and small shares presented to the other natives in accordance with the usual custom.

In the morning, Ahnalka harnessed six dogs to his sledge and went to look for Henson. He found him shoveling snow against the outside of the corridor and, when he looked up, Ahnalka pointed to the dogs and the sledge. Henson, who understood that he was about to receive a driving lesson, walked alongside while Ahnalka, swinging his whip, cried "Huk! Huk!" and off they went to a smooth stretch of snow beyond the igloos.

Driving dogs, Eskimo fashion, is a very difficult art. The dogs are fastened to the sledge by a toggle from which separate traces extend to each dog. When they are pulling, they spread out fanwise behind the king dog, which has earned its position by fighting the rest of the team. The driver has no reins. He walks or runs behind the sledge, holding to the upstanders, by which he controls it as a farmer controls his plow, and guides the dogs entirely by the tone of his voice, and a whip with a short stock and a lash thirty feet long.

The proper use of the whip is the hardest to learn. It must strike a dog lightly, for the purpose is not to punish but to encourage him to do his share of the pulling. Furthermore, the lash must be swung so that it will hit a particular dog on the tip of the ear.

Ahnalka handed Henson the whip and, shouting "Huk! Huk!," he gave it a swing, the lash whirled out, missed the dogs, and came coiling back around his shoulders. Ahnalka released him and once more Henson cracked the long whip, but only succeeded in showering the dogs with snow. Not knowing what was expected of them, they settled down on their haunches.

Henson, nothing daunted, bellowed "Huk! Huk!" but the dogs didn't move. Ahnalka repeated the command deep in his throat, and the dogs, hearing the tone to which they were accustomed, got up. Imitating Ahnalka's voice, Henson tried

Swinging the whip correctly is the most difficult part of driving a dog team (from a model)

again. This time the lash flew back and circled Ahnalka's neck.

Matt decided he'd better stop before he did any more damage. He helped Ahnalka uncoil the lash, handed him the whip and, in spite of Ahnalka's protest, started for the house.

On the way he saw two twelve-year-old boys, Sipsu and Ahnidloo, lashing away at mounds of snow arranged like a dog team. "So that's how they learn the trick," he said to himself. He arranged a set on the other side of the house where there was plenty of room, and every light day he swung his whip until, by spring, he could hit the mark every time.

Ever since their arrival, Josephine had been the cook, roasting venison, baking bread, pies, and cakes, making stews, puddings, and doughnuts for six ravenous men. But now that the hunting season had ended, she turned the job over to Henson except for the daily batch of bread on which her husband insisted because he believed it prevented scurvy, a miserable disease and sometimes fatal, from which all previous Arctic expeditions had suffered. Holiday dinners also remained her specialty.

For Thanksgiving she gave them a feast equal to any they might have enjoyed at home—broiled seafowl with green peas, venison pie, hot biscuits, plum pudding with brandy sauce, apricot pandowdy, apple pie, pineapple, candy, coffee, whiskey cocktails, and Rhine wine.

It was a happy occasion for all of them, but Peary, more than anyone else, had much to be thankful for. That morning he had walked five miles without his cane, and though his leg swelled a little, it was not painful. The hunting season had yielded all the skins he needed, and he was surrounded by Eskimos whom he described as his "faithful servants." The only part of his program not achieved was the establishment of food depots on the icecap, but he knew that, with the help of the natives, everything would be up there in time to make the early start he had planned.

VII

ACROSS THE FROZEN DESERT

After Thanksgiving, the main room was turned into a workshop where the boys and the Eskimos made sledges and skis. Peary constructed an odometer. This was a wheel to be attached to the rear of a sledge, where its revolutions measured the distance traveled. Until now, bracket lamps had given enough light. But on December first, a big lamp, which the Eskimos called the "*mickaninny sukinah*" (baby sun), was added, and kept burning from eight in the morning until ten at night. It took some time to adjust to the endless darkness. Every now and then one or another would think, "It's hard to do this by lamplight. I'll wait until tomorrow," forgetting for the moment that there would be no daylight in the morning.

The Eskimos were drawn to the lighted room, and the hours slipped pleasantly away as they stood by watching the boys use tools the like of which they'd never seen, while the boys used their growing knowledge of Eskimo words to talk and laugh with their guests.

In her small bedroom, the society belle from Washington sat on the edge of her bunk basting up sample garments of outing flannel to be tried on and fitted before the precious skins were cut. On the floor, at her feet, two Eskimo women and a girl sewed industriously—Ahnalka's wife, so skillful that Josephine called her "The Daisy"; Ikwa's wife, Mane, and twelve-year-old Tooky who had come back with Ahnalka and

"The Daisy" when they brought their household goods down from the North. "The Daisy" and Mane each had a baby boy in her hood, and rocked gently back and forth, sometimes crooning softly if the child became restless.

With the steel needles and thimbles Josephine gave them, they could work faster than with the bone needles and clumsy sealskin thimbles they'd always used. But the stitches had to be so close together that no icy wind could find its way between them, and Josephine examined each seam to make sure it was airtight. If she found that it was not, the seamstress had to go over it again and make it so.

The thread the *Kabloonas* had brought was not strong enough to hold the tough skins together, so the women made their own, Eskimo fashion, by splitting deer sinews, which little Annadore chewed until they were flexible. As the pretty child crouched beside her mother, chewing as contentedly as

Eskimo woman chewing sealskin for the sole of a boot

if she were chewing gum, Josephine often wanted to take her on her lap, but was afraid of the consequences.

Although her native helpers were good-natured and surprisingly gay, she disliked having them in her room, for their bodies had a strong odor, due to their diet of blubber and seal, and their hair and clothing were full of lice. She kept them as far as possible from her bed, and when their work for the day was over, swept the floor with her silver-handled whisk broom lashed to an alpenstock, for she'd forgotten to bring a broom. Then she sprinkled the floor with a solution of corrosive sublimate Dr. Cook had provided, and this, plus an alcohol rub before going to bed, kept Peary and herself free of the pests.

The Eskimos also had a method of delousing which, though not entirely successful, left them with no more of the parasites than are harbored by sixty per cent of the white race. Every few days the women took clothes and bedding outside for an hour, after which the lice had frozen and could be beaten out. On the whole, the Eskimos were reasonably clean. It was impossible for them to bathe because the only pots in which ice or snow could be melted held little more than a cupful of water. But they slept naked, the dirt rubbed off on the skins on which they lay, and the women cleaned the bedding by laying it on the ground and kneading snow into it with their feet, a process which made the furs as fluffy and fresh as if they'd just come from a store.

As for their body odor, it was not unpleasant once you got used to it. Peary and the boys even found it welcome when they traveled from village to village in the winter months, for it meant warmth, food, and happy laughter in the igloos where they stopped for the night.

Due almost entirely to these "faithful servants" who worked nine or ten hours a day without complaint, three pairs of skis were ready for use by December 21; also a second sledge with ivory-shod runners and ivory and horn braces fashioned by Ikwa and Ahnalka from narwhal and walrus tusks. In Josephine's department, a complete outfit of clothing had been finished, consisting of a hooded deerskin jacket, or *kooletah*, and knee trousers of deerskin together with the sealskin boots, or *kamiks*, into which the trousers were to be tucked.

In such a costume, with a skirt modestly covering the trousers, and woolen stockings inside the *kamiks*, Josephine went out to inspect her fox traps in temperatures as low as forty-five degrees below zero. "Yet I have felt much colder out shopping at home when the temperature was only a little below the freezing point," she wrote in her diary.

In preparation for Christmas, Josephine decorated the family photographs on the wall of their bedroom with red, white, and blue ribbons, and felt for the first time how far away they were from those they loved. The boys removed all lumber and tools from the big room, scrubbed the floor, made candelabra to light up the corners, and hung flags along the walls.

As she looked at the flags, bright and gay in the lamplight, Josephine suddenly remembered what Astrup had said about cloudy days on the icecap. Using a white silk handkerchief and a piece of blue silk, from one of her tea gowns, cut in the shape of a star, she made a small flag, or guidon, such as the Army used to show the position of the leader or guide.

At nine o'clock on Christmas Eve, she put cakes, cookies, nuts, and raisins on the table. Peary added a big bowl of milk punch, which, as he had hoped, served to offset any pangs of homesickness the members of his party might feel. Each assistant received a book from him, and for Josephine he had carved two ivory hairpins to hold her heavy braids in place. In return, she handed him a small parcel tied with red ribbon.

When he saw what was in it, he gave an exclamation of

pleasure, and waved the guidon above his head. Astrup, quick to realize that this would take care of that lost horizon, led the boys in three cheers for Mrs. Peary.

On New Year's Eve, the Eskimos were invited to join in the celebration, and stared with open-mouthed astonishment at Josephine, who was wearing a low-cut black and yellow taffeta tea gown and waving a fan, while outside the wind howled, and snow swirled in blinding sheets about the nearly buried house.

Throughout the winter, groups of Eskimos came to visit friends who were living at Red Cliff, and to see Marri Palook, the Eskimo brother of whom they had heard. A few of them stayed, among them Ikwa's brother, Kyo.

Ikwa did not want Kyo living in their peaceful colony, and only brought him because Kyo threatened to kill him unless he did so. But Kyo behaved himself and took pains to make himself useful. He made a broom out of the wings of eider ducks, used it whenever he saw shavings or sawdust on the floor, scooped the ashes out of the stove pit, and worked like such a willing slave that Peary called him "Uncle Tom." When he complained that Ikwa's igloo was too small, he was allowed to sleep in the room with the boys. Only later did Peary discover that Kyo claimed to be an *Angakok* whom the natives feared, and was given to violent outbursts of temper during which he had committed more than one murder.

Their many visitors made it possible to begin work on the anthropological exhibit ordered for the Chicago World's Fair. Every Eskimo was measured by Dr. Cook and photographed by Peary. While Henson manipulated the flashlight, Peary took front, rear, and side views of men, women, and children, all naked except for a loin cloth.

The natives couldn't understand why he wanted to see them without clothes, and hesitated to strip until finally they got it into their heads that Pearyaksoah wanted to make more people like them. After that, each new arrival was told the important part he would play in this great enterprise, and when his photographs had been taken, he bragged about them to an attentive audience.

To their surprise, Peary's party discovered that the Great Night was not the long period of gloom and boredom they had dreaded. For one thing, they were kept busy on work that was new to them and held their attention. Each one tried to outdo the others in building the most practical sledge—light, yet strong enough to bear the loads required.

When it was moonlight, they practiced traveling on skis and snowshoes under Astrup's expert instructions, or had wrist-pulling matches and tugs of war with the natives who for generations had enjoyed such contests.

All these activities made the time pass so quickly that before they realized it, the winter was almost over and soon the sun would rise again. To celebrate that great event, Peary, Astrup, and Dr. Cook climbed to the icecap the night before, and used the occasion to try out their camp stove and sleeping bags.

Unfortunately none of them knew how to construct a domed igloo, so the walls of their shelter were laid up in a rectangle with skis across them to support blocks of snow for a roof. This done, they had supper, then took off their fur clothing, and crawled into their sleeping bags.

During the night a heavy snowfall crushed the roof and wall at one end of their igloo, so that they woke to find themselves, their clothing, and all their food and equipment completely buried. Peary and Cook at last managed to force their way out, but Astrup couldn't free himself. Peary, still in his sleeping bag, rolled outside, got the shovel, removed the snow around Astrup and, with Cook's help, released him. By nine o'clock in the morning, Peary had dug out a *kooletah*, trousers, and *kamiks* which Astrup, more warmly dressed than Peary, who wore only his undershirt, put on after getting out of his sleeping bag. Then he dug out another set for Cook.

While his two assistants warmed themselves by trotting up and down, Peary dug out tea, sugar, milk, the stove, and a kettle. By the time the stove was lit and the kettle filled with snow and put on to boil, the southern sky was aglow, and a dazzling spot of yellow showed where the sun was about to rise. Peary took the guidon and two American flags from the pocket of his bag, fastened then to an alpenstock and two skis driven into the snow, and the banners blew out in a bright salute to the God of Day.

For many minutes the three men watched with exultant joy as the golden orb began its journey around the horizon. Then they turned to their hot tea and, as soon as Peary had drained his cup, he crawled out of his bag.

It was no fun standing in the biting wind with nothing on but an undershirt while he worked his way into frozen drawers, socks, jackets, and trousers. Then and there he made up his mind that this was the last time he would expose himself to such an ordeal. On the way back to Red Cliff, he devised a method by which, with drawstrings added to jackets and trousers, they could sleep in their clothes. He never used a sleeping bag again.

The work of sledging supplies for the twelve-hundred-mile trip on the icecap began early in April. Gibson went up to Tooktoo Valley with the first load, taking Kessuh along to drive the dogs. Kessuh was one of the "dudes" from Cape York, so called because of the fine clothing they wore on their first visit to Red Cliff.

A few days later, Henson and Astrup followed with three loads, accompanied by Kyo and Kuku, a young hunter who was courting Josephine's twelve-year-old seamstress, Tooky. Leaving Astrup and the Eskimos to move everything further up the valley, Henson brought back his sledge with its eight-dog team, filled it with cans of pemmican, and drove off again.

The dogs they were using belonged to the natives, and Peary needed at least twenty for his own use on the icecap. Kessuh sold him five, and his friend Tala-ko-teah, who arrived at Red Cliff soon afterward, sold four.

Before Tala-ko-teah left, to return to Cape York, Peary handed him two letters to be passed on to the first Dundee captain who dropped anchor there, so that he, in turn, could mail them when he reached London. No previous explorer ever had given a native such a responsible job, and thus Tala-ko-teah became the first Eskimo mail carrier, with the gift of a hatchet as postage. He proved to be worthy of Peary's belief in his honesty. A year later, the letters were delivered in Philadelphia, and thereafter Tala-ko-teah was called "George Washington."

By carefully questioning every native who came to Red Cliff during the winter, Peary had discovered who owned the best dogs and what he would have to pay for them. Taking Josephine along for companionship, and with Kyo as driver, he started off to visit all the settlements in the vicinity. Panikpah, one of the Eskimos who had built an igloo in the fast-growing colony around Red Cliff, went with them until he came to the trail that went across Inglefield Gulf to his father's home.

At the first village where Peary stopped, he found Ahng-odo-blaho, known as "the dog man" because he had three dogs trained to fight polar bear, the "tiger of the North." Peary was able to get all three in return for a saw and a rifle with ammunition. Angh-odo-blaho, like Panikpah and twelve-year-old Sipsu, proved to be among Peary's most valuable allies in his effort to reach the Pole.

At the next village, Peary made a point of calling on Merk-to-shar, the one-eyed hunter whose praises had been sung by every visitor to Red Cliff. Merk-to-shar himself had never condescended to come there, and Peary was curious to discover whether he regarded the white men as intruders. The two men were soon on the best of terms, however, and Peary secured two dogs from Merk-to-shar's famous pack.

Farther along the coast, he stopped at the hamlet where Panikpah was visiting, and was received with great ceremony by the father, who was headman of the little community. Young Sipsu also was staying there, and from him Peary learned that his father had dogs and sealskins he was willing to sell. His igloo, Sipsu said, was near the shore several miles beyond. As a result of this information, Peary returned to Red Cliff with eleven new dogs and a sledge load of sealskins in prime condition.

There Astrup reported that during his absence most of the food and equipment had been taken to the valley and carried up the half-mile bluff at its northern end. The steep, stony path made the use of sledges impossible, and each man bent his back under whatever weight he could bear until everything had been deposited on a small plateau at the top. After such exhausting work everyone needed a day off—natives as well as the white assistants.

The icecap was fifteen miles beyond the plateau, but the Eskimos refused to go farther. Fierce winds had blown against them on every upward trip—a sign, they said, that Kokoyah, the Devil of the Icecap, was angry and trying to drive them back.

Kyo explained their fear by saying that the Devil ate men who invaded his territory.

Henson, who had read Peary's account of his experience with crevasses in 1886, realized that these were the basis of the Eskimos' superstition, and sympathized with their fear of a danger that was real. But when Kyo began to terrify the natives by telling them that Kokoyah would punish the white men by destroying Red Cliff and all who lived there, Henson was angry and did his best to prevent their leaving. He finally persuaded half a dozen to wait until everything needed for the trip was on top of the bluff. The others hurried away, with the exception of Kyo, and the fact that he stayed revealed him as the fraud he was. His only purpose had been to keep the Eskimos in subjection by showing that he was in touch with the spirits that controlled their destiny.

On the third of May, Peary and Henson placed the last hundred pounds of food on the eighteen-foot sledge, and followed the well-worn trail to Tooktoo Valley. At the foot of the bluff, they emptied the sledge, Peary took it on his back, Henson tucked a twenty-five-pound tin under each arm, and they made their way to the top. There they found the boys asleep, and their dogs, which they'd led up the day before, tethered nearby. Peary swung the sledge to the ground, and the sound woke them. They said everything had been backed up to the foot of the ravine through which they could be sledged to the Cache Camp, two and a half miles above. Peary, knowing that they must be exhausted, told them to go back to sleep while he and Matt went down for the rest of their load.

It took two days to move the half ton of supplies up the steep trail to Cache Camp. Henson and Gibson went up with the first load, and stayed to build an igloo to shelter the party while provisions, fuel, and equipment were sorted and the weight distributed among the sledges.

Henson's heel had been frozen a few days before, and Peary, noticing that he was limping, asked Dr. Cook to look at it. When the doctor decided that it wouldn't be safe for Matt to go on, Peary frowned. He had counted on Henson's going all the way, for he had had more experience than the others in handling the fierce Eskimo dogs, and was the only assistant who could drive.

On the other hand, it would be a comfort to know that he was at Red Cliff with Josephine. Peary commissioned Henson to act as her guardian, and to see that she got safely home if he did not return.

The other assistants went on with Peary to help with the dogs until they got used to their new masters, and would obey them. For the first ten days, the pain in Peary's leg was almost intolerable, due to the unaccustomed exercise involved in snowshoeing and chasing the unruly animals. Night after night, they got loose by gnawing through their traces or the strap by which they were tethered. Sometimes they could be lured within reach by bits of pemmican scattered on the snow. Then while one boy made a lunge for the dog's neck and pressed his nose into the snow, another put on its harness. By that method a man might escape without being bitten more than once or twice.

Other dogs had to be caught with a double lasso, and the ropes tightened by two boys before the brute's head could be forced to the ground by a third, while a fourth harnessed him. "Talk about lassoing wild steers in Texas," said Gibson, "it doesn't compare with rounding up Eskimo dogs!" Muzzles designed by Peary at last put an end to the worst part of this exhausting performance.

In order to make the dogs go, Peary, followed by three that knew him best, and holding a line attached to the sled to help them pull, walked at the head of the procession, while Astrup ran beside the dogs carrying a whip to urge them on. The other sledges were lashed together and driven by Gibson, Verhoeff, and Dr. Cook in the same fashion.

By the time they had covered a hundred and thirty miles, the system was working fairly well, and Gibson, Verhoeff, and Cook turned back with two dogs and a sledge carrying enough food for twelve days. Astrup, because he was an expert on skis, went on with Peary.

They traveled in what they called night, when the sun was behind them. At the end of each march, they rubbed vaseline into their faces, chapped by the wind that always blows on the icecap, put drops of opium solution into their eyes, aching from the glare of the sun on the snow, and covered them with a strip of fur so that they could sleep in darkness.

They had neither tent nor sleeping bags. A trench in the snow with their alcohol stove at one end, protected by a tarpaulin, served as a kitchen. They tightened the drawstrings around waist and knees, pulled their arms through the wide armholes, and slept with their hands folded on their chests. When it snowed, they snuggled against their sledges, as Peary and Maigaard had done years before.

There was plenty of hardship, all of it new to Astrup and some of it to Peary, but no serious danger threatened them until they came to headlands overlooking inlets along the north coast into which great glaciers were flowing.

Peary knew that under the broad expanse of snow, crevasses were hidden, but although he went farther inland and changed direction again and again hoping to avoid them, four dogs dropped out of sight and only their traces saved them from falling to the bottom of the abyss. Then a sledge, carrying all their hardtack and a hundred pounds of pemmican, sank in, but fortunately caught on a ledge of ice and was hauled to safety.

As they toiled cautiously onward, the sun's path around the horizon moved upward. At last the temperature rose to seventy-seven degrees. They stopped, and stripped for a refreshing rubdown with snow. The next day was equally warm, and they tossed their fur clothing on top of the sledges. Soon afterward the sky became clouded, the horizon disappeared, and the bright blue star on Peary's guidon was a welcome sight to Astrup. Even the dogs traveled faster because of it, for they too felt the depression caused by unbroken whiteness.

Victoria Inlet lay ahead of them, and Peary kept to the

southeast in order to flank the glacier and the circle of crevasses at its head. Three days later, a wide opening to the
northeast caught his eye. Through it he could see no blink
from the icecap, nor vapor indicating land. Perhaps it looked
down on the East Greenland Sea. He changed their direction,
and they headed toward it.

From the top of a moraine that extended a long distance
into the icecap, Peary saw a summit that appeared to command a view through the gap and, stopping only long enough
to put on his snowshoes, he left Astrup to care for the dogs
and slid down to the land. Here a conglomeration of sharp
stones made snowshoes impossible, and he went ahead wearing only his sealskin *kamiks*.

Within a mile he saw traces of musk oxen, and some distance beyond stopped to examine a patch of grass where bits of
their wool were scattered. From here on, their trails were as
thick as sheep paths in a New England pasture, and he re-
joiced, not only because this was a chance for them to get
fresh meat, but because by following the trails he no longer
had to walk over rocks which already had cut through his
kamiks and bruised the soles of his feet.

He kept going for five miles, but the summit from which
he had hoped to see the northeast coast of Greenland seemed
to recede as he advanced, and the condition of his *kamiks*
made it unwise to go further. He patched them with his sealskin mittens and knitted skullcap, but long before he reached
the camp on the moraine he had to use whatever part of his
clothing he could spare to protect his feet. "It was," he writes,
"with the feeling of one who is suddenly relieved from an
excruciating toothache, that I stepped from the ragged rocks
up onto the Inland Ice and strapped on my snowshoes."

After a hot meal and a short sleep, the first Peary had
had in twenty-three hours, he prepared for a week-long trip
with Astrup and the dogs, which couldn't be left unattended.

Sledges would be useless on the rocky route, so, with packs on their backs, they descended the moraine.

After the clear, cold air of the icecap, the almost tropical heat below sapped their energy as they toiled along like beasts of burden. When at last they climbed the summit that was their goal, it was only to find that the view to the east was blocked by other summits.

Footsore and exhausted, they ate a little hardtack, washed it down with hot tea, fed the dogs, and slept for a few hours. Then, keeping along the crest of the ridge, they finally made out, far ahead, what appeared to be the headlands of an inlet from the sea. With renewed hope, they pressed on, but summit after summit intervened.

Peary had begun to worry about food for his dogs, especially Pau, the leader of the team, who was dragging along, eyes dull, tail down, showing that he was far from well.

The men began to look for musk oxen as keenly as they looked for an opening to the coast, for the loss of even one of their dogs would be a calamity.

They rested a few hours. Soon after they started again, Peary stopped and looked closely at a couple of brown spots in the valley. Maybe they were rocks. But presently they moved. He pointed them out to Astrup. Full of anticipation, they led the dogs down between the banks of a ravine that hid them until they were within half a mile of the oxen. Here Peary dropped his pack, took his Winchester, and telling Astrup to keep the dogs quiet, crept cautiously toward the animals. So much depended on success that Peary had an attack of buck fever. His first shots only wounded the ox at which he aimed. It came charging toward him, but his third shot brought it down, and its companion dropped soon afterward.

The dogs had heard the shots and were wild with excitement. Astrup tied the dogs to keep them out of the way while

Musk oxen

the great shaggy beasts were being skinned. As soon as one of
the huge hindquarters was ready, Peary took it down to the
dogs, and watched with sympathetic pleasure as they devoured
the warm, bloody meat.

Meanwhile, the skins had been spread on a patch of grass,
close to a little stream. While Peary stretched himself out on
the fur couch, Astrup set up the stove and broiled sirloin
steaks until they could eat no more. Neither dogs nor men
were in any condition to travel after such a meal, and they
rested several hours before continuing their journey.

They climbed a few more summits, always expecting the
next one would give them the long-desired view, until at last
they found themselves on the edge of a towering cliff, and saw
"stretching away to the horizon the great ice fields of the
Arctic Ocean."

Peary's keen eyes swept westward, and he thought he saw the outlet of the channel of which they'd caught glimpses on their left, ever since they had left Victoria Inlet. He assumed that it was a continuation of the inlet and, therefore, marked the northern coast of Greenland. In that case, the mountains beyond rose from islands, and he was burning with a desire to find out how far they extended toward the Pole. But for the present he had to be satisfied with what he already had discovered. (See map, page 134.)

Years later, other explorers found that Peary's conclusions were wrong. It was not the Arctic Ocean he had seen from the towering cliff. He was a hundred miles from the coast; what he had seen was the broadening of a long fjord. The channel of water he thought marked the north coast of Greenland was above sea level, and whatever water he saw in it was drainage from the slopes above. But explorers who discovered these errors found his conclusions justified by the conformation of the landscape within sight, and had nothing but praise for the surveys and sketch maps he made of the immediate vicinity.

Putting further speculation aside, Peary made the observations necessary to establish the latitude and longitude of the point they had attained. That done, he got out a flask of brandy, poured some for Astrup and himself, and christened the bay "Independence Bay," because they had reached it on the fourth of July. A glacier on their right was named "Academy Glacier" in honor of the Academy of Natural Sciences of Philadelphia and, being a Naval officer, naturally he called the spot where they were standing "Navy Cliff."

Here a cairn was built; an account of the expedition, its aims and members, placed inside; the pole from which his guidon was still flying was set among the stones on top; two American flags were added, and they spread their colors triumphantly as a token of hope fulfilled.

Stopping only long enough to remove the flags, and put a

handful of flowers between the stones where the flagpole had been, they took one last look at the magnificent panorama, and turned toward home.

The prize was won, the first flush of success faded, and the trip back was tedious and uneventful.

At Red Cliff, on the contrary, there was plenty of excitement, and Josephine had reason to be thankful that Henson was there. The shouts of "Matthew has returned," that had wakened her one morning soon after her husband's departure, had dispelled one anxiety, for she knew that the presence of this man whom the Eskimos loved would prevent any unwelcome advances.

The Eskimos, especially Kyo, did not love Dr. Cook. Kyo resented the presence of another medicine man as a threat to his prestige.

Their dislike became fear when the doctor, while cleaning his rifle, accidentally sent a shot through the roof, where Eskimo mothers had taken their babies to play in the sun. Josephine herself was frightened, for she knew that Henson also was sunning himself up here. His heel, which at first had threatened to develop into a chronic running sore, had improved under Dr. Cook's care until it was almost healed, and Josephine was planning to take him with her to Tooktoo Valley and camp there so that she would be on hand to welcome her husband as soon as he came down from the icecap. She was greatly relieved, therefore, to learn that the shot missed him; also that no one else had been hit.

But Kyo used the accident as a means of adding to the Eskimos' terror. On the side of the house toward the igloos, there was a window that had been closed all winter. Now that the weather was warm, the sash was raised, and Kyo claimed that the doctor was preparing to fire his rifle through it. Bullets would not hurt him, he said, because Kokoyah was his friend, and would not let him die. But if the doctor killed a single Eskimo, Kokoyah would, if Kyo asked it, sink the big ship on its way home and all the white people on board would drown.

Peace was restored when Cook gave him some wood he needed to repair his kayak, but then he went on to tell Josephine that he had had a dream in which he saw only one man returning from the icecap, and it was not Pearyaksoah. The other Eskimos, who believed Kyo's claim that his dreams foretold the future, shook their heads and said mournfully, "The great Peary is dead."

To escape such gloomy forebodings, Josephine, already anxious enough about her husband, decided to leave Red Cliff at once.

The next morning, she sent Henson and Ikwa ahead with camping equipment and enough food to last until August 6, expecting her husband would be back by then at the latest, for he'd told her he would return around the first of the month. She spent the rest of the day cleaning the little bedroom and washing the curtains so that it would look homelike and cozy. In the evening, Dr. Cook walked the fifteen miles to the valley with her. It was raining and the tent was too small to offer shelter, so he went back on Ikwa's sledge.

As soon as the weather cleared, Josephine decided to start for the hut on the crest of the bluff where her husband had left a small cache of food. She wrote a note, telling him she was waiting to greet him a few miles below, put a can of fruit and a small flask of brandy in her bag, and covered them with an American flag. Then she and Henson started out.

To reach the trail to the icecap they had to cross a swift river, and they timed their departure to reach it at low tide. Even so, the icy water came above Josephine's knees, and all that saved her from being swept off her feet by the strong current was a boat hook she'd brought, on which to raise the flag over the hut.

Once across, they put on dry stockings, and followed the trail up the bluff. There they hoisted the flag, left the fruit and brandy with Josephine's note propped against it, and started back. But they found that the tide had risen, and wading the river was out of the question. So they went upstream to a lake and, as she sat beside it, looking down on the valley gay with yellow poppies, Josephine felt that no harm could befall them in such smiling surroundings. But when they again reached the crossing place, they saw to their dismay that the tide was a high low tide and the rocks were still under water.

A cold fog had blotted out the sun, and to get above it they climbed the bluff, stopped at the hut for a small drink of brandy to take the chill out of their bones, and went several miles up the ravine beyond. There they found warm sunshine, but their enjoyment was marred by the swarms of mosquitoes it had attracted. Peary and Astrup, coasting down the western slope of the icecap, were far more comfortable.

Just before noon, Josephine and Matt went back down the river, where they were met by the welcome sight of the rocks that marked the way across. Numb with cold, from the waist down, they got to the other side, ran the three miles to the tent, and, after all, suffered no ill effects from their adventure.

Two days later, Josephine was awakened by a shrill whistle followed by footsteps. It was an Eskimo.

"The big ship has come," he said.

"Not so," Josephine answered, and reached for her rifle.

"Me not lie," he said, as he pushed his shaggy head into the tent, tossed her a bundle of letters, and went off. They were all from her family, begging her to come home on the *Kite* even if her husband had not returned when it was ready to sail.

What were they thinking of, she wondered? Didn't they realize that her husband's heart would be broken if he came back and found she had deserted him? She'd wait all winter, if necessary. She was sure Matt would wait too, and what the Eskimos could endure during the winter months, they could endure also.

Finally she did consent to go back to Red Cliff because Dr. Cook had come up in the whaleboat and reported that the Eskimos were quarreling among themselves and even knifing each other, and Henson was needed to keep them in order. Acting on Henson's advice, she stayed in a cabin on board the ship, but she told Captain Pike and Professor Heilprin, who had come on the *Kite*, that when the ice in the bay made it necessary for them to leave, she would go ashore and wait with Henson until her husband returned.

On August 5, the Professor led a relief party to the icecap in order to give the two explorers any help they might need. Early the next morning, the door of Josephine's cabin banged open, and she found herself in her husband's arms.

On deck there were cheers and congratulations as Astrup followed and, on the shore, the Eskimos were shouting derisively at Kyo for, in spite of his prophetic dream, Pearyaksoah had come back alive.

But there was another man in the party who was not so lucky. When it was time for the *Kite* to sail, there was no sign of Verhoeff. Gibson said he had left him at Five Glacier Valley, which he planned to cross to visit an Eskimo village on the coast. Gibson had gone to meet him there, but no one had seen him. (See map, page 112.)

While Peary and one party examined every mile of the coast in both directions, Gibson, with five Eskimos, climbed to the edge of the nearest glacier and walked down beside it.

Here, at last, traces of Verhoeff were found. Ikwa discovered footprints, and followed them onto the glacier until they disappeared. Further search showed no tracks leaving it. The conclusion was inevitable. Kokoyah had swallowed him.

But Peary clung to the hope that the young man was still alive. He left a supply of food beside the glacier, and gave Red Cliff to Ikwa and his wife, who promised to make a home for Verhoeff if he returned.

With heavy hearts, Peary and Josephine finished their packing, gave the Eskimos everything they didn't want to take home, together with wood, knives, iron kettles, and other prized articles that had been sent on the *Kite* by friends in Philadelphia.

The voyage started under a cloud of sorrow that was only partially dispelled by the uproarious welcome they received when they arrived in New York. The man who had been ridiculed for the audacity of his undertaking was now hailed as a hero, and his crossing of North Greenland won acclaim from the President of the Royal Geographic Society in London as "an achievement second only to the attainment of the Pole."

VIII

TEMPTING THE DEVIL

Discovery of the Pole was, of course, Peary's primary aim, but he wasn't ready to admit it yet, fearing that if his purpose were known, some other explorer might steal the honor from him as Nansen had done when he made the first crossing of Greenland. In spite of his effort to avoid competition, however, he soon learned that he had a rival, and again it was Nansen, who was about to start for the Arctic in a ship designed to float in the icepack on a current which he believed would carry him across the top of the world.

Peary was equally certain that he could get there by way of the chain of islands that he believed stretched a long distance in that direction. But if he were to reach the goal ahead of Nansen, he must start as soon as possible. Already the Norwegian government had provided two-thirds of the money Nansen needed, and the balance had been raised with the help of a generous donation from the King.

Not daring to count on any such help from his own government, Peary continued to play his cards close to his chest. His application to the Navy for a three-year leave stated only that he intended to return to Navy Cliff, and from there send one party south to close the five-hundred-mile gap on present maps of the Greenland coast, and another party north to discover how far the archipelago extended. He had reason to believe that the prospect of locating America's northeast shore line would appeal to the Navy. But it did not.

"You're going to stay right here and do your duty!" exclaimed the head of the Civil Engineer Corps, banging his fist on the desk.

Again the Academy of Natural Sciences of Philadelphia came to the rescue. Its president, General Isaac Wistar, questioned Peary as to the probable cost of the expedition, and was especially interested in the possibility that Greenland might extend far to the north and that a study of glacial deposits might yield information as to the past history of the region.

"Peary," he said, "I believe you should have the opportunity to carry out your project."

General Wistar called on the Secretary of the Navy, B. F. Tracy, who had arranged for Peary's leave in 1891. Two other members of the Academy went to Grover Cleveland, recently elected to the presidency, though not yet inaugurated, and convinced him that the expedition, if carried out, would make an important addition to geographical knowledge. As a result of this double-barreled assault, the leave was granted.

This accomplished, Peary was faced with the problem of financing his undertaking. Widespread interest in his Arctic experience, which had been shared by his wife, the first white woman to venture so far north, suggested that lectures would be well attended. He consulted the head of a leading lecture bureau, only to be told that it was too late in the season to arrange a successful tour. Too late, also, Peary realized, to raise the money he needed by any other means. He outlined what he had to offer; his enthusiasm was contagious; the manager notified his list of sponsors, and the number who wanted to add the name of the famous explorer to their lecture series broke all records.

Peary's plan for his tour revealed unexpected talent as a showman. He had brought back the six dogs that survived the trip across the icecap, and was keeping them tethered next to his office in the Navy Yard. He was fond of them and hadn't wanted to leave them behind. Now he thought of a way to use them.

He asked Henson to accompany him on the tour, and, wearing his fur suit, drive the dogs around the city for an hour or two before each lecture. Henson was highly amused by the suggestion, but a little skeptical as to how the dogs would react. However, the hubbub that developed whenever they gave chase to a cat provided many a lively story for the press, and aroused curiosity that brought people to the lectures who otherwise might not have come.

In his first Philadelphia lecture, Peary experimented with a program that was so highly praised by press and public that he continued to use it. Setting the stage to look like an Eskimo village, and wearing his Arctic costume, he entertained his audience by throwing on the screen pictures of Red Cliff where his party had enjoyed such warmth and good cheer, of the moonlit landscapes that relieved the darkness of the Great Night, of Eskimos at work and play, of flowers growing among rocks beside the glaciers, magnificent views from Navy Cliff, and pictures of the cairn with his guidon and the Stars and Stripes flying above it.

When the applause died down, he showed pictures of Mrs. Peary who, he explained, had made the guidon that led the way across those twelve hundred miles.

"Here," said a man in one of the audiences, offering his opera glasses to the woman beside him, "don't you want to have a look at his wife's face? She's the one I'm interested in. Think of a woman going up there!"

"I enjoyed every minute of it," said Josephine, with a smile, as she accepted the glasses from her startled neighbor.

The climax came when the lights were turned on, and Henson drove his team on to the stage. Peary explained that

Painting, by Arthur Jansson, of Eskimo Village, designed by Peary and on display at the American Museum of Natural History. At right rear is shown frozen meat, raised on stone pillars to keep it away from the dogs

these were the dogs that had crossed Greenland, and invited the audience to come up and see the wolflike animals. Many did so, and those who had enough courage to pat their heads never lost a chance to brag about it.

Within three months, Peary had delivered 168 lectures and, after deducting the manager's commission and other expenses, had $13,000 toward the cost of his expedition. He had kept two secretaries busy sending letters to wealthy men asking for contributions, and was assured of the balance needed. But just as success was within his grasp, came the Panic of 1893, and many promises were withdrawn.

Again Peary showed himself the master of his fate. He put his equipment and his ship on exhibition in Philadelphia, New York, Boston, and Portland, and the quarters paid for admission gave him the required amount.

He sailed from Philadelphia aboard the *Falcon* on June 26, 1893. Nansen left Norway the same day, and as far as Peary was concerned, the race was on, for although he had not admitted it publicly, in private he had told at least one of his supporters that if the islands stretched as far northward as many believed, he would go on to the Pole.

Nansen, however, did not regard his own effort as a sporting event. He was the last of a group of explorers whose primary aim was not personal aggrandizement, but extension of knowledge about the Polar region. Any desire he felt to stand on the mathematical point that marks the top of the world, he dismissed as a remnant of childish vanity.

The expedition Peary had outlined was, in fact, two expeditions, each of which meant a round trip of seventeen hundred miles, five hundred more than Peary and Astrup had covered in 1892. Of the nine men he chose for assistants, only two—Henson and Astrup—had had any experience in the Arctic, and everything depended on whether or not the seven tenderfeet could adapt themselves to the conditions they would have to face.

Also among the newcomers was a nurse for Mrs. Peary, who was expecting a baby, a secretary for Peary, and an artist who paid his own way.

As he had sped down the last slope of the icecap the year before, Peary had caught sight of a sheltered cove in Inglefield Gulf. Before leaving for home, he had explored it with Josephine. They spent their wedding anniversary in the cove,

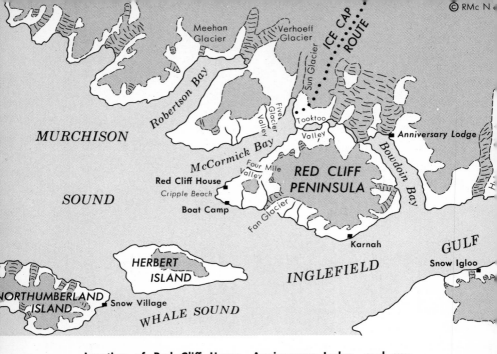

Location of Red Cliff House, Anniversary Lodge, and surroundings, as well as the icecap route described on page 74

and decided that its southern exposure made it a perfect site for a house. Accordingly, the *Falcon* dropped anchor there on August 3, and Peary went ashore to find the best place to build their base. The ring of stones used to hold down the tent where he and Josephine had camped was still there, and the site he chose was just fifty feet away. When the house was up, he named it "Anniversary Lodge." The harbor he named "Bowdoin Bay," in honor of his college.

As soon as lumber and other supplies had been put ashore, the work of building began, and, within four days, the frame was up and a start had been made on the first shell of tar paper covering. Peary now left his assistants to continue the job and went off on the *Falcon* after walrus to feed the sixty-eight dogs he had bought on the way up. Josephine and Myah, one of his best native hunters, went with him. They stopped at Karnak to pick up Ahnalka, and were shocked to hear that his wife, "The Daisy," who had been the best seamstress at Red Cliff, was dead. Peary found the bereaved husband sitting in his igloo, staring straight ahead and apparently unaware of what was going on around him. He gave no sign that he had heard Peary's words, and there was nothing to do but to leave him alone with his sorrow.

By afternoon, the *Falcon* was in the midst of a walrus herd, and by midnight twenty-four hefty beasts were in the hold. On the way home, Peary, Myah, and members of the crew went ashore, and between them shot seventeen deer. The hunting season was off to a fine start.

By August 20, the house was finished, Josephine moved in, and the *Falcon* sailed for home, taking letters for friends and relatives in the States. Three members of the party sailed with her, taking one of the whaleboats in which to bring back Eskimos to transport five thousand pounds of provisions from the coast to the icecap.

They came back with a boatload of Eskimos, followed by a procession of kayaks, and while some of them climbed the four-mile path to the moraine with heavy packs on their back, the others skinned the walrus and deer and cut up the meat. By the end of the month, the job was finished. In return for their labor, Peary gave them hunting knives and shafts for their harpoons, and they left for home.

Immediately afterward, four assistants were assigned to the job of moving supplies out on the Inland Ice, while four others hunted walrus and deer. Henson, however, was not among them. A studio for the artist was needed, and when that was finished, sledges must be made. Henson had made five sledges but that wasn't enough and Astrup, the only other assistant who knew how to make them, had been put in charge of the important task of establishing depots of food along the route toward Independence Bay. So Henson worked steadily on by himself and was beginning to wonder if he'd finish the job in time to have sledges ready for Astrup and the others before darkness brought their work to an end, when unexpected help arrived. Ahnalka, whose period of mourning was over, had come from Karnah with his friend Kyutah and wanted Marri Palook to hunt reindeer with them. Henson shook his head, and pointed to the half-finished sledge beside him. The two friends nodded, took what they needed from his tool chest, and worked with him until five more sledges were ready for use.

A new member of the party arrived on September 12— Marie Ahnighito Peary. Her middle name was that of the Eskimo woman who had chewed the bird skins from which she had made soft, warm clothing for the first white baby to be born so far north. Natives brought their entire families all the way from Cape York, two hundred miles to the south, and from Etah far to the north, to see the wonderful "Snow Baby," as they called her, even though fingers, laid gently on her skin, told them she was warm and not made of snow as they thought when they first saw her.

Josephine and the baby had come through the ordeal safely; enough venison was in the larder to last until the December moon; nearly twenty tons of walrus meat were on hand for the dogs; and Peary faced the future with confidence. The fine weather they had enjoyed for the last six weeks gave him reason to hope that by the end of October all the provisions would be deposited along the first hundred miles of the icecap.

But now the demons of wind, snow, and darkness began to relieve each other as guardians of the frozen desert over which Kokoyah presided. Astrup was only twelve miles from its border when he was seized with cramps, and was brought down to the Lodge in such a state of collapse that Peary was forced to take over the job.

When he reached the moraine, Peary found that every

sledge left there had been blown away. He went back for more and, with the help of two assistants, managed to move the supplies fourteen miles ahead. Here they spent the night, intending to return to the Lodge in the morning for more men, dogs, and sledges in order to advance the depots another twenty-four miles.

But a howling gale and flying snow held them in their tent for two days. A week later, every available man went to the moraine with dogs and sledges. The demon of the storm was still on duty. A boulder, picked up by the wind, struck one assistant in the middle of the back and injured him so badly that he was unable to join the icecap party in the spring. Another was thrown on his face, and a hundred-pound tin of pemmican struck Peary a glancing blow that disabled him for over a week and might have sent him over the edge of the cliff to the rocks below. Against such an onslaught they were helpless, and beat a hasty retreat to the Lodge.

Next the Lodge itself was attacked. The entire face of a nearby glacier fell into the bay, raising an enormous wave that broke through the ice in the harbor, surrounded the house, rolled the launch over and stove her in, dashed a whaleboat a hundred yards up the valley, leaving her in ruins, and as it receded carried away the dory and all the barrels of oil on which the Lodge depended for heat. The dory was lost, but after struggling for hours in the freezing waters, the men managed to recover most of the barrels.

They were now in the shadow of the Great Night. It was too late in the season to advance the supplies beyond the insignificant distance already attained and Peary realized that the expedition he had planned with such optimism allowed no leeway for accidents or delays. The twelve-hundred-mile trip to Navy Cliff had taken three months. Nearly twice that distance would require close to six months on the icecap, possibly more. Could his men endure it? Or the dogs? Would their food hold out? Should he leave a couple of hunters at Navy Cliff to lay in a supply of musk-ox meat? Should he take Henson instead of Astrup? He was reliable; his help with the dogs would be valuable; he was good at mending sledges; and he knew how to build igloos that were windproof. But would it be safe to leave anyone else with Josephine and the baby?

He wondered if Nansen, locked in the ice pack that could crush his small ship as if it were an eggshell, was suffering moments of anxiety equal to his own. Nansen's plan, too, was overly optimistic and equally hard to accomplish.

To escape such useless worry—useless because he had announced the plan and had to go through with it—Peary hunted whenever there was moonlight, or sledged to Eskimo villages to buy walrus meat for the ninety ravenous dogs. He chose natives to go with him instead of assistants, whose presence would remind him of the problems he faced. His favorite companions were Koo-loo-ting-wah, who had been with him at Red Cliff, Ootah, a lad of eighteen who had hauled supplies to the icecap and was living nearby with Panikpah, and Nooktah, whose daughter was helping to care for the baby so that the nurse could cook for the crowd.

The child was pale, but healthy and happy, and when, in February, the first ray of sun she'd ever seen crept through the window, she reached for it as if it were a wonderful toy.

The return of the sun was the signal to start for Navy Cliff. Hugh Lee, a newspaper reporter and Peary's youngest assistant, was sent ahead to dig out the supplies. But he lost his way in a blinding snowstorm and wandered about for a day and a night, until at last two Eskimos found him twelve miles beyond the Lodge and brought him back. The surgeon found that one of the boy's toes was frozen, but in spite of the fact that it hadn't healed, Lee started with the rest of the party two weeks later, on March 6.

Peary started two days afterward and, as he said good-by

to the natives who were still at the Lodge, he was startled to hear Ootah answer "good-by" in perfect English. Josephine walked up the valley with Peary until they met Koo-loo-ting-wah who was waiting for him with a sledge. They parted with no sign of the emotion they felt, and, if Josephine's eyes filled with tears, it was not until she turned toward home.

Peary and Koo-loo-ting-wah climbed the rough trail across the moraine. There Peary seated himself on the sledge, and Koo-loo-ting-wah drove him swiftly over the glazed snow until they reached the camp where Astrup was preparing supper while three Eskimos, Ahng-odo-blaho, Pooblah, and Pe-wah-to were tethering the dogs.

Pooblah, Pe-wah-to, and Koo-loo-ting-wah had not taken part in early preparations for the trip, but when Peary called for volunteers to accompany his party for the first twenty-five miles into the Devil's territory, all three had agreed to go, and eventually, like Ahng-odo-blaho, they went with Peary and Henson on two record-breaking expeditions.

The sun was still too low to give any warmth, and the Devil of the Icecap made full use of this opportunity to defeat them. At the end of the first day, Lee's toe had been frost-bitten again and was in bad shape, but he thought he could push ahead. Astrup said he felt the symptoms of another attack of cramps and couldn't go on.

The possibility of losing his two best men gave Peary a sleepless night. He could only hope that morning would find the condition of both improved. But after an initial effort in the face of the biting wind, during which they advanced only two miles, it was evident that both boys must return. Peary went with them, and noted that while Astrup rode all the way, Lee gritted his teeth and walked the last ten miles.

When Peary rejoined the party after the seventy-mile trip to the Lodge and back, he found that they had pushed five miles ahead. Here they were held four days by wind and drifting snow, and when they started on, were able to make only three miles before another storm descended upon them. By morning, there was a screaming gale, the temperature dropped to sixty below zero, men who walked fifty yards in the open had fingers and toes nipped, and one of them froze his heel and had to be sent back. Dr. Dedrick, the surgeon, went to help manage the dogs and sledge, and would remain at the Lodge to look after the other disabled men.

Left with only three assistants, Peary decided to concentrate all his efforts on reaching the chain of islands and following it to the Pole. Supplies no longer needed by the small party were cached to be picked up on their return.

For ten miles they enjoyed fair weather, but the Demon of the Icecap had only begun to play his cards. The storm had blown the snow into ridges which had frozen into sharp peaks of ice, difficult to see in the eternal whiteness. As they passed over them, one sledge after another was broken, and they had to stop and repair them. The assistants were too discouraged to tackle the job at once, and they made camp.

Next morning, in a piercing wind, with the temperature fifty-two degrees below zero, they went to work. Fumbling clumsily with mittened fingers, they untied the lashings and removed the loads. With braces and bits they bored new holes in the runners, slowly, because in such cold the steel might break. That done, they took off their mittens in order to thread sealskin thongs through the holes and attach them to the crossbars of the sledge.

Peary warned them to pull their hands up through their sleeves and put them under their armpits whenever their fingers stopped smarting, and keep them there until they began to burn, and if their feet began to feel like blocks of wood, they should stop whatever they were doing and jump up and down until they stung.

The time lost in all these maneuvers dragged the job out for ten wretched hours and, in spite of their precaution, all ended with frostbitten fingers.

After a hasty supper of pemmican and tea, Peary ordered the dogs harnessed, and they headed into the wind, accompanied by clouds of frost formed by the breath of the panting dogs. Whiskers, which had made a luxuriant growth since their last shave a month before, froze to each side of their fur hoods as soon as their breath moistened them, and the men had to stop and pull them loose in order to move their heads.

With the sledges running easily over a smooth surface, they began to average fifteen miles a day. Hope replaced Peary's despair, for at this rate they could reach Navy Cliff within a month of the date he had set, which was far from satisfactory, but still might give him time to go to the Pole.

Then came another violent storm, and by the time it was over, all three assistants were in bad shape. They were willing to go on, but as a result of their long exposure to bitter cold, dogs which hadn't frozen to death were going mad. Foaming at the mouth, they had bitten their teammates until the contagious and fatal disease, *piblokto* (Arctic hydrophobia), was spreading through the pack, and it was certain that few dogs, if any, would survive. With a heavy heart, Peary faced the fact that he must turn back. The Devil of the Icecap had won.

It was a knockout blow, but Peary rose with the count, ready to go on fighting. Here, 124 miles out on the frozen desert, he cached over half a ton of pemmican to be used by another expedition the following spring, marking the spot with a fourteen-foot pole on the top of which he wired a tin can that would reflect the sun and be visible several miles away.

With sledges lightened and the wind at their backs, they covered eighteen miles on the first day of their homeward march. As they went on, the death of more dogs made it necessary to lighten the loads again and two more caches were made, each marked with a tall pole, and containing between them a ton of supplies.

Early on the morning of April 21, Henson caught sight of a man laboriously working his way down the slope from the moraine. He ran to meet him, and when he saw that it was Peary, he knew the expedition had failed.

He looked into the haggard face, blistered by wind and sun. The eyes squinting between sunburned lids indicated snow blindness, and Henson took Peary's arm so he could close them. But Peary shook him off and, erect and defiant, strode into the Lodge. Telling the nurse to have something hot ready for his assistants who were not far behind, he went into the room he shared with Josephine and the baby, and for several days no one except the surgeon saw him.

In about an hour, the other men limped in. Henson helped the doctor undress them, and tears of pity filled his eyes as he saw that their bodies were covered with lice which, they said, had caused them more suffering than the cold.

Warm baths and alcohol rubs brought relief to all of them. After frozen feet and fingers had been cared for and opium solution dropped into eyes aching from the glare of the sun, they sipped hot tea, swallowed some pea soup, and dropped off to sleep.

But Peary found it hard to sleep. Worse than his bodily distress was the mental distress that began to torture him. He had found some consolation in planning another attempt for next spring. But now that he was here with Josephine and the baby, it dawned on him that her family would be uneasy until both of them were safely home, and that probably a ship would arrive this fall, instead of next year as scheduled.

In that case, what could he say to the men who had shown enough belief in his success to finance the expedition? Nothing, except that he would try again. And after this flash in the pan, what did such a promise amount to? Again, nothing. Who would contribute toward the expense of hiring a ship to bring back a man who had failed once, and doubtless would fail again? No one.

By morning he was sitting on the edge of the bed with his head in his hands. Josephine brought him his breakfast and, after two cups of coffee, it occurred to him that a ship to take him home next year wouldn't be necessary. He and his assistants could walk to Cape York, sail on a Dundee whaler, and cross to the United States from England.

When the doctor came in to look Peary over, he found him cheerful, and needing only drops in his eyes and a few days' rest to make him as well as ever. To his questions about the condition of other members of the party, the doctor reported that Lee was still confined to his bunk, but should be up and about in a week or so; Astrup was as fit as a fiddle and had gone off two weeks before with his favorite hunter, Koo-loo-ting-wah, to explore Melville Bay.

The mention of Melville Bay gave Peary an inspiration. He could blunt the edge of his defeat by finding the "iron mountains" that dozens of explorers had searched for in vain ever since 1818, when Eskimos at Cape York had shown Captain James Ross tools made with the iron chipped from them. Two of his Eskimos, "George Washington," his mail carrier, and Kessuh, the Cape York "dude," had told him they knew where the great irons were. If he could find them and send them back on the ship with Josephine, she could sell them to a museum and so get enough money to send a ship for him next year.

His belief that a ship would arrive in August was well founded. It was not only Josephine's family who wanted news; Peary's mother was equally worried, and so were Professor Heilprin and other members of the Philadelphia Academy of Science who realized the difficulty and danger of Peary's ambitious plan. Again the professor made arrangements for a party of scientists to go north, and their passage money, supplemented by a check from Peary's mother, made it possible to charter the *Falcon* for another voyage.

There was no way of letting Peary know that a relief ship was on the way. The knowledge would have gladdened his disabled assistants; also the physician who knew that three of them needed hospital care. But Peary's only worry was whether he could get to Cape York, locate the "iron mountains," and return before a ship arrived.

Astrup would be the logical man to take with him; he was in prime physical condition and had just been over the route. However, he decided to take Lee. Astrup was able to carry out a project he planned himself, but always turned out to be ill when Peary needed him. Lee, on the other hand, could be counted on to go ahead no matter how much pain he suffered. Peary's appraisal of the young man was accurate, but Lee almost lost his life because of it.

To pass the time until Lee should be able to go with him, Peary spent hours making a small sledge, selected two gentle dogs that he named "Laddie" and "Lassie," tied his baby daughter to the upstanders, and drove her up and down the coast while she shouted with delight.

Sometimes he took along her favorite playmate, Kood-lóok-too, who was "The Daisy's" son by her first marriage. She had brought him with her when she came to Red Cliff and, now that she was dead, Ahnalka had no way of taking care of him. He was a merry little fellow, willing to do whatever he could to be helpful, and wandered from igloo to igloo, staying wherever he was welcome. Recently he had come to the Lodge, where he slept under Henson's bunk. His courage in fending for himself aroused Henson's fatherly instinct. He hired two women to give him a scrubbing, cut his hair, and dressed him up in made-over clothes of his own. Kood-lóok-too means "little orphan boy," but usually he was called "Good luck to you." For years he and Ahnighito remained fast friends, and when she came north they greeted each other with shouts of joy.

As soon as his dogs were fit to travel, Peary sledged miles up the coast to buy walrus meat for them, and was relieved when he returned to find that Lee was ready to start.

In return for a gun, Panikpah drove them across Inglefield Gulf to an Eskimo village east of Cape Parry. There they found "George Washington" in his igloo, and while his wife cooked seal meat for their support, he told them the legend of the Great Irons.

There were three of them, he said—a woman, her dog, and her tent. Long ago Tornarsuk, the all-powerful Devil of the North, had hurled them down from the sky in a fit of rage. The woman and her dog had fallen near the coast. The tent, much larger, had landed on a small island beyond. This was an encouraging bit of information, for it meant that it would be easier to get them aboard ship than it would have been if they'd been inland.

Peary loaned Panikpah three dogs to take him home, and since the "Washingtons" had two children and therefore no room for guests, Peary and Lee slept until midnight in the igloo of one-eyed Merk-to-shar, the famous bear-hunter. Then they started for Cape York, "George Washington" ahead, with Peary on his sledge, drawn by ten dogs, Lee following with a team of six.

It was the middle of May. The shore ice was beginning to melt and, under the newfallen snow, there were several inches of slush and wide cracks into which they stepped without warning. By the time they reached Cape York, they were wet to the hips. That night Peary and Lee slept in the igloo of the oldest man in the settlement, who had no children to disturb them. A storm that held them there the next day was wel-

Hugh Johnson Lee

comed by Lee, who, although he had endured the hardships of the trip without flinching, was completely exhausted.

On May 26, with all sixteen dogs hitched to "George Washington's" sledge, they drove down to the ice foot on the northern shore of Melville Bay. After a few miles they crossed to an island where Kessuh lived, for he also had seen the Great Irons, and Peary wanted him to come along. The igloos in the little settlement were empty, but fresh sledge tracks led them to a cave where Kessuh was staying. He harnessed his dogs, Lee got on his sledge, and they went on at a swift pace.

At four o'clock the next morning, the Eskimos turned toward the coast, tethered their dogs, and "George Washington" led Peary up a narrow valley, peering right and left until he spied a bit of blue trap rock projecting above the snow. Kicking the snow aside, he exposed more pieces, and with a satisfied smile explained that this was the pile of stones used to hammer flakes of iron from "the woman."

He hurried back to the sledge for his shovel and ice saw, and began digging a few feet away from the trap rock. By five-thirty the "woman's" shoulder was exposed to the view of a white man for the first time since she had fallen from the sky. Kessuh and Lee worked away with their shovels until they had dug a trench three feet wide and five feet deep around her.

"George Washington" scraped the snow and ice from her shoulder, and Peary, to show that he was the discoverer, scratched the letter P on her dark brown surface.

Meanwhile, "Washington" knelt in the pit and pounded off bits of iron, as his grandfathers had done. Then he borrowed Peary's knife, opened it and, where the blade had been, inserted a row of the iron chips. This, he said, was how, in the old days, his people had made their knives.

After erecting a cairn near "the woman," in which Peary placed a record of his discovery, they hunted about for the "dog" but it was so deeply buried in the snow that there was not time enough to dig around until they found it. Instead, they sledged across to the island, hoping to locate the largest of the three meteorites, the "tent," but snow also covered it and Peary had to content himself with knowing where it was.

They said good-by to Cape York at midnight, Peary setting a pace that left little time for eating or sleeping. The first day they traveled through heavy snow and Lee, bending over the upstanders and straining every muscle to push his sledge along, lost his sunglasses. Again and again, open water forced them to climb the bluffs and cliffs that lined the shore, sometimes carrying sledges and equipment on their backs, and once pulling and pushing dogs and sledges up a long slope of ice so steep that steps had to be cut. When they neared Cape Parry, they found that in order to get around it, they must climb a glacier, which they succeeded in doing as flies crawl up a wall.

From the head of the glacier, a steep slope led down to the coast three thousand feet below, ending a few miles from "George Washington's" village. The only way to get down was to sit on their sledges and coast.

With "Washington" to steer, and Peary seated behind him, the big sledge started first, while the dogs whirled and tumbled after. To Peary it was "one of the grandest and most exhilarating of toboggan slides."

To Lee, who followed, it was torture. Without his dark glasses to protect his eyes, which by now were almost useless, the least ray of light gave him excruciating pain, and he started the descent with his eyes shut, opening them only now and then to catch a glimpse of the trail ahead. In one of these momentary glimpses, he saw the tracks of Peary's sledge veer sharply to the left and, using his whole body as a brake, he managed to stop on the very brink of a deep crevasse.

Shielding his eyes with his hand, he saw the coast still far below, but the track appeared to be straight. He squinted until his eyes were narrow slits, got safely down, and half an hour later was met by an Eskimo who drove him on to the village. From here, after a few mouthfuls of food and with fresh dogs, borrowed from "George Washington" and old Merk-to-shar, they drove rapidly across the gulf and up the bay to the Lodge. In the face of incredible difficulty and danger, they had covered, in four days, two hundred miles from Cape York.

The doctor treated Lee's eyes and advised him to stay in his bunk until further notice. Peary, buoyed up by success, needed only food and a night's rest.

Immediately after breakfast, he seated himself beside his stenographer and dictated an account of his discovery. Then he consulted the doctor as to how many assistants he could count on for an expedition the following year. The doctor's report was not encouraging.

In the evening, Peary told his assistants why he expected that a ship would arrive this year instead of next, and said that although they had agreed to stay two years, he would let anyone leave who felt he must do so. Most of them welcomed this offer as if they were prisoners who had narrowly escaped a death sentence, and through the rest of June and all of July they waited in a fever of impatience for the arrival of a ship.

They were beginning to despair, when, on the last day of the month, Koo-loo-ting-wah brought word that the *Falcon* had come and was fast in the ice off Karnah. A day and a half later, Josephine's brother, Emil, and Professor Bryant, leader of the scientific party, sledged to the Lodge. But for three weeks, ice made it impossible for the ship to enter the harbor.

The scientific party took advantage of the delay to make the investigations they had planned, and all those who were leaving hastened to pack their belongings. When at last the *Falcon* anchored in front of the Lodge, Nooktah and Koo-loo-ting-wah began to put boxes and trunks aboard. The sight of Lee following them with a bag in each hand filled Peary with dismay, for he had been sure that the boy had enough grit to remain. Hoping he could be persuaded to change his mind, Peary walked out toward the ship. They met halfway, and Peary was relieved to learn that it was not his own baggage Lee had been carrying.

Peary told him he'd asked the other assistants if they would stay another year, and all had refused except Henson. When Lee said that since that was the case, he would stay too, Peary was elated and they shook hands to bind the bargain.

IX

THE DEVIL TAKES HIS DUE

The *Falcon* weighed anchor on August 26, leaving the Lodge empty except for Lee, who stayed to guard it and help Nooktah's family move into the abandoned studio. Peary sailed with the rest of the party, but only to guide the ship to the meteorites. He took Henson, Nooktah, whose daughter was going to Washington to look after Ahnighito, four other Eskimos, and the largest whaleboat to bring them back.

They found Melville Bay full of heavy ice that made it impossible to get anywhere near the meteorites; impossible, also, to realize Peary's expectation that money to charter another ship could be raised by selling them. But he had made up his mind to stay, and stay he would, for he knew that his career as an explorer would be ended if he returned before he had accomplished what he came up to do.

His decision filled Josephine with despair. He tried to comfort her by saying that if no ship came, he'd walk down the coast and get home on a whaler by way of London. There was no time to argue whether or not such a plan was feasible. To avoid being frozen in for the winter, the *Falcon* must push ahead without further delay. Seamen lowered the whaleboat; Henson and the Eskimos followed; Peary kissed Josephine and the baby as casually is if he were leaving on a pleasure cruise, and also went over the side. With Henson as coxswain, and the Eskimos at the oars, they pulled away.

Standing in the stern, Peary watched the *Falcon* as she gathered headway, forced her way southward between floes and icebergs, and disappeared beyond the horizon. Then he turned and looked into the faces of his wild, fur-clad crew, pulling for the shelter of Cape Athol, and as eager as he was to reach the Lodge before they were caught in one of the gales all too frequent at this time of year.

When the wind was favorable, they stepped the mast, shook out the sail, and raced ahead. When the wind died, the crew bent to the oars, smiling and cheerful except for a bit of seasickness when the swells were high. Otherwise everything went well until, halfway back, they were about to round a glacier that projected far out from the land. As they came nearer, Peary caught sight of a tunnel running through it, and couldn't resist the temptation to pass beneath its crystal roof. Pointing to the archway, he told Henson to go under it.

A flood tide was swinging cakes of ice toward the shore, and Henson, hoping that Peary would change his mind, took pains to see that his crew nosed the boat into every one that obstructed their progress toward the glacier. As they neared it, there was an ominous rumble, followed by an explosive crack, and a huge block of ice fell from the keystone of the arch into the passage beneath. Violent waves rushed out, the boat was tossed like a cork, and the Eskimos, gray with fright, needed no order to pull away. Their backs strained until the oars bent like whalebone. Henson, seizing a boat hook, faced forward and shoved aside the drift ice in their path, until at last they were out of danger.

A week later, they reached the Lodge, where Lee was waiting for them, sick and, for once in his life, discouraged.

September was spent getting deer, walrus, and other game for their winter supply. By the first of October they had over five hundred pounds of venison and two tons of walrus stacked against the walls of the big living room in the Lodge. The meat, already partly frozen, had to be dealt with before it became as hard as a rock, and chunk by chunk it was piled around the glowing stove, where half a dozen natives cut it into small pieces and packed it in tins for future use on the icecap.

The next important job was to find the food that had been cached up there. Henson, Lee, and Nooktah made the first attempt, and got to the vicinity of the nearest cache. But new snow, unusually deep for this time of year, completely hid the tall pole set up to mark it. Thoroughly alarmed, Peary himself went up, with Henson and the Eskimo known as "Flaherty." For two days the weather was clear, but not one signal pole was seen. A gale and driving snow followed and "Flaherty," panic-stricken by these signs of Kokoyah's wrath, deserted. Peary and Henson struggled on, but soon had to take refuge in their tent.

Five days the storm held them there; after the first three, Peary couldn't sleep. The infernal whistling of the wind as it drove the snow against the tent, destroying all chance of finding the caches, seemed to be taunting him for his effrontery in attempting the impossible. He thought of the precious hours he might have spent with Josephine and the baby, hours he had thrown away because the "Devil of Arctic Exploration" had taken possession of him.

When at last the wind died down, he wrenched his thoughts back to the task at hand. All that day and the next, he and Henson crisscrossed the white blanket, peering through the dim light in every direction. There was no sign of a pole.

By the time they reached the Lodge, under the shadow of the cliffs, only an hour or two of daylight remained, and Peary, who had never minded the long darkness before, felt they were in the shadow of death.

By the end of the year, his foreboding seemed likely to become a certainty. His assistants were seriously ill, and there was no doctor to care for them. Henson was down with the grippe and, if it developed into pneumonia, he might die. Lee's malady hadn't yielded to Peary's efforts to cure it, and he also might die. The future, like the sky above, showed no spark of light, and Peary developed a bad case of the blues.

But that night Peary dreamed he was back in his boyhood, facing the future with no fear of defeat and, when he woke to find New Year's day clear, Henson better, and Lee more like himself, he took it for a good omen.

Everything possible had been done to ensure the success of the expedition across the icecap. Meat had been ground and mixed with fat as a substitute for the pemmican that might never be found. With great patience and ingenuity Peary had devised a cooker in which kerosene could be used instead of alcohol, should that cache also be lost. Four sledges had been built; he had bought enough dogs; and fur outfits had been made by the cheerful Eskimo women. Four natives—Ahnalka, Nooktah, and Kardah and Kah-dah-su of the whaleboat crew— had been persuaded to travel the first 124 miles into the Devil's country in order to help locate the caches. They were the first Eskimos brave enough to go so far from the coast that its cliffs and mountains were invisible.

Peary's party was small, but he considered this an advantage. If, as seemed likely, food gave out and they were forced to depend on finding musk oxen, as he and Astrup had been, there would be enough meat for Lee, Henson, himself, and the dogs, but certainly not enough for dogs and men in a party of nine such as he'd had the year before.

He felt, therefore, that his chance of success was good, barring illness or accidents. The dogs might be wiped out by another outbreak of Arctic hydrophobia. As for accidents, it was impossible to foresee what was in store for them, and moods of anxiety often replaced the confidence with which he faced the future.

Henson, who had learned many things from the Eskimos besides how to drive a dog team, removed one source of discomfort that had tormented the previous party. Two weeks before they were to leave, he took all their fur clothes outside and left them there until every louse was frozen; thus peaceful sleep at the end of a hard day was assured.

They started on the first of April. Lee, even then in no condition to handle a sledge on the steep upward slope, led the way, followed by the Eskimos and their dogs pulling heavy loads. Henson came next with the largest sledge, pulled by thirteen dogs and carrying about a thousand pounds of food and equipment. Peary, with Lee's sledge, brought up the rear.

At the edge of the icecap, two Eskimos, who had agreed to help get supplies across the moraine, turned back. The other four marched courageously forward, quartering the surface around each cache, the approximate location of which Peary determined by compass and by pacing the distance. They succeeded in finding only the smallest, from which they dug out two cases of hardtack and a case and a half of milk. All the pemmican—chief necessity for the journey—was lost.

Peary asked Henson and Lee if they were willing to take a chance without the pemmican. Both said they were willing to go ahead with the food they had.

The Eskimos prepared to leave. They had kept their promise; they could do no more. Alone in the white wilderness, they must find their way back before a snowstorm wiped out the sledge tracks that were their only guide to the familiar landmarks of the coast.

Peary gave them a letter to Josephine, which they were to pass on to a captain who would forward it from his home port. "We have only ourselves and the All-Powerful One to rely on," he wrote, "and in the event of mishap no human help can reach us." It was a harsh and merciless message, but kinder after all than one that would have raised false hopes.

From the first, Fate was against them. By the end of three days Lee was so ill that Peary dosed him with medicine and put him to bed. While they waited for him to recover, snow and a murderous wind fell upon them. Peary and Henson did their best to care for forty-two howling dogs that tangled their traces, tore up the stakes to which they were tethered, and dashed for the pile of meat with such fury that the two men had to jump away to save their sealskin boots from being torn to bits. One dog, mistaking Peary's red mitten for a hunk of meat, snapped at it, but unsuccessfully, for the mitten quickly disappeared behind Peary's back.

Progress was slow. Neither walrus meat for the dogs nor venison for the men was as nourishing as the scientifically pre-pared pemmican. The men, in fact, rarely ate enough meat, for it was raw and frozen, they could get it down only by warming it in their tea, and even so found it repugnant.

Dogs wore out and had to be shot. Within two weeks Lee's sledge was abandoned, and all possible equipment dis-carded in order to lighten the loads.

Henson suggested that icing the runners of the sledges would make it easier for the dogs to pull them, and when Peary agreed, Henson unloaded one of the sledges, turned it on its side, and went to work. It was his first attempt, but he had watched Ikwa and knew what to do. He lashed a strip of walrus hide to the runner, left it to freeze, and then coated it with an inch of snow dipped in warm water. Quickly he shaped and pressed it with his hands until the hide was covered. When this had frozen solid, he chipped and smoothed it with a knife, then rubbed it down with a hand dipped in water.

The job held them up for an hour or more, and had to be done once or twice every day, but in spite of the delay, the sledges ran so much more smoothly that the dogs made better mileage until they neared the summit of the icecap. Now they

were a mile and a half above sea level, and the rarefied air made the dogs gasp if they were driven faster than two miles an hour. The men, who had to get into the traces and help pull, could walk no faster. Every extra effort, such as stopping to tie a boot or pick up a mitten, left them panting and with bleeding noses. Lee gave out entirely; his toe was frosted again and he had to ride.

Finally, after three hundred miles of arduous toil, they reached the crest and began the descent toward the east coast, which should have been swift and easy, but was not. A runner on the largest sledge broke under the heavy load. Henson replaced it with a runner from one of the trailers, but this too gave way twelve miles farther on. Everything was removed from the sledge, and Henson strengthened it from side to side with a pair of skis, and added the other runner from the trailer. Thus converted into a three-runner sledge, it carried its thousand pounds without mishap.

When they started for the icecap, this sledge and its heavily loaded trailer had been pulled by sixteen dogs. Since it carried supplies for the return trip, the weight of its load had not been reduced, but now, instead of sixteen dogs to pull it, there were only seventeen left in the entire pack. Again the men had to get into the traces with the dogs, drag one sledge ahead, and then go back with the dogs for another.

After a few days, Lee's toe was worse and, to ease his pain and enable him to keep going, Peary gave him frequent doses of morphine. This was the same toe that had frozen the year before, causing Lee's return to the Lodge. Then, in spite of the pain, he had insisted on walking. Now he did the same, gritting his teeth until his jaws ached.

rosses show Nansen's route in 1888; the dots show Peary's
>ute in 1886; solid line with arrows shows his route out
nd back in 1891–2; and dashes show his route in 1893–5

Since they were going downhill with the wind at their backs, they made good time. They were now more than four hundred miles from the Lodge, which meant that before long they should escape from this frozen desert and get down to the land. It was none too soon. The last of the walrus meat had been fed to the exhausted beasts, and from now on it would be a case of dog eat dog.

Peary ordered the three-runner sledge dismantled, cached its load, except for a week's supply of rations and their camping gear, which was transferred to a smaller sledge, and they hurried on. By evening, they saw what appeared to be mountains. Not daring to trust their snow-dazzled eyes, they reached the rim of the icecap and saw beneath them land that Peary recognized as being just west of Navy Cliff.

With a light heart, Lee pitched the tent, but his face fell when Peary told him that he must stay in the tent, rest, and take care of the dogs, while he and Henson went after musk oxen.

Early in the morning, Peary and Henson started down the four-thousand-foot slope to the moraine, taking their rifles, a trailer, a small stove, and provisions for three days. Suddenly the snow gave way under Henson, and he plummeted downward. By flinging out his arms, he managed to hold himself waist-deep in the crevasse until Peary pulled him to safety.

Soon Peary himself dropped into a crack, and it was Henson's turn to come to the rescue. After that, it was one or the other of them until they got hardened to the danger and walked straight ahead, though always on the alert and ready to throw themselves forward whenever the snow sank under them.

Once safely down, they started eastward through a narrow trench between a wall of ice and towering rock. For twenty-five miles they walked over sharp stones and climbed jagged rocks only to discover at the end that they were completely hemmed in.

"Evidently the guardian demon of this land is opposed to our examining it or making any havoc in his musk-ox herds," said Peary.

Lee, watching for them from the rim of the icecap and still nauseated from the horrible business of butchering another dog, choked back a sob as he saw them coming up the slope with an empty trailer.

They ate what, by courtesy, was called a meal, then pulled the hoods of their *kooletas* over their eyes to shut out the light, and Henson and Lee went to sleep. Peary closed his eyes and concentrated on the dilemma that confronted him. They had enough food to get most of the way back, and when that was gone, they could eat the dogs. If they went ahead they might find musk oxen, but again they might not. For himself, there was no choice. Failure and death were identical. But he had no right to risk the lives of his boys. He must let them make their own decision.

After breakfast, he laid the situation before them, and asked whether they wanted to start back, or whether they were willing to stake everything on finding musk oxen on the land ahead. "We have talked it over," Henson said. "We know and we have known for days the chances we are taking. We want to go on."

They broke camp and went back to the spot where food for the return journey had been cached. Taking everything except the big sledge and a few rations, they turned their backs on the five hundred miles that separated them from the nearest human beings—three exhausted men and nine starving dogs, pitted against a relentless foe.

"I felt then, as I feel now," wrote Peary, "that in that

cool, deliberate moment we took the golden bowl of life in our hands, and that the bowl had suddenly grown very fragile."

Instead of retracing their steps, Peary led the way upward toward the northeast, hoping to catch sight of the place where he and Astrup had started their descent. With keen eyes, and a memory equally keen, he recognized it. Within a few hours they came to the cone of splintered rock from which Peary had left the icecap in 1892, and pitched their tent behind it just as a Niagara of snow swept down on them.

"The demon angel of the land is evidently still on the alert," said Peary.

He examined Lee's toe, and for two days kept the boy off his feet. He did what he could for it, but after examining it on the third day, he told Lee he'd have to stay in camp while he and Henson went down. Peary promised that as soon as they found meat, Henson would come back with a load.

The land at the foot of the moraine was almost bare of snow, and they helped the dogs pull the sledge over miles of rubble. Ahead they could see the mountain ridge that Peary and Astrup had followed when they were looking for a view of the coast. Now the object was to find meat.

They succeeded in reaching Musk-ox Valley, crossed it, but saw nothing to indicate that a herd had been there. Weak and hungry from a diet consisting of only hardtack and tea, they walked a few miles farther until Peary spied a fresh hare track, and then the hare itself.

He called to Henson to tether the dogs and come up with his rifle. Henson, though a good shot, was trembling with eagerness at the prospect of food. His first two shots went wild, but the third was successful. They cooked the animal—all ten pounds of it—the first full meal they had had since the Eskimos had left them five weeks before.

Two days later they came to a valley in which Peary, on his way back from Navy Cliff, had seen musk-ox tracks. They went down and found tracks only a few days old. Rapidly following them up the slope, they spotted the herd on a little terrace just below the crest of the mountains. They fastened the dogs to a rock, muzzled them so they couldn't chew themselves loose or make a racket to disturb the musk oxen, and climbed to the terrace. There they lay down to regain their breath behind a big boulder about two hundred yards from their prey.

Their eyes were too weak from the blinding glare of the sun to shoot from that distance. So, one from each side of the boulder, they dashed straight toward the herd. There was a snort and a stamp of the foot from the big bull standing on guard, and the next instant every animal was facing them in a close line, with lowered heads and horns. They waited until the men were within fifty yards. Then the bull lowered his head still more, and Peary, suspecting it was a signal to charge, and knowing that the black avalanche would crush them if once it started, raised his Winchester.

Heart, soul, brain, and eyes were behind the stinging bullet that went straight between the horns and into the vital spot at the back of the neck. As the bull went down, the herd wavered, Henson's rifle cracked, and a cow fell. Without raising his Winchester above his hips, Peary got another, Henson another, and they followed in pursuit of the retreating herd.

Suddenly a cow wheeled and made for Peary with lowered horns. He turned and ran, but the snow was deep and he heard the ox closing in on him. As he passed Henson, he saw him raise his rifle.

Peary heard a shot, followed by a heavy thud, and looking back he saw the shaggy animal lying dead less than twelve feet behind him.

"Matt," he panted, "you saved my life."

"A lucky shot," said Henson. "It had to be. It was my last."

Like famished wolves, the men ate chunks of the raw, warm meat as fast as the skin was cut away. Then Henson brought up the dogs, and they too gorged themselves on the rich, steaming food. By the time the shaggy pelts were removed, it was midnight, and the happy hunters threw themselves down on the soft fur and slept.

For two days they followed the herd without coming close enough for another shot. So Peary sent Henson with a sledgeload of meat to the camp where Lee was waiting, told him to cache the meat there for the return trip, and bring Lee and the camping gear back with him. Meantime, he would continue to hunt.

His main objective, however, was to find a practicable route to the coast and the islands that stretched toward the Pole. A ravine running down from a high plateau gave him a ray of hope and, with Henson and Lee, who had rejoined him, he followed it. They took the tent and food for Peary expected that they would camp on the shore that night. But like other approaches he'd tried, this one ended on a vertical cliff several hundred feet above the sea.

Disheartened, they made their way back to the moraine and up the steep slope to the icecap. As they crossed the area where snow masked the network of crevasses, Lee, watching Peary stalking ahead, apparently heedless of danger, was convinced that he wanted to die rather than face the consequences of another failure. When they reached Cache Camp, Lee seized the first opportunity to remove the cartridges from all the rifles.

His concern was unnecessary. Peary shoved his despair aside, and devoted all his energy to the immediate task of getting his little party safely home. With the precision of a mathematician he took stock of their food supply. If they could get along on half rations, there was enough to last thirty days. The outward trip, when men and dogs were fresh, had taken them forty-three days. But now their sledges were lighter, and he felt confident the men could make it, provided no storms delayed them. He was equally sure the dogs could not.

Determined to gain every possible mile while the dogs lasted, he set a rapid pace. In a day and a half, they reached the camp thirty-six miles away, where a little food for the return journey had been cached. Loading the musk-ox meat on the big sledge that had been left there, and everything else on a small one that Henson made from a pair of skis, they started up the ascent to the crest of the icecap.

They traveled, Peary says, "with the grace of cripples," for the soles of their feet were horribly sore from tramping over stones and rocks on the land below. Nevertheless, by the end of the day they had marched twenty-five miles and, on the next day, the odometer recorded twenty-five and a half.

It was too much for Lee. With nothing to eat but a small portion of hardtack and tea, he became so weak that nothing would stay on his stomach. Retching and aching all over, barely able to drag one foot after the other, he started grimly off on the third day, but collapsed after three and a half miles. Peary gave him quinine and brandy, and extended a line from the sledge to help support him. They stopped twice to brace him with hot tea, peptonoids, and more brandy, making it possible for him to go on for fifteen miles.

But the labor of pulling Lee, added to the heavy going through new snow, exhausted the dogs. Two gave out entirely and had to be shot. With only seven dogs left, the large sledge was abandoned and, after Henson had iced the run-

ners, everything was transferred to the small one, Peary praying that it would hold up until they got back.

The next day, both Lee and the dogs were done in by
the high altitude they had reached. The dogs again were able
to make only two miles an hour and, after four miles, Lee,
dizzy and bleeding from the nose, sank into the snow and
lay there watching the others plodding on a mile ahead. At
last, Peary, looking back, saw him and turned to retrace his
steps. But Lee staggered to his feet, motioned him to stop,
and managed to reach him.

For a day and a half, Lee was given a cup of warm milk
with peptonoids and brandy every hour. This, plus a fifteen-
hour rest, enabled him to travel for a week, during which
they made over twenty miles a day.

One by one, the dogs were giving out. As Henson
crushed another skull with his hatchet, and butchered the
faithful beast, he began to hate this life in the Arctic where
hunger drove you to kill the weakest in order to save the
strongest. By the time they were halfway home, only four
dogs were left, and all of them so nearly used up that in spite
of Henson's constant icing of the runners, he and Peary had
to help them pull the sledge.

It was hard work and almost beyond their capacity, for
by now both men were suffering from scurvy, due to lack of
fresh meat. Their legs were swollen from ankle to knee and
pressed against their sealskin boots with agonizing pain, until
they were forced to lie beside the sledge now and then to ease
the throbbing. Their gums were ulcered and shrank away from
their teeth, leaving them so loose it was impossible to chew,
and they could get their hardtack down only by soaking it
in their tea.

Lee, after staggering drunkenly for hours, collapsed again.
Henson, half delirious from hunger and the pain in his legs,
walked back and, as he raised Lee to his feet, grim pictures

flashed through his mind of men he had read about who died as they walked or, starving, were driven to cannibalism as Greely's men had been.

But although they were on the outskirts of hell, they were still able to defy the devil. Peary brought up the sledge, and they put Lee on it. Henson wrapped a fur robe around him, then fastened two traces to the toggle, and the one remaining dog and the two men dragged Lee toward home.

When, two days later, they saw the summits of the land, Lee told them to go ahead and cook a meal. He could go on without help, but would want something to eat when he got there.

Peary and Henson ate their two remaining pieces of hardtack, drank some tea, fed the dog a sealskin boot and a few yards of walrus line, and began what seemed an endless march to the moraine. But, after a few hours, they reached it, and followed the rough path down to the Lodge.

Fearing that Lee couldn't make that last lap, Henson hastened to light the stove and stir up a kettle of mush. He handed a bowlful to Peary, swallowed a few mouthfuls himself, and dumped some in a pail to take up to Lee. But when he opened the door, there was Lee crawling up the path on hands and knees. Squatting beside him, Henson gave him a few spoonfuls of mush. Then he lifted the emaciated boy, and carried him into the house.

X

SMALL VICTORY AT GREAT PRICE

They were home, but death was still close behind them. Lee was suffering from dysentery and unable to keep anything on his stomach. Peary and Henson could eat only soft food, and there was no meat for the broth they craved. When they put on their boots and walked to the brook for water, the pain in their feet was almost unbearable. They needed help, and Nooktah's house was empty.

For five days they waited in an agony of suspense for his return, or the arrival of some hunter who might see their tracks and come in. By now, Lee was delirious with fever and, in order to sponge off his burning body, Henson went for water. As he lay beside the brook waiting for the swelling in his legs to go down so that he could carry the pail back to the Lodge, he heard dogs and a sledge approaching. He sat up, and saw that it was Nooktah bringing his family home.

They greeted Henson with surprise and joy. They were sure, Nooktah said, that Kokoyah had destroyed Pearyaksoah and his companions, and since hunting was no good around here, they had gone to visit his friend Kah-dah-su, hoping he might have some meat to spare. He had given them two slabs of venison and a chunk he'd cut from a frozen walrus. Nooktah said he would be glad to share the meat with Marri and the *Kabloonas*.

Henson picked up his pail and, supporting himself by

the upstanders, walked to the Lodge. He went in first, and Peary gave a sigh of relief when Nooktah followed with the venison. He dropped it into the pot of water on the stove and, while it was coming to a boil, Lee enjoyed a sponge bath with the rest of the water Matt had brought.

As soon as Henson had had a bowlful of stew, he went outside, seated himself on the sledge, and told Nooktah to tie him to the upstanders so that he could drive across the gulf and send hunters out for deer. While he was gone, Nooktah was to try to get a hare or two, and his wife was to take good care of the *Kabloonas*.

Before long, Henson met Kah-dah-su with more meat on his sledge for Nooktah, and thought how lucky they were to be living among people who shared food and shelter as a matter of course. As he approached the settlement for which he was headed, Eskimo friends ran to meet him, and welcomed him as a man returned from the dead.

They untied the rawhide lashings, helped him to his feet, carried him into old Merk-to-shar's igloo, and laid him on a soft bed of furs. Henson told them that Pearyaksoah needed deer, and soon heard the crack of whips as the best hunters in the village started off to get some.

While they were gone, Merk-to-shar's wife nursed Marri Palook back to health. When she found that his loose teeth made it impossible for him to chew, she brought him a bowl of dark red liquid. He gulped it down, felt a glowing, stimulating warmth spread through his body, and held out the bowl for more.

For ten days Henson drank pint after pint of the liquid, which Merk-to-shar told him was seal's blood, the Eskimo cure for scurvy. His gums hardened, his legs no longer swelled, and when the hunters returned with as much venison as his sledge could carry, he was able to drive back to the Lodge, running behind the upstanders as usual.

Although Peary had improved on the diet of broth and stew, his face was still pale and shrunken. Henson offered the skinful of seal's blood he had brought him, but Peary shuddered and said he was doing all right without it. What worried him was Lee, whose failure to improve indicated that he needed a doctor's care and, on July 21, Peary sledged to Karnah to discover whether the ice was breaking up so that a ship could get through to the Lodge. His anxiety was increased when he found that the pack was still solid.

The twenty-five-mile trip had left him stiff and exhausted, and he realized that any idea of going a couple of hundred miles south to a port where they might board a whaler was impossible. Neither he nor Lee could make such a journey, and he doubted if either of them could survive another winter in the Arctic.

Everything depended on whether or not Josephine had managed to raise enough money to charter a ship in time for it to reach them while there was still a chance of finding open water. He knew that she would do her best, and that is exactly what Josephine had done.

The previous fall, while Peary had been making pemmican to replace the half ton that had been lost on the icecap, she had written letters to every prospect she could think of. By December, $8,000 had been pledged, but by Christmas, due to various circumstances, $3,000 had been withdrawn.

She consulted Judge Charles P. Daly, a family friend, who was President of the American Geographical Society. The Society had contributed $1,000 to each of the expeditions of 1891 and 1893, and now promised the same amount provided other learned societies and institutions would also contribute. Judge Daly suggested that Josephine call on Morris K. Jesup, President of the Museum of Natural History.

Josephine had found it very distasteful even to write

letters asking for money. To ask for it face to face was humiliating. But necessity gave her courage, and she made an appointment to see Mr. Jesup. She arrived at his office to find the Board of Directors waiting to hear what she had to say, and was filled with dismay. But Mr. Jesup had been thoughtful enough to invite his wife to the interview, and the presence of another woman restored Josephine's poise.

She told briefly how her husband had found the meteorites, the legends about their origin, and how cleverly the Eskimos had used them to escape from the Stone Age. Her husband had expected to send them back, she said with a rueful smile, but ice had prevented the ship from getting near them. This time, he would try again.

The directors, impressed, agreed to contribute $1,000.

When the meeting adjourned, Mr. Jesup introduced her to his wife, who invited her to have lunch with them. During the meal, they asked her to tell them about her two years in the Arctic. Mr. Jesup, who already admired the pluck with which this sweet and modest young woman had shouldered the burden of a financial campaign, was stirred to further admiration by the calmness with which she had faced the experience of living farther north than any white woman ever had ventured.

When she was about to leave, he said: "I believe that you are doing all you can to raise this money and I don't want you to do any less, but if you do not succeed in raising it all, come back to me again."

She thanked him on behalf of her husband, at which he smiled and said that he was not especially interested in exploration. He just wanted to do what he could to bring her husband back to her.

To Josephine, this sounded like charity and she hoped she could get all she needed from organizations that considered exploration important. Professor Heilprin, now President of the Geographical Society of Philadelphia, arranged to send a member to map an uncharted coast, and $760 was paid for his passage; Professor Henry G. Bryant of the Academy of Natural Sciences of Philadelphia sent a contribution; his wife sent another; Peary's admirers gave what they could afford; Josephine added the royalties received from the publisher of the diary she had kept at Red Cliff; but the total was still far from enough.

At this point Josephine agreed to lecture under the auspices of the National Geographic Society. Since she had long been prominent in the social life of Washington, the lectures were preceded by receptions, and the hall was crowded. A stereopticon and screen had been provided which made it possible for Josephine to do most of her talking in the dark. Even so, at the first lecture stage fright got the better of her, and the hand holding the signal to let her brother know when to put in a new slide trembled so much that the buzzer never stopped. Luckily Emil knew the story well enough to go ahead without any prompting. The affair was such a success that another followed.

By spring Josephine realized that it was foolish to expect to meet the cost of a ship by continuing to collect the money in small amounts. In order to get up and back before the ice blocked the channels, the ship must sail in June. So she went again to Mr. Jesup. As he had promised, he contributed the balance needed, and she hired the *Kite*.

On August 3, Peary was awakened shortly after midnight by someone shaking his shoulder. He turned over and saw Josephine's brother. A stranger was standing beside him, whom Emil introduced as Professor Rollin Salisbury, who had been sent by the University of Chicago to examine the meteorites. Emil said the ship was in McCormick Bay, and he and the professor had walked across from Tooktoo Valley, wading two rivers on the way.

Peary asked if Josephine had come with them, and was bitterly disappointed to learn that she had not. The news that a doctor was on board, however, relieved his anxiety about Lee.

By the time Peary had pulled on his boots, Henson and Lee, who had waked when the door burst open, had hot coffee ready and benches near the stove so that the two men could dry their clothes.

Nooktah, who also had heard the arrival of midnight guests, surmised that a ship had come and hurried in to ask if his daughter was on it. Emil said she was, and Nooktah left to tell his wife the news. After a long sleep and a big breakfast, Peary, Emil, the professor, and Nooktah started for the ship, reaching it at five o'clock the next morning.

Peary had assumed that it would be the *Falcon*, and was shocked to hear that she had been lost with all on board soon after landing Josephine and the rest of the party. He was relieved to see, however, that it was not an untried vessel that had come for them, but the *Kite*, which had brought them safely up in 1891 and returned for them in 1892, commanded this time by Captain John Bartlett, brother of the captain who had gone down on the *Falcon*.

Among the scientists on board was the collector for the Museum of Natural History to whom Peary had promised walrus hides for the taxidermy department. The next two weeks, therefore, were spent hunting walrus, and the number secured was much more than enough.

By that time it was possible to get through the Bay to the Lodge. Nooktah and his daughter went ashore, Henson and Lee boarded the *Kite*, and off they went. The doctor gave Lee a thorough examination and prescribed a special diet. Peary and Henson were pronounced in good shape, and at once Henson began skinning the walrus.

On this trip, the ship was able to get within a mile and a half of the meteorites before ice stopped her. Henson collected

Eskimos at Cape York to help move the heavy stones, and with Emil's engineering skill added to Peary's, they were put aboard. The strongest jack they had was unable to move the "Tent," largest of the three, but a hole drilled several inches deep showed that it contained nickel, and Professor Salisbury said there was no longer any doubt that the Eskimos were right when they said the stones had fallen from the sky.

When the Eskimos had been put ashore and rewarded for their labor, the *Kite* steamed across to Jones Sound, where the scientists carried out their assignments. With these obligations fulfilled, they turned homeward, and reached St. John's, Newfoundland, late in September, 1895. Here Peary learned that a second expedition was on its way to the Pole, sponsored by Alfred Harmsworth, owner of a London newspaper, and led by Frederick Jackson, a British explorer. Since nothing had been heard from Nansen, Canadians were betting on Jackson to win the prize.

With two polar expeditions in the field, Peary felt sure that one or the other would succeed, and that he had lost his last chance to make his name famous by being the first man to stand on top of the world.

Grimly he went ahead with his present task of transferring the meteorites, walrus hides, and the large collection of valuable specimens to the steamer that was to take the party on to New York.

When they arrived there, the curator of the Museum of Natural History came aboard to examine the hides. He admired the skill with which they had been handled and, when he learned that Henson had done the work, offered him a job in the museum's taxidermy department. There, for three years, Henson assisted in skinning carcasses and preparing them for exhibit.

As soon as the meteorites had been delivered to the museum, Peary and Emil left for Washington, where Josephine was living with her family. She was alarmed when she saw her husband's gaunt face, his body little more than a skeleton, and saw also that, in addition to being a physical wreck, he was mentally depressed.

But he rejected her advice to take a good rest, and the next morning reported to the chief of the Civil Engineer Corp who assigned him to the Brooklyn Navy Yard, where he had worked in 1889 and where he again was to supervise the building of a dry dock.

When they were settled in their new home, Josephine took her husband to call on Mr. Jesup. Peary thanked him for the generous gift that had made the relief ship possible, and Jesup replied that the two meteorites more than repaid him.

Jesup, like Josephine, thought Peary needed time off to recuperate. He wrote to the Navy Department, and Peary was granted a short leave. After that the two men saw each other often, and the relationship that developed between them was like that of father and son. Together they planned an exhibit of Eskimo villages, showing the conical skin tents where they lived in summer, the stone and sod houses that were their winter homes, and the snow igloos they used on hunting trips. (See picture, page 110.)

By summer, Peary's work on the dry dock was so nearly finished that his supervision was no longer essential, and he asked for a three-months' leave in order to bring to the United States the largest meteorite ever found. When his request was refused, Mr. Jesup, who was eager to add this historic treasure to the other two Peary had brought him, sought the help of his friend William C. Whitney, who had been Secretary of the Navy under Cleveland and influential in bringing about the president's nomination for a second term. Whitney, therefore, had no difficulty in persuading Cleveland that Peary's purpose was important, and the leave was granted.

Henson, when he was about thirty, in 1896

Peary had raised, through a series of lectures, most of the money needed to charter a ship, and the passage money of scientists and students had made up the rest. Henson got a leave of absence from the museum, and they sailed on the *Hope* in July, 1896. Hugh Lee went with them, and they were glad to see that he had fully recovered from the ordeal of the previous year. The scientists and students were left at various ports along the Greenland coast, to be picked up on the homeward journey.

At Cape York they took on board all the able-bodied natives, who worked day and night, with picks and shovels, to clear the ground around the base of the meteorite. Inch by inch the "iron mountain" was lifted by hydraulic jacks from its frozen bed, and pulled slowly down toward the coast by a wire cable attached to the chains that encircled the unwieldy mass of metal.

But before it could be lifted to the natural rock pier alongside the ship, the weather, until now calm and clear, took a turn for the worse, as if confirming the Eskimo's superstition that the Devil of the North opposed the removal of the "star stone." Pack ice began to crowd into the bay, threatening to crush the ship against the rocks, and she hastily steamed away.

Another failure, this time when he was on the verge of success, sent Peary's spirits plunging. But the news that greeted him on his return filled him with elation. Nansen had not reached the Pole. Moreover, he had seen no land between the northernmost point he had reached and Jackson's base on the Franz Josef Archipelago. That meant that Jackson would be defeated also, and proved that if there was a land route to the Pole it was on the American side of the hemisphere. This was territory that Peary regarded as his bailiwick, and he was determined to take advantage of the situation as soon as possible.

But there is no fence across the top of the world. In August, while Peary was still struggling with the big meteorite, three Norwegians, who had contributed generously to Nansen's expedition, had offered to finance another and asked Nansen to lead it. Nansen was unwilling to leave home so soon

Very sincerely
R E Peary
Civil Engineer, U.S.N.

Peary, when he was about forty, in 1896

after his return, and suggested that Otto Sverdrup be chosen in his place. Since Sverdrup had been captain of Nansen's ship, the *Fram*, during its long drift in the ice, and had proved his ability as a navigator, the suggestion was approved.

"There were still many white spaces on the map," writes

Sverdrup, "which I was glad of an opportunity of colouring with the Norwegian colours," and he gladly accepted the leadership of the expedition. Sverdrup, with Nansen and the sponsors, charted a route up the west coast of Greenland, and as far along the north coast as they could get before wintering. Then they were to sledge to its most northern point and down the east coast until they reached the part already explored. (See map, page 186.)

Their plan did not include an attempt to reach the Pole. Nansen's discovery that it was not surrounded by land, as some had supposed, nor by open water, as others had assumed, had removed whatever scientific value might have been gained from its discovery, and Sverdrup's expedition, like Nansen's, had an objective that was primarily scientific. With this end in view, it was agreed that if ice in the channels compelled Sverdrup to change the route, he might substitute any explorations that were feasible. By the middle of September, preparations for the voyage were underway.

Four months later, on January 12, 1897, the American Geographical Society awarded Peary a gold medal for his explorations in Greenland and, in accepting it, he made the first public announcement of his plan for an expedition that was to continue until he had reached the Pole. He would use a ship, he said, powerful enough to force its way through Robeson Channel and land his party on the north coast of Greenland. In the moonlight nights of winter, they would sledge supplies east, and by spring would be ready to start toward their goal by way of the archipelago that extended from the northern tip of the coast. This chance duplication of Sverdrup's route was to prove disastrous.

Mr. Jesup, now President of the American Geographical Society as well as the Museum of Natural History, appointed a commission to study the campaign Peary had submitted. He would need, he said, "a fund sufficient to insure the continuation of the work of exploration for five years, if necessary; say $150,000 dollars."

It was a bold proposal, but Mr. Jesup, whose admiration for the unswerving determination of the Peary family, won in the first place by Josephine's gallant struggle to charter a relief ship, urged the commission to accept the plan. "I trust Peary," he said. "I believe he will find the Pole."

In April, 1897, Peary received orders to report for duty at the Naval Station on Mare Island in San Francisco Bay. Promptly he mailed a reply asking for a five-years' leave, and warned Mr. Jesup of the threatened collapse of his plans. By evening, Jesup had asked a dozen prominent men to write the Secretary of the Navy on Peary's behalf. All received courteous refusals, and a second letter to Peary told him he must leave for California without delay.

Luck saved him. A day or two before he was to start, he happened to be introduced to a prominent Republican, Charles A. Moore. Moore knew nothing about the Arctic, and cared less, but Peary's fighting spirit won his admiration.

"How much leave would you like?" he asked when Peary had explained his difficulty.

"Five years," said Peary.

"Very well. I'll get it for you," replied Moore.

He went first to the Secretary of the Navy, who was willing to grant any request from a man who had done so much for the party, until he learned that Peary's leave was the object of Mr. Moore's visit.

"Anything but that!" he said.

"Then I'll get the President to order it," said Moore.

President McKinley, in return for Moore's effective support, was willing to grant any favor the politician asked. Two days later, the Secretary of the Navy notified Peary that the leave had been granted.

In July Peary went to Cape York to round up the Eski-

mos he would need for his expedition for the following summer, and to enlist their help in getting the big meteorite.
Again Henson went with him. Mrs. Peary and her daughter,
Ahnighito, also were members of the party, and Hugh Lee
and his bride sailed with them as far as Godhavn where they
spent their honeymoon.

At Cape York a swarm of kayaks came out to meet the
Hope, and while they were giving Marri Palook an uproarious
welcome on the forward deck, Kood-lóok-too ran to Ahnighito
and gave her a bag of ivory beads he had carved from walrus
teeth. In the sailors' quarters someone started the phonograph,
and the two children clasped hands and danced up and down
with excitement.

Since the weather was favorable, no time was lost in
anchoring the *Hope* alongside the pier on the edge of which
the Great Iron had been left. The ship's hold was reinforced
with heavy oak timbers, cargo was shifted and ballast added
to insure her stability under the extra weight of the meteorite,
and a bridge of tough oak, reinforced by steel cables, was
built from ship to shore. Meantime, the Eskimos had leveled
the lower edge of the pier and tamped down a stretch beyond
to make a seat for the bridge.

Now the heaviest steel rails available were laid on it,
and the track was continued across the ship to the hatch. A
massive timber car was placed on the rails, jacks lifted the
thirty-four-ton meteorite aboard, where it was lashed by steel
chains and wedged with oak blocks to hold it firm. In order
to move the car, hydraulic jacks were placed behind it, heavy
tackles attached, and the ends carried to the drum of a steel
winch which would begin to move when the car started its
descent to the ship.

As soon as the tide placed the *Hope* at the proper height,
Peary lifted Ahnighito in his arms, and put a bottle of cham-
pagne in her hand. Her mother and Captain Bartlett started

The three meteorites discovered by Peary in 1894, now in the American Museum of Natural History. The Eskimos called them "Dog," "Woman," and "Tent" (christened "Ahnighito"), which is the largest meteorite in the world on exhibit

the jacks, and as the car, with its precious burden, began to move, her father told her to break the bottle against it. For a moment she hesitated, unable to understand why she should do something she'd been taught not to do. But she was an obedient child, and after more urging from her father, she smashed the bottle against the star stone and christened it "Ahnighito."

By the middle of the next afternoon, the meteorite had been lowered into the hatch, and the *Hope* steamed away to Cape York where most of the Eskimos went ashore loaded with guns, ammunition, and other rewards for their labor.

On October 2, a floating crane hoisted the meteorite from the *Hope*, and cheering crowds lined the streets of New York as twenty-eight horses pulled the heavy dray that carried it to the Museum of Natural History, where, along with the "Woman" and the "Dog," it is now displayed in the Hayden Planetarium.

In December, 1897, Peary went to London to receive a

gold medal from the English Royal Geographical Society. To the large audience that gathered in his honor he spoke not only of his work in Greenland that had prompted the award, but also of his plan for reaching the Pole. In doing so, he was careful to mention his need for a ship strong enough to get through the ice to the Polar Sea (Arctic Ocean).

Soon he received the offer of a ship from the Dundee Whale and Fishing Company, but cables to New York failed to bring the amount needed for deposit. A wealthy American, who was visiting in London, also refused his request. "They tell me you don't know when to stop, Mr. Peary," he said. "I am always loath to help such a person."

But Alfred Harmsworth, later known as Lord Northcliffe, saw in Peary the type of man he admired just because he was a fighter who wouldn't give up. He called on Peary and offered to give him the *Windward*, used by the British Polar expedition that he had sponsored, and because Peary's plan called for a ship powerful enough to smash her way through the ice, he promised to have new engines installed in time to get the *Windward* to New York before summer.

This stroke of good fortune was offset by news of Sverdrup's forthcoming expedition to North Greenland. Although his plans had been widely known in Europe for a year, apparently little was known of them in the United States. Now Peary learned that the preparations were well along. Nansen's ship, the *Fram*, had been completely rebuilt for the voyage with funds voted by the Norwegian government; equipment and ample supplies for five years had been provided by contributions from leading citizens; and a party of fifteen had already been selected. Peary had nothing but promises. It was a dismal prospect that grew worse instead of better.

In February, 1898, the U.S. battleship, the *Maine*, was blown up in Havana Harbor. The American public, convinced that the Spaniards were responsible, flooded Congress with demands for war. In March, $50,000,000 was voted for national defense, and men who had promised to contribute to Peary's expedition withdrew their offers.

In April, war was declared. Peary's services as a civil engineer would not be needed, and his five-year leave was not canceled. But time was running out, and he was getting nowhere. In fact, he was slipping backward. In that same month came a cable from London saying that a machinists' strike had prevented installation of new engines in the *Windward*. Since purchase of another ship was out of the question, Peary sent word to send her along as she was.

"The Fates and all Hell are against me," he said to Josephine, "but I'll conquer yet!"

In the spring, a few men, following a suggestion by Mr. Jesup, had organized the Peary Arctic Club to finance Peary's efforts. Now Peary went to Mr. Jesup with the news about the *Windward*, and asked whether there was enough money in the treasury to pay for the installation of stronger engines. There was not. Only eight men had sent in the $1,000 promised, less than enough to carry him through one year.

During the next six weeks, Mr. Jesup, Herbert L. Bridgman, business manager of the Brooklyn *Standard Union*, and Henry W. Cannon, President of the Chase National Bank, who formed the nucleus of the club, found several men who believed that capturing the Pole was an American enterprise, and fearing that the Norwegians might get there first, agreed to subscribe. Mr. Jesup felt sure that as soon as the war was over, those who had withdrawn their support would fulfill their pledges, and urged Peary to go ahead and spend what money they had, saying that he would underwrite the expense of sending a relief ship in 1899.

Peary had decided to limit his party to Henson and a surgeon, Dr. Dedrick. Some of his supporters questioned the wisdom of taking a Negro, and suggested he either be replaced by a white man, or that Peary should take a white man also. But Peary replied that Henson's ties with the Eskimos made him irreplaceable and, further, that no white man would give him four years out of his life unless he was ambitious to be an explorer himself, which would mean conflict and insubordination.

As soon as Mr. Jesup had assured him of his continuing support, Peary sent for Henson. He had assumed that Henson would be willing to go, and sending for him was a formality. But the situation was not as simple as he had imagined. Ever since the sinking of the *Maine*, Henson had realized that a war with Spain might upset Peary's plans and force him to postpone the expedition indefinitely. This would be a disappointment to Peary, but Henson saw it as an opportunity. He'd had a chance to make friends, and was a welcome guest in many homes. He'd done well at the museum and could go on working there, which would make it possible for him to marry and have a home of his own before he went north again.

Therefore, when Peary told him that all obstacles had been overcome, and he was counting on him to sail with the expedition in July, Henson was taken by surprise, and it took him a minute or two to adjust himself to this unforeseen development. Peary was equally surprised by Henson's silence, and hastened to add that no other assistant was to go with them, and that whether or not he reached the Pole depended entirely on Henson and the Eskimos.

Henson was no longer in a dilemma. If a Negro made it possible for Peary to get to the Pole, the prestige it would bring to the Negro race would more than offset the postponement of the family life for which he longed. He said he would be glad to go and do his best to help Peary succeed.

Josephine was to be left behind this time. To keep from thinking about the four years of separation and the possibility that she might never see her husband again, she bought some red, white, and blue taffeta and made an American flag, with stars stitched in the blue corner. The day before Peary sailed, she gave it to him, and asked him to keep it near him as a reminder that she was with him heart and soul, though not in person as she'd like to be.

In order to beat Sverdrup to Greenland and to secure the best dogs and Eskimos for himself, Peary needed a faster ship than the Windward, which was little better than a sailing vessel. So he hired the swift little Hope to meet him at Sydney, and left New York on the Windward with John Bartlett as captain and his nephew, Bob Bartlett, as first mate. He stopped in Portland long enough to say good-by to his mother, and sailed from Sydney July 7 on the Hope, leaving the Windward to follow and join them at Etah. He took it as a good omen when, just before they steamed away, a cablegram brought word that the Spanish Navy had been defeated, the war was practically over, and efforts to finance his expedition were bound to succeed.

Further good news awaited him at Cape York: Sverdrup had not arrived. The Eskimos welcomed Henson as if he were a brother who'd been away too long. They greeted Peary with reverence, but when he told them he wanted twenty drivers, their families, and their dogs to winter on the north coast of Greenland, and sledge over the Polar Sea in the spring, they asked for time to talk it over.

They gathered around old Merk-to-shar, the one-eyed hunter who was now the head man of the settlement, and talked all night. In the morning, Merk-to-shar reported that they were afraid to go where they never had hunted, but if Peary would take them on the big ship and care for them while they were gone, they were willing to risk it.

Four hours later, the ship was crammed with restless dogs and terrified women and children. The Windward joined them at Etah toward the end of the month. Coal, brought from Sydney to lighten the load of the slower ship, was transferred, and the *Hope* left for home.

As Peary had feared, the *Windward* was not powerful enough to push her way through the heavy ice, and by the middle of August was imprisoned by a floe off Cape D'Urville on Ellesmere Land. But he had planned for such an emergency: he would add to his reputation as an explorer by surveying and mapping the unknown region to the southwest. Another consoling thought was the probability that Sverdrup's ship also would be held back by the ice. But where? Off Ellesmere Land like himself? What then? Would he too start to explore it? (See map, page 186.)

Determined to be the first in the field, Peary left the *Windward*, climbed a summit from which he saw that the channel to the north was still closely packed, and taking a chance that his ship would be unable to advance in his absence, explored two uncharted bays.

By the middle of September, it was plain that they would be held here until spring, on the wrong side of the channel and three hundred miles below the Greenland base he had wanted. He was prepared for that emergency also. By sledging some two-hundred-fifty miles north he could reach Fort Conger, Greely's old headquarters on Lady Franklin Bay, which had been abandoned fifteen years before. By now it might be a total wreck, but it could be rebuilt, and was close enough to the Arctic Ocean to give him a base from which to start for the Pole. (See map, page 186.)

Supplies were landed, and Henson began the work of transporting them to the fort, while Peary, having a premonition that his rival was in the vicinity, left on another exploring trip.

Since fresh meat was needed to tide them over the winter, he took along Pe-wah-to and Myah, his old hunters, and during the week they were gone, they got two bears, saw walrus in Buchanan Bay, and fresh traces of musk oxen along the shore. Peary promptly returned to the ship in order to add more hunters to his party, and to get a report as to the possibility of sledging north along the coast.

Henson told him that the sea ice and the ice foot were so rough that only thirty miles of roadway had been cut. Peary sent him off again with instructions to take more Eskimos, choosing those who were the strongest and most willing workers.

After a few days' rest, Peary led a large hunting party to Buchanan Bay, and while the Eskimos followed the musk-ox tracks, he crossed the bay in search of walrus or another bear.

During this trip, the premonition that had hastened his exploration of the territory became a certainty. He caught sight of a tent on the southern shore, and presently a man appeared who watched his approach through binoculars. Peary left his sledge and went up to meet him.

"Are you Captain Sverdrup?" he asked.

"I am," said Sverdrup, extending his hand.

They walked up to the tent, which Sverdrup explained was the base for their surveying and mapping activities. Inside, one of his assistants was grinding coffee, and Sverdrup invited Peary to come in and have some.

But Peary answered that he must go back and join the hunting party that had come out with him. Sverdrup walked with him to the sledge, and they parted amicably. As he drove away, however, another premonition took possession of Peary. Sverdrup doubtless knew about Fort Conger, and might be planning to use it as a base. No matter what it might cost in time and effort, this must be prevented.

He found the Eskimos had killed fifteen musk oxen during his absence, and as soon as they had been skinned and the meat cut up and stacked, they returned to the ship with sledges loaded to capacity.

Henson was ready to report the result of his second ordeal on the ice foot, and said that he and the natives had cut the trail for another twenty miles. Peary told him they must do better than that, and sent him back with orders to make all possible speed with the road, and establish depots of food along the way.

Sledging up the coast was infinitely harder than sledging on the icecap had been. There the surface was usually smooth. Here a smooth surface was rare. Heavy floes, driven by wind and tide into the narrow channel between Greenland and Ellesmere Land, were piled up mile after mile in towering ridges that completely blocked their way. Sometimes they could get around them by driving out onto the sea ice. Otherwise, Henson scouted along the base until he found a spot where the ascent was easiest, and they took out their pickaxes and gouged out a track winding up one side and down the other. Then began the arduous work of getting the sledges across. Pushing with their toes so as to throw all their weight forward, they urged the dogs upward with voice and whip, at the same time straining every muscle to keep the sledge on the track. Sometimes the dogs would give up, and the drivers had to dig in their heels and brace themselves against the upstanders to prevent the sledge from sliding backwards. Usually, when they reached the top, the sledge would begin to coast down, and in spite of all efforts to hold it, would crash on the ice below. Then the poor dogs, trembling with fright, would be released from their tangled traces, and the next hour would be spent unloading the sledge and making the necessary repairs.

Between the ridges, soft snow held them back, or jagged hummocks of ice, which had to be removed by pickaxe and shovel before they could go ahead. When the loads were too heavy to be pulled up the steep peaks, the men carried them over, and climbed down again for the dogs.

Two of the Eskimos in Henson's party, Sipsu and Ah-nidloo, were the boys who, at Red Cliff, had swung their whips at mounds of snow arranged like a dog team. They were nineteen now and expert drivers, and their strong young bodies were an enormous help in packing heavy burdens over the upended floes. Like other Eskimos, they often were discouraged, but the friendly "Adolo, Adolo," with which Henson roused his helpers for another hard day on the trail, filled them with hope and courage.

By the middle of October, they had extended the road to Cape Fraser, and since this was the beginning of the Long Night, they returned to the ship. Peary, who had been busy helping the Eskimos bring in the rest of the musk-ox meat, now had a chance to inspect Henson's work. On October 29, he made his first trip over the trail, and in two days reached the rocky cape that Henson and the Eskimos had gained after five weeks of back-breaking labor.

As he looked at the huge floes forced up by the tide and stretching like Alpine peaks beyond Cape Fraser, Peary was appalled, and went on foot to see what chances they had of going ahead. An examination of the sea ice convinced him that it would be impossible to sledge around the obstructions, but he told Henson that a good deal of hard work with picks and shovels would get them through.

During the November moon, Henson, with Ahnidloo, Sipsu, and a sturdy giant, Ahng-ma-lokto, cut a trail across the peaks that had seemed impassable, and succeeded in reaching Cape Wilkes, ninety miles from the ship. Peary had followed with Myah, Ootah, and Pooblah, to build igloos at selected stations along the route. (See map, page 186.)

He had hoped to move on to Cape Lawrence, thirty-five miles beyond, but Myah had had a dream in which he saw much open water and rough ice ahead, and decided to go back to the ship. So Peary turned over to Henson the loads he had brought, took the best driver and eight picked dogs, and overtook the deserter. To prevent any other Eskimos from following his example, he gave him a whipping, and drove him back to his igloo in disgrace.

With Ootah and Pooblah added to the three Eskimos he already had, Henson succeeded in finishing the road to Cape Lawrence in the last days of moonlight, and they sledged 125 miles down to the ship with a bitter wind in their faces, and with the temperature at fifty degrees below zero.

Henson assumed that the winter would be spent as usual, mending sledges, making new ones, and hunting. But he soon discovered that Peary had other plans. As soon as the December moon rose, they were to advance all their supplies to Cape Lawrence, go on from there with light loads, and take possession of Fort Conger.

Henson, who had just traveled over a well-worn trail in the dark, didn't like the idea of going beyond Cape Lawrence where there was no road and, for most of the way, there would be no moon. He suggested that it might be safer to wait until February, and start in the twilight of the rising sun so that the unexplored half of the 250-mile journey could be made in the daytime.

But Peary, knowing that Sverdrup had dogs and sledges, and easy access to a route through the back country, feared that he might already be on his way to Fort Conger, and insisted on leaving as soon as the December moon rose. Accordingly, on December 20, he started off, and Henson, Sipsu, Ahnidloo, and two other Eskimos went with him.

He succeeded in capturing the Fort, but the effort left him crippled for life.

XI

LIMPING AHEAD

To have reached Fort Conger at all was something of a miracle. The sledge road ended 125 miles below, and for six days they hewed their way northward. To escape a piercing wind, they burrowed into a snowdrift, and one of the Eskimos was so numb with cold that they left him there with a companion and nine of the dogs.

The moon had set, and they traveled in total darkness. Judging their position by the number of inlets they crossed, Peary knew by the end of the second day that they were on the edge of Lady Franklin Bay, within striking distance of the fort.

They slept a little, and then for eighteen hours groped their way across the bay, stumbling and falling on the rough surface until they came to the north shore. Here they camped in a cave under a cake of ice—cold comfort, for the temperature was sixty degrees below zero. They had eaten the last of their food fifty miles back, so Henson killed a dog, they divided the carcass, drank enough tea to give them some warmth, and after several more hours of groping reached what Peary took to be an island below the fort. He knew that somewhere above there was a marker giving the mileage and the direction, and he asked Henson to go up and look for it.

Henson slipped a box of matches into his pocket, took several lengths of lashing from his sledge and, tying one end around his waist, he handed the other to Ahnidloo, telling him to keep hold of it so that he could find his way back.

An hour later, a tug on the line told Ahnidloo that Henson was coming. He reported that he found the marker, and that Fort Conger was two miles west of it. Peary, who was lying against the upstanders of a sledge beating his feet together, ordered the Eskimos to get ready to march. Henson, noticing that Peary's feet struck each other with a dull thud like blocks of wood, asked if they were all right. They were a bit frostbitten, he said, but when he rose, he staggered and would have fallen had not Sipsu caught him and helped him onto a sledge.

Henson led the way up the slope, stopping occasionally to peer at objects that showed dimly against the snow. At last he saw the shape of a building that looked more like a barn than a fort, and as he came nearer he was relieved to see that it was still covered with a roof.

There was no lock on the door and Henson walked in, using his sledge cooker for a light. The first thing that caught his eye was a kitchen range on one side of the large room that was perfectly dry, but in wild disorder as if it had been left by people in a hurry. Open trunks, empty boxes, buffalo robes, piles of paper, rags, and castoff clothes covered the floor, and on the table were overturned coffee cups, cigar butts, and a half empty tin of hardtack. He smashed a couple of boxes with his foot, picked up a wad of paper, and started a fire in the stove. By midnight, when the rest of the party arrived, the room was reasonably warm.

While the Eskimos were gorging themselves on hardtack, Peary examined the label on the tin and, finding that it was from an American firm, concluded that it was not Sverdrup's party, but Greely's that had eaten the last meal there. Greely had reported that when he left Conger in accordance with orders to do so in case no ship reached him, he'd abandoned

a lot of food. Peary therefore sent Henson out to look for
it in the sheds outside.

The oil in the sledge cooker was almost gone, so, before
leaving, Henson lifted it and examined the shelf behind the
stove, where he found half a bottle of olive oil. He poured
some into a saucer and, twisting a rag into a wick, made a
lamp, Eskimo fashion. Telling the boys to keep the fire burning, he went out to the leanto and, by the tiny flicker of
flame, saw two barrels, one marked "Salt Pork," the other
"Beef," and a keg of rum.

He called Sipsu to give him a hand and, while they
were outside, Peary dragged his chair over to the stove, tried
to pull off his boots, gave it up and, opening the stove door,
placed his feet inside. Presently Sipsu came back rolling the
barrel of salt pork, and Henson followed with the keg.

"Rum!" he exclaimed.

"For that kindness," said Peary, "I could forgive Greely
his sin of being an Army man."

Henson asked about his feet. Peary said they were still
numb and, putting them on the floor, told Henson to take
his knife and rip off the boots. Carefully Henson slit one
and then the other, and held the heels while Peary pulled.
The feet did not move. Henson made another slit, inserted
a finger, and said that the pads of hay that lined the soles
were blocks of ice and the socks were frozen to them.

Peary gave a powerful jerk on the boot Henson was
holding, told him to grab the other, jerked again, and his
feet came out. But the tips of eight toes stayed behind in
the socks.

He drew his quivering lips between his teeth and, for a
moment, Henson was too horrified to move. Then he grabbed
a bucket, handed it to Ahnidloo, and ordered him to fill it
with snow. Peary plunged his feet into the bucket. They were
as white as the snow, and so were his legs. While the boys

rubbed them, Henson searched for a medicine chest. Not finding one in the house, he took Sipsu and went back to the
leanto. There he handed Sipsu the little lamp, and pried open
box after box until he came to the bottom of the heap.

He was praying desperately for success, because he knew
that, unless he found an antiseptic, gangrene would develop
and Peary's feet, and possibly his legs, might have to be
amputated. The last box was coated with ice, but a blow with
his hatchet loosened the lid, and he took out a small chest.
His prayers had been answered. Inside he found iodoform and
rolls of bandage. Thanks to his years as loblolly boy on the
Katie Hines, he had known what to look for and what to do
with what he had found.

The color had come back in Peary's legs, but his feet
were bluish-black from stagnant blood. With Sipsu's help,
Henson carried him across the room and laid him gently on
a buffalo robe that covered one of the cots. Spreading the
powder on the gauze, he bandaged the toes and placed a pad
under the feet so the blood could flow toward the heart.

He chipped off chunks of frozen rum and, when it had
melted, filled a cup, which Peary took in hands that trembled. The warmth spread through him and, in spite of the
excruciating pain in his thawing legs, he slept. Henson and
the boys spread buffalo robes on the other cots and slept also.

The next morning, a search of the shed brought to light
not only kerosene, but quantities of food that was still edible
—cornmeal, hominy, molasses, a case of evaporated milk,
boxes of canned beans, soup, more hardtack, coffee, and tea.

But when the Eskimos saw that the diet of salt pork and
frozen beef was killing the dogs, fear overcame their loyalty.
The food is not good, they told Henson. It has killed the
dogs; it would kill them also. They were going to leave at
once, while there were still enough dogs to get them back
to the ship.

Henson asked them whether they would stay if he got musk oxen. They shrugged, and said nothing.

While he was changing Peary's bandages, Henson asked whether Greely had found musk oxen in the neighborhood. Peary said a few had been found to the southwest, and added that fresh meat would be a welcome change.

Henson didn't tell him how much more was at stake. Without Ahnidloo and Sipsu and their dogs and sledges, it would be impossible to get Peary down to the ship in time to save his legs. He selected a rifle from the rack, cleaned it, slipped in a round of ammunition, and went outside to give it a try. It worked perfectly.

Full of apprehension, but outwardly confident, he led the boys southwest until at last he made out black dots against the snow. Once more his prayers had been answered. It was a herd of musk oxen. They piled the sledges with the carcasses, and there was no more talk of desertion.

In their absence, Peary, undaunted by his toeless feet, wrote on the wall beside him: "*Inveniam viam aut faciam*" (I shall find a way or make one).

By February 18, there was enough light to make a return to the ship feasible. Peary had paid a high price for this strategic base from which he still was determined to start for the Pole, and he didn't intend that a Norwegian or anyone else should take it from him. Before they left, he asked Henson to look for some cardboard. A piece was found, and Peary printed a notice on it in big, bold letters, saying that he had taken possession of the fort and everything in and around it in the name of the United States government.

His toes were still so painful that he was unable to stand for more than a moment, but thanks to Henson's constant attention, gangrene had not spread to his feet. Sipsu and Ahnidloo wrapped his legs in a musk-ox hide, and as they lifted him to carry him outside, he told Henson to tack the notice of ownership on the outside of the door. When it was up, Peary eyed it with stern satisfaction.

Henson covered him with a buffalo robe and lashed him securely in place to make sure he wouldn't roll off if the sledge slipped sideways on the edge of a ridge. But nothing could prevent the torture he endured as the sledge jolted along over the rough ice, nor the pain he suffered as Henson and the boys wedged him through the narrow entrances of the igloos where they spent the night.

At the far end of the trail, Bob Bartlett was waiting in a fever of anxiety that made sleep impossible. Peary's failure to return with the two Eskimos had filled him with foreboding, especially as they had reported wild storms and Peary's decision to go ahead in total darkness. When the February moon rose, he began his long vigil. One week passed, then another. It was the last day of moonlight, and the temperature was sixty-five degrees below zero, when he heard dogs in the distance. Soon he saw the sledges and, as they came nearer, he noticed with surprise that Peary, the champion walker, was riding.

But, as he passed, Peary greeted Bob with a smile and a wave of the hand, and Bob, reassured, grasped the upstanders and trotted along beside Henson to the ship. Only when Henson called for help, and members of the crew carried the sledge aboard with Peary on it, did he realize that something was seriously wrong. Two weeks later, Bob administered the ether while eight of Peary's toes were amputated.

He was still convalescing when a party, headed by Captain Bauman, Sverdrup's second in command, arrived at the *Windward*. They had been guided to the ship by Koo-loo-ting-wah, who had learned its location from the Eskimos Peary had sent to Whale Sound for more dogs and hunters. Koo-loo-ting-wah had started immediately for Peary's base, to tell the natives there that some of their relatives had been killed while walrus hunting. On the way he passed the *Fram* and had stopped, hoping to receive hospitality and gifts from the white men.

Sverdrup invited him to dinner, and asked him his name. When he answered, "Koo-loo-ting-wah," Sverdrup was delighted, for he recognized it as the name of the Eskimo who had been Astrup's guide when he explored Melville Bay. Astrup's admirers had sent a marble tablet to be placed at Cape York as a memorial to his achievement, but ice had prevented a landing there. Now Sverdrup asked Koo-loo-ting-wah to do it, but was unable to make him understand.

Captain Bauman had often spoken of going north to see Peary, and took advantage of this opportunity to do so. The first mate went with him and, on the way, Koo-loo-ting-wah told them he'd heard Peary had frozen his feet while hunting to the southwest. Bauman, therefore, was not surprised to find Peary in bed.

Carefully guarding the secret of his northern base, Peary explained that his toes had been frostbitten on a trip at the end of February, and he'd had to have them amputated. Bauman expressed his regret, and said Sverdrup also would be sorry to hear of such a serious mishap.

"You must take your chances up here, you know," Peary replied. "I'll be walking around in a few days."

"The main purpose of my visit was to invite you to come down and spend Easter with us on the *Fram*," said Bauman, handing him visiting cards from Sverdrup and other members of the expedition.

Peary thanked him, regretted that the trip was impossible, and invited him to dine with the ship's officers and spend the night. In the morning, Bauman discussed the other purpose of his visit, which was to find out how much of the country Peary had mapped so that his own party would not duplicate it.

"I haven't worked out my maps," Peary hold him, but added that he had made no surveys beyond their headquarters, nor above or below them.

Bauman was relieved to know that all danger of collision was removed and the possibility of cordial relations established. Peary again asked him to thank Sverdrup for his invitation, sent him a box of cigars, but would not promise to visit the *Fram*.

As soon as Peary's left foot had healed, the ship's carpenter made him a pair of crutches, and in the middle of April Sipsu drove him to Fort Conger. Henson had gone ahead with a party of Eskimos to finish the road and move the rest of the supplies up from Cape Lawrence. When Peary joined him, they started north to discover whether it would be possible to cross over to Greenland.

The ice in the channel was covered with deep snow. Peary tried to go ahead on snowshoes, but the exertion broke open the stitches in his right foot, and he had to go back to Conger. Here he rested, while Henson and the natives secured enough musk oxen to provide meat for the future, and then Peary rode back to the ship. Henson and the Eskimos continued to transport supplies and, by the end of May, fourteen tons had been deposited along the route.

Slush and water had replaced the winter ice and snow, which meant the end of the sledging season. So Peary sent Henson across to Etah, where he was to wait for the relief ship Mr. Jesup had promised to send, and tell the commander of the expedition where to find the *Windward*.

The next day Peary made preparations to continue his exploration of Ellesmere Land. Dr. Dedrick protested, but Peary ignored him. He took with him Ahng-ma-lokto, a sturdy Eskimo named Seegloo, and Koo-loo-ting-wah, who had come back to the *Windward* a few days before. With these able assistants Peary traveled some 2,500 miles, during which they climbed a glacier and crossed the Grinnell Land icecap. (See map, page 186.) He returned to the ship soaked to the waist from wading in icy water, his feet bleeding, and the stumps of his toes in frightful condition.

In Etah, meantime, Henson had found Eskimo friends, some of whom he hadn't seen since Red Cliff.

"Where is Ahnalka?" he asked, as they crowded around to welcome him.

Their smiles faded. For a moment there was silence.

"It is sad," said Ahnalka's friend, Kyutah. "Ahnalka hated the *Angakok*, Kyo, and would not hunt for him. So Kyo kill him."

Suddenly the crowd parted and Matt saw fear in their eyes as a man with an air of supreme authority strode up to him. "I Kyo," he said, "I powerful *Angakok*. Kyo afraid of no man."

As an *Angakok*, Kyo had the right to demand food in return for his services as a magician. Knowing this, Matt replied scornfully, "I have no fear of you. I am not lazy. I hunt and kill my own meat."

The taunt hit where it hurt. Kyo agreed to go hunting with other men in the tribe, and the natives made good use of this chance to get rid of their evil neighbor. A few weeks later, Kyutah reported that "Fourteen, perhaps fifteen, brave hunters each put one bullet in Kyo."

True to his promise, Mr. Jesup had sent the *Diana*, with Sam Bartlett, John's brother, as captain, and Mr. Herbert L. Bridgman, Secretary of the Peary Arctic Club, in command. They anchored off Etah early in August. Henson went aboard immediately and gave Mr. Bridgman Peary's message.

Since the club had decided that the *Windward* must return with the *Diana* in order to have new engines installed, Mr. Bridgman said there was no point in trying to reach her while she was fast in the ice. The delay would give sportsmen who had come on the *Diana* a chance to hunt walrus, to which their passage money entitled them.

He gave Henson a package of letters for Peary, and said he also had letters for Captain Sverdrup but didn't know where to find him. Henson suggested that he might try Payer Harbor.

Thus it happened that when Sverdrup left his winter quarters in the hope of pushing northward, he caught sight of the smoke from a steamer off Payer Harbor. He tried to get near her, but only managed to come close enough to see her signal that she'd left letters for him.

A week later, the *Windward* broke out of the ice and crossed to Etah. Peary was delighted to hear that the *Diana* had come and that Mr. Bridgman was on board. Quickly he went through the letters Henson handed him, which were full of good news. Mr. Jesup wrote that the club had arranged to finance every expedition Peary embarked on until he reached the Pole. Peary hastened to reply that he had succeeded in getting a base that could be reached by land, and that if his luck held, Sverdrup would be unable to force his ship through the ice and would return to Norway with nothing to report but defeat.

Sverdrup already had found the ice too much for his ship, and that same evening the *Fram* dropped anchor not far from the *Windward*. Captain Bartlett and Dr. Dedrick hastened over to pay their respects, brought a bundle of newspapers, and said that Peary was preparing to spend the winter in Etah.

In the morning, Captain Bauman called on Peary and congratulated him on having recovered sufficiently to make the long journey that Koo-loo-ting-wah had mentioned. The *Fram*, he said, had been unable to get through the ice, and they'd been forced to change their plans.

Peary invited them to send letters by way of his ships,

but only to their nearest friends, and on condition that nothing should be reported about the expedition itself.

The next night the *Diana* returned, and Mr. Bridgman, seeing no lights in the *Windward*'s cabins, went over to the *Fram*. He found Sverdrup on deck, introduced himself, and said he'd left letters for them at Payer Harbor. He promised to let the *Fram*'s owners know on what date the club's ships would sail so they could bring any letters received for Sverdrup and his party.

Since they were in Peary's winter quarters, Sverdrup gave up the walrus hunt he had planned, and sailed away before morning. Although he'd had to abandon his plan of rounding Greenland, he was content. The north section of Ellesmere Land, which he had left to Peary, and the land they'd seen to the west of it, was now open to his own party, and for the next three years they explored it with marked success.

Mr. Bridgman found Peary in his cabin shortly after breakfast writing up his report of the year's work. They greeted each other warmly and Mr. Bridgman said it must have been a disappointment when the *Windward* had to land him so far south. But Peary assured him that the year hadn't been a total loss, and Greely's old headquarters, which he was using for a northern base, offered two possibilities for the next year —either an advance on the Pole or the exploration of the north coast of Greenland—whichever seemed better under the conditions encountered in March or April.

Mr. Bridgman congratulated him, and left him.

"Peary told you about his feet, did he?" asked the captain as Bridgman came on deck.

"Not a word," he said. "What was there to tell?"

Captain Bartlett told him.

Bridgman was stunned by the news. "I'll fix it," he said, firmly, and went down to Peary's cabin. In ten minutes, he was back.

"You fixed it, sir?" asked Bartlett.

"Fixed it, hell!" exclaimed Bridgman. "Might as well talk to a stone wall. 'When my furlough has expired or I have reached the Pole, I shall be ready to go,' he said."

Peary had decided to spend the winter in Etah, using for shelter a caboose presented by the president of the Erie Railroad and used on the *Diana* as a deck house. Now it was hoisted over the side and taken ashore. Supplies and several tons of walrus meat for the dogs followed, and both ships sailed away.

Already the fierce winds for which Etah is noted were sweeping down on the settlement, and the work of transforming the caboose was started immediately. A workroom was added, both were buried in snow, and the natives built igloos alongside with entrances arranged so that they could enter without going outside.

In January, Henson and the Eskimos sledged food across to Cape Sabine, cut a new trail for fifty miles, and in February began transporting supplies to the fort. Peary followed in March, and found that the process of breaking in his feet to the manner in which he now had to walk was agonizing. The pulling and straining of tendons and muscles unused to such treatment made his legs ache until it seemed that another step was impossible. But by the end of the three-hundred-mile trip, he was able to go ahead with reasonable comfort.

After discussing the situation with Henson, who told him that the Eskimos were terrified at the thought of traveling over the Polar Sea, he decided to explore the Greenland coast, where for most of the way they would be on land. He started on April 11, with six natives and Henson.

At the first camp, Sipsu, who had agreed to come in spite of stomach cramps that had plagued him for several days, was seized with such griping pains that Peary took him back to the fort. The rest of the party crossed the channel and, when Peary rejoined them, they cut a road up the coast until, at the end of ten days, they were stopped by open water at the foot of the Black Horn. Cliffs. They waited two days and, on the second night, the temperature dropped to twenty-five degrees below zero, forming a thin coating of ice. Sliding, with feet wide apart, they rounded the cliffs, and returning, used their feet like brooms to brush the snow aside and give the ice a chance to harden.

Now two Eskimos were sent back in accordance with the system of support Peary had adopted. The food on their sledges had been used to feed the entire party up to this point, and there was only enough left to get them to Fort Conger. The others went on around the cliffs and started along the north coast of Greenland. Ten days later, Ootah and Poo-blah, the second supporting party, turned back, and Peary, Henson, and Ahng-ma-lokto went on with full sledges.

When, on May 13, they reached the most northern point on the coast, Peary found that the archipelago, which he expected would give him steppingstones to the Pole, stopped short of it by over six hundred miles. An experimental trip of fifteen miles due north over the polar ice brought them to a wide stretch of water, and they returned to their starting point, which Peary named Cape Morris Jesup.

From there, Peary led them eastward to complete his exploration of the north coast. In the face of a wind that burned their faces until they cracked, and in a glare of sun almost unendurable even through their dark glasses, they rounded the most easterly cape. Peary named it Cape Bridgman, and went southward until he recognized a mountain he had seen from Navy Cliff in 1892. Thus having nearly closed the gap between Independence Bay and the North Coast, he turned back and camped again at Cape Morris Jesup.

While Henson and Ahng-ma-lokto built a cairn, Peary stripped to the waist and unwound from his body the flag his

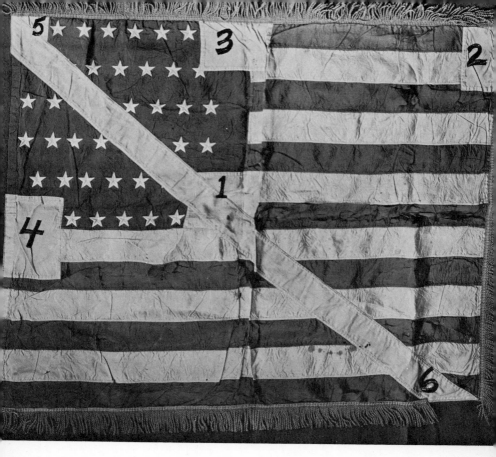

The silk flag made by Josephine Peary in 1898. The pieces were left by her husband as follows: 1 and 2 at Cape Morris Jesup in 1900; 3 at Cape Thomas Hubbard in 1906; 4 at Cape Columbia in 1906; 5 at the nearest approach to the Pole in 1906; 6 at the North Pole in 1909

wife had made for him. Carefully he cut out a small square showing bits of the red, white, and blue, and enclosed it in the records left in the cairn: the date when he discovered this northern terminus of Greenland, the latitude he had reached over the sea ice, and the names of his companions.

By June 10, they were back at Fort Conger, wet from head to foot as the result of spending the last week almost continually in water. "Yet," writes Peary, "I never felt before,

I never expect to feel again, the same exhilaration of spirit, the same mental exaltation . . . This whole grand coast, fronting the central Polar Basin, never before seen by human eye, was mine . . . by the great right of discovery. A mild form of lunacy, perhaps, yet the feeling has been in the heart of every man who has trodden for the first time on new lands, and will be in the hearts of a few more men yet, before the earth yields up its last unknown mile."

Peary had observed while camping on the ice pack north of Cape Jesup that the floes were drifting rapidly eastward toward a southerly current. Obviously conditions here were not favorable for an expedition to the Pole, and he decided to make the attempt from Cape Hecla on the north coast of Grant Land. (See map, page 186.)

In order to avoid the preliminary trip from Etah, which would add three hundred miles to the distance that lay between the fort and the Pole, he prepared to spend the winter at the fort. If the re-engined Windward could get to them, well and good. In case it could not, they began bringing up supplies cached along the route and, when that was done, they hunted musk oxen.

Early in April of the next year (1901), with Henson and Sipsu, who was the only Eskimo with courage enough to go along, he started for Cape Hecla. But Peary, sledges, and dogs were not in any condition to travel the ninety miles to the cape, let alone the five hundred miles each way to the Pole. Peary shuffled bravely along in the track Henson tramped out through the soft snow, but they had caught only their first glimpse of the sea when his strength gave out.

Within eight days they were back at the fort, and the next week started south for Cape Sabine, where Peary hoped the Windward had left provisions for another year.

Ten days later they were met by a party of Eskimos sent north to look for them. They said the big ship had come many moons before, and was still waiting at Cape Sabine. Mrs. Peary was on board, also Ahnighito.

"And they were there all the time we wintered at Conger," Peary groaned. "If I'd only known . . . if I'd only known!"

Motioning to the Eskimos to step aside, Peary and Henson started for the ship at a speed that left them far behind, and reached the *Windward* on May 6, Peary's forty-fifth birthday.

Ahnighito saw them first and, with a shout of joy, threw herself into her father's arms. Holding her tight against his shoulder, he drew his wife into the same embrace. Charles Percy, the steward, came forward from the galley to add his greeting. He was devoted to Peary, who had picked him up in Newfoundland where he was known as a ne'er-do-well. But Peary had seen in him possibilities hitherto not recognized, and had hired him as a man of all work. "Old Charlie," as he was affectionately called, had made good. He was an excellent cook, and proved it by making a birthday cake, which Mrs. Percy topped with frosting and canned cherries.

Henson had felt a pang of loneliness as he watched the joyful reunion. In all the world there was no one who cared whether he lived or died. Why had he shut himself off in this bleak land of eternal ice, wind, and snow, with its long months of darkness? What good was it doing? He was sick and tired of living like an Eskimo. He wanted a home of his own.

He went to his cabin, looked with disgust at his fur clothing and, opening the porthole, dropped it out on the ice. Then he laid out clean clothes, took a hot bath and, feeling more cheerful, joined in the celebration.

But the warmth of family life had not softened the hard core of Peary's ambition. Three days later, Henson had his furs on again and was sledging up the coast with a party of Eskimos to prepare Fort Conger for another assault on the Pole. In spite of Josephine's warning that he should give his feet a chance to recover from the effects of the rough trip down, Peary went with them. But by the end of a month, his feet were breaking down, and he returned to the ship, where the work of establishing winter quarters awaited him.

The caboose had served that purpose so well that he decided to use the *Windward's* deck house. To make a foundation, stringers were laid, and stones set between them, topped by a thick bed of hay. The deck house was placed on it, and with snow heaped around it, was comfortable even on the coldest days.

The Peary Arctic Club, much disturbed because the *Windward* had failed to return as expected the previous fall, sent the *Eric* north to see what had happened. Again Mr. Bridgman was in command, and Dr. Cook, Peary's former assistant, was with him. They reached Etah in August and, learning that the *Windward* was icebound at Cape Sabine, they crossed over.

Bridgman's first question when he met Peary was about his feet. Peary told him they had taken him 150 miles along the unexplored coast of Greenland, and out on the sea ice farther north than anyone had gone from the American side of the polar basin.

Such an achievement under such a handicap amazed Bridgman. It also relieved his mind about Peary's ability to win the Pole, and he brought him up to date by telling him that the Duke of Abruzzi had tried for the pole in 1900, but had fallen short by 220 miles. (See map, page 186.) On his return, however, he had said that another expedition, starting from the coast of Grant Land, would succeed.

Peary, knowing that ice-filled channels could be counted on to prevent an invasion of his country, was not dismayed. He reminded Bridgman that the only base from which to reach that coast belonged to the United States government, and was occupied by himself.

Bridgman laughed, and said that the club would be pleased to know that he was holding the fort against all rivals. Then he gave him a handful of letters, and left him to read them in peace.

But peace was not what the letters brought him. Among them was a note from his cousin Ella, saying that his mother had died in November. When Josephine came to tell him lunch was ready, she found him with his head in his arms.

She had invited Bridgman and Dr. Cook to eat with them, and the doctor's unexpected visit helped turn Peary's thoughts away from his sorrow. Cook was just back from the Antarctic, and full of amusing anecdotes about his experiences in Patagonia where, as he told it, he had been the life of the party. He had brought his camera, and after lunch Peary posed for him with Ahnighito on his lap.

Before the end of the month, both ships sailed away, leaving only "Old Charlie" who was to cook and tend camp for Peary and Henson.

In September, an epidemic swept through the Eskimo settlement around the deck house. Although Peary dosed them with everything he thought helpful, six had died by the middle of November, and the rest were too weak to hunt. Henson shot ten musk oxen a few miles above Cape Sabine, and thus fortified, the natives began to regain their strength. But they looked at Peary with eyes full of suspicion, and he couldn't understand why they continued to resist all his efforts to gain their confidence.

It was Seegloo's wife who finally explained. "The Almighty Devil was angry that we joined Peary again, to help the white men travel across the great ice," she said.

But the epidemic had run its course and, by spring, fourteen Eskimos had mustered up enough courage to help sledge supplies to the fort, but half of them refused to go any closer to the Devil's heart land on the Polar Sea.

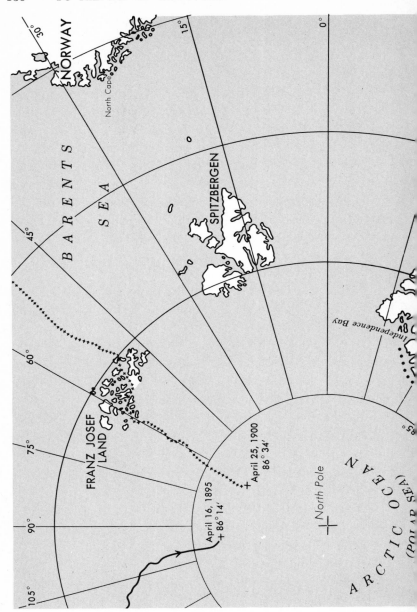

Dotted line shows Peary's route from 1898–1906, showing point reached on April 21, 1902; solid line shows the Arctic Ocean part of Nansen's route and the farthest point he reached; line of dashes (---) shows Sverdrup's route to Land's End, reached in 1902; line of crosses (xxx) shows part of Abruzzi's route and the farthest point he reached

The rest started off with heavily loaded sledges, Henson leading and Peary bringing up the rear to make sure there were no deserters. From the first they encountered violent resistance in the shape of furious gales and blinding snow. When these obstacles did not force them to retreat, their lives were threatened. Peary's sledge slipped on the tilted trail, and the two Eskimos ahead found their sledges slipping also, and saved themselves by a hairsbreadth with their feet already dangling over a vertical cliff fifty feet high. After that, the only way to get ahead was along a shelf of ice so narrow that the slightest deviation would plunge them onto the ragged ice below. At this point, three Eskimos balked, convinced that Tornarsuk was determined to destroy them.

From Cape Hecla, the four who remained took one look at the chaos of floes cracking and piling up into ridges under the pressure of the tide, leaving streams of water between them. Even Ahng-ma-lokto, who'd gone out on the frozen ocean from Cape Jesup, was dismayed by the prospect and, like Ootah, Sipsu, and Pooblah, refused to go farther.

"I've practically promised everything I've got," said Peary. "Isn't that enough?"

Henson shook his head. "It's that damn devil of theirs, Tornarsuk."

He went to the sledges on which the Eskimos sat with their backs to the devil's stamping ground. Trying to see the situation as they saw it, he said a few words that brought them to their feet, and they took their places at the upstanders, ready for the order to march.

Peary had watched the colloquy with interest, and asked what had made them change their minds.

Henson smiled a little sheepishly. "I told them," he said, "that in the South was the greatest and most powerful devil in the sea, the United States Navy."

"This is a fine time to be insulting the Navy," said Peary.

"Well, it sounds foolish in English," Henson admitted, "but I let the idea sink in that the United States Navy devil was feared by Tornarsuk, and that you are the highest honored son of the Navy and also feared by Tornarsuk."

Peary laughed. "Believe me, I'm highly flattered."

On April 6, they climbed down from the Cape, and as their sledges slid from the solid ice along the shore onto the moving ice pack, their noses were buried in snow, and the dogs sank in so deep that they had to be lifted out. The men walked in advance, stamping out a trail for the dogs and returning to dig out the sledges. It was slow work, but worse was lying in wait for them. On the second day out, they had to cut their way over or around hummocks of ice as high as their shoulders, sometimes lifting the sledges bodily over the barrier. At the end of a week, they were stormbound by a gale, and the floe on which they were camped split with a report like the crack of a rifle. Using cakes of ice as a ferry, they moved to the next floe. It was easy to understand now why the Eskimos called this the Devil's Domain.

A short distance beyond, they were stopped by a band of water so broad that Peary called it the "Grand Canal." From here, Ootah and Pooblah were sent back. They had accomplished their task of supplying food for the party, and must get to land as best they could with the provisions left.

As soon as the canal froze, Peary, Henson, Sipsu, and Ahng-ma-lokto crossed and forged ahead through fog and stormy weather. Again a trail had to be cut over high ridges of ice and, at the end of sixteen hours, they had made only two or three miles. And so it went for another week, each march bringing them only a few miles nearer their goal.

On April 21, Peary took one last look at the pinnacles and domes of ice that separated him from the Pole, and wrote in his diary: "The game is off. My dream of sixteen years is ended."

XII

ONE LAST HOPE

Under the circumstances, Peary's effort to reach the Pole was indeed only a dream. In reality the four sledges he had couldn't carry enough food to last until his party got there, to say nothing of getting back again. They had barely enough to take them to Fort Conger.

But Peary's character was full of contradictions. Sometimes he was misled by his overweening ambition. More often, common sense prevailed and he carefully analyzed the problems he had to solve. This quality, plus his courage and determination, won him the support he needed for success.

The difficulty of finding their way back to the coast gave him no chance to brood on his failure. Their outward trail was buried under snow, blocked by new pressure ridges, or broken by streams of water where the floes had split apart. It was not until they reached land, and the hazards of the ice pack no longer presented a challenge, that Peary gave way to despair.

Two days later, they rounded Cape Sheridan and camped just below on the shore of the Polar Sea. In 1875, this had been the winter quarters of the *Alert*, a British ship that had dropped anchor farther north than any vessel before or since. The sight of the cairn that marked her achievement led Peary out of his black mood into renewed hope.

The Peary Arctic Club had agreed to finance him until

he reached the Pole. With this end in view, they had bought more powerful engines for the *Windward*, but the engines weren't powerful enough to get her to his base at Fort Conger. She had other faults, too. Her hull wasn't slender enough to squeeze through narrow leads; her prow wasn't designed to break the floes that blocked her way. Plans for a more adequate model began to race through Peary's mind, and he reached Cape Sabine in good spirits. While waiting for the *Windward*, he hunted or did further surveying of the back country. When the *Windward* arrived, with Josephine on board, his first words were not about his failure, but about the new ship and his certainty that his next expedition would be a success.

Josephine didn't have the heart to remind him of his promise that this expedition would be his last. Instead, she smiled and said that with such a ship as he described, she knew he would reach the Pole.

As usual, two or three weeks were spent hunting walrus for his Eskimo helpers, and it was late in August, 1902, when they arrived in New York.

Henson telephoned to George Gardner, one of the friends he had made while he was working in the museum. Mr. Gardner invited him to come for dinner and stay as long as he wished. While Henson was packing his bag, Peary came in. He said he wouldn't be needing Matt for a year or two, and asked where a letter would reach him. Henson gave him his friend's address. Peary walked to the gangplank with him and wished him good luck until they met again.

In his voyages on the *Katie Hines*, Henson had seen many countries, but very little of the United States. He decided, therefore, to take a railroad job and become acquainted with his own country. He spent the night with Gardner, who promised to keep mail for him, and by noon had a job as Pullman porter on the Pennsylvania Railroad.

Peary, back at his post with the Civil Engineer Corps in Washington, found himself among strangers. Even those who had worked with him in the past seemed to have forgotten him.

"I felt," he said to Josephine, "as if I'd wandered back like a lost cat."

In October, he went to a surgeon in Philadelphia who, after an inspection of Peary's mutilated feet, amputated the little toes, which extended behind the stumps of the others, slit the skin in front, and drew forward the tissue from underneath and behind the toes, thus making a cushion for the stumps. The operation made it possible for Peary to go ahead easily on snowshoes, but otherwise he walked with a sliding gait which, on ice, was a handicap, and very tiring.

Because of his many years in the Navy, two grades of promotion were due him and, after passing the examination required, he had been raised to the rank of Commander. This meant a small increase in pay that was welcome and, as soon as he returned from Philadelphia, he rented an apartment for his family, who had been living with Josephine's parents.

In spite of his long absence, his work for the Navy was skillful and inventive and, in July, 1903, he was made a member of the Naval Examining Board. The next month, his family was increased by the birth of a son, who was named for his father. On October 20, he was sent abroad as president of a Naval Commission to study European types of barracks. Until now he had been forced to keep a tight rein on his ambition to reach the Pole. Although he had made a new record for the American side of the Arctic, it was not enough to offset the triumph of the Abruzzi expedition, and even some of his supporters in the Peary Arctic Club had lost confidence in him.

"I told you," one of them said to Mr. Bridgman, "that the British had proved a generation ago that the Pole couldn't be reached through Kennedy Channel. Why should we throw good money after bad by letting Peary try that way again?"

In London, however, Peary found the Admiralty waiting in suspense for news of Robert Scott's attempt to reach the South Pole, and this put new life into his determination to make his dream come true. By New Year's Day he was back in Washington, and immediately began sending letters asking support from men who, he believed, might still have faith in his ability to succeed. Among the replies he received, the one from the President of the Academy of Natural Sciences of Philadelphia, was typical: ". . . after hearing your lecture and reading your article in *McClure's* . . . I am more than ever impressed with the almost insuperable obstacles to be overcome by anyone attacking the Pole over the shifting floe ice and open leads which characterize the region north of Cape Helca. . . . To put it briefly in my humble opinion, the chances of success are not promising even under your experienced and resolute leadership."

But Mr. Jesup and Mr. Bridgman still believed that if Peary had a ship that would give him a base on the edge of the ice pack, he could reach the Pole. Therefore they rallied old subscribers to the Peary Arctic Club, added new ones, and in April the club was incorporated.

Peary submitted his plans for the ship, and Mr. Jesup and Mr. Thomas Hubbard each agreed to give $50,000 if Peary would raise the money for the expedition itself. In July, Peary and Captain Charles B. Dix, a shipbuilder from Buckport, Maine, whose firm had been chosen for the work, met with Mr. Jesup at his cottage in Bar Harbor and, in order to avoid delay, the captain agreed to assume the risk of ordering the lumber needed. Soon afterward, James C. Colgate made a contribution that completed the amount necessary to build the vessel. At the meeting where this was announced, the Assistant Secretary of the Navy was present, and was so impressed by the support Peary received from men of standing and wealth that he arranged to have the expedition sponsored by the Navy, although without financial backing, and Peary was granted a three-year leave.

When it came to naming the ship that was to battle with the ice until it reached the coast of the frozen ocean, Peary chose "Roosevelt," a name which, to him, symbolized the persistence and victory over all obstacles that characterized the President of the United States. The keel was laid in the middle of October, 1904, and Peary moved his family to the Maine coast, where he supervised the building of the ship, and also the building of a summer home on Eagle Island, thus realizing an ambition he'd had ever since he discovered it during his last year in high school.

While he had been struggling ahead on what he called "the Black march" toward his financial goal, Henson had been enjoying glimpses of America from parlor cars on the Pennsylvania system.

After two years of travel in the East, he wanted to see the Far West, and took a job that would get him there by the southern route. Before he reached New Orleans, rotten oranges had struck him as he helped passengers off the train, while the farmhands shouted, "Git back on them thar cars, nigger!" Another night, when the train stopped to take on water, a shot through the window, where he sat reading, just missed his head. "Thet'll teach 'em we don't like niggers down here," his attacker yelled as the train began to move.

New Orleans also was inhospitable. Disgusted, Matt took the first train leaving that city for the North.

A letter from Peary was waiting for him in Mr. Gardner's apartment, saying that the new ship would dock in Brooklyn some time in April, and he hoped that Matt would be on hand to help him get ready to sail in July.

That gave Matt a few weeks to enjoy his friends. He made the most of it, and so did they. Word spread that he was staying with George Gardner, and not only friends but other Negroes who wished to meet the first Arctic explorer in the history of their race, gathered in Gardner's living room. One evening there were two women among them, Mrs. Ross and her daughter Lucy.

Mrs. Ross asked him what Eskimo women were like, and he told her they were industrious and trained from childhood to make good wives and mothers. Gardner reminded Matt that he'd also said earlier in the evening that an Eskimo had wanted to trade wives with Peary, and asked if that was customary. After a moment's hesitation, Matt turned to Mrs. Ross and said perhaps they were talking too freely in front of her daughter.

"I'm no child!" said Lucy. "I guess if I'm old enough to earn my own living, I'm old enough to hear about Eskimos."

She spoke with such spirit that Matt was surprised to discover she was not the mild and gentle young thing he had thought her. Her readiness to view unusual customs as the natural outgrowth of primitive life and to understand the Eskimos as he did, gave him a feeling of warmth and security. After that, they saw each other often, and before the *Roosevelt* sailed, they were engaged to be married.

"I'll bring you the North Pole for a wedding present," said Matt as he kissed her good-by.

They parted with a laugh that drowned out the sadness of the moment, and filled Matt with hope and good cheer whenever he thought of it in the dark months to come.

The *Roosevelt* was not an impressive sight as she cast off and backed into the East River on July 16, 1905. She was not much larger than a sea-going tug, and was equipped with sails so that she could use the wind and save the fuel needed to stoke her powerful engines.

Her captain was Robert A. Bartlett, who had been his uncle's first mate on the *Windward* in 1898. In the meantime he had been captain of several sealing vessels, which had given him much experience in ice navigation, and the crew, mostly from Newfoundland like himself, had complete confidence in him.

There were only two assistants in addition to Henson: Ross G. Marvin, a graduate of Cornell University, and Dr. Louis J. Wolf, attending physician at the Cornell University Medical College.

Peary had found that a deck house, where it was possible to have glass windows and sunlight, was far superior to the dark and damp rooms below. Therefore all the *Roosevelt's* cabins, including the crew's quarters, were on deck, and Peary's, which was next to Henson's, was large enough for the pianola and the collection of records given him by members of the club.

Only one catastrophe marred the voyage to Etah. After leaving Sydney, it was found that several sections of the water-tube boilers were leaking. Efforts to repair them were fruitless, and the ship was reduced to half her horsepower. Fortunately, the sea was calm, and Melville Bay was free of ice, which gave rise to hope that the northern channels would present fewer difficulties than usual.

Peary and Henson visited the Eskimo settlements around Cape York and Inglefield Gulf, and collected thirty-three families, their dogs, sledges, and whatever else they had. When they overtook the *Eric*, which was loaded with additional coal for the *Roosevelt*, Peary, Henson, and Marvin went aboard to hunt walrus. Eighteen of them were piled on deck when they reached Etah.

The coal put ashore by the *Roosevelt* was left at Etah for the return trip, but even so she was lower in the water than Peary wished, for in addition to four hundred tons needed to get them to their northern base and back, food enough to feed his large party for a year, plus half a ton of walrus meat, there were two hundred dogs on deck and almost half a hundred Eskimos on the fo'c'sle and tops of the deck houses.

Soon after midnight on August 18, they steamed into the ice pack which, contrary to Peary's expectations, was wedged in the narrow channel more tightly than he'd ever seen it. Captain Bartlett, whose experience in ice navigation had been in sealing vessels, proceeded cautiously as was customary when they were heavily loaded. But Peary, eager to see what the ship could do, ordered full speed ahead.

With some misgivings, the young captain obeyed, and Peary was elated as he saw the *Roosevelt* split the ice with her steel-shod stem and rise on it like a horse taking a fence, while her steeply sloping sides, also encased in steel, slipped from its grip and the pressure lifted her until the floe smashed under her weight and she shoved it aside. Again and again, she rammed and rebounded, then gathered speed for another rush forward, while the Eskimo women shrieked and the dogs howled.

"She fights like a gladiator!" Peary exclaimed with justifiable pride, for he had put all his knowledge of engineering into designing her to win just such a battle. Bartlett, reassured by the ship's buoyancy, in spite of her heavy load, was full of enthusiasm as he saw how easily, because of her narrow width, she wheeled and twisted through every opening.

But in spite of his confidence that the *Roosevelt* would give him a base on the Arctic coast, Peary had ordered her headed for Cape Sabine, where he intended to put ashore food, coal, and a few boats in case the ship should be damaged and they would have to make an overland retreat. However, heavy ice blocked the approach, and he established his sub-base at Victoria Head some miles farther north.

As they steamed on past Cape D'Urville, their head-quarters in 1898, Henson lounged against the rail, thinking of the many times he'd cut a road and sledged provisions over the rough ice foot, laborious work that the *Roosevelt* was now doing for them.

Marvin, looking across the deck and seeing Henson's carefree posture, decided he was the laziest man on the ship. But presently a strong wind from the north bore down upon them. "All hands! Douse the sails!" ordered the mate and, to Marvin's surprise, Henson was the first man aloft. As he watched him reefing the frozen canvas with the poise and knowhow of an old salt, Marvin's interest in the Negro was quickened. When at last they anchored in the lee of a cape, he asked Henson how many years he'd been at sea, and how much he knew about navigation. Henson said he'd had five years on a windjammer back in the eighties, but that his knowledge of navigation consisted only of what he called "knot and splice seamanship," and he needed to master the mathematical end. Marvin, who had spent three years on a Navy schoolship, offered to teach him, and during the winter Henson tried to fill that gap in his education.

By evening, the *Roosevelt* once more was hammering and squeezing her way ahead, but by morning she had to creep under the shelter of Cape Wilkes. Apparently the ice on this side of the channel was unbroken, and Peary decided to cross to the Greenland side where he'd noticed, in previous years, that there was more open water.

The next afternoon the *Roosevelt* headed eastward into the channel pack. Like a fifteen-ton battering ram she hurled herself at the ice and smashed her way through, while the deck heaved upward and rocked from side to side. When the ice resisted, she retreated, gathered headway, and attacked again until the ice split with a savage snarl.

Bartlett, aloft in the crows'-nest, at last sighted a stretch

Captain Robert Bartlett in the crows'-nest of the *Roosevelt*

of loose ice. He shouted to the helmsman, but couldn't make himself heard above the howling of the terrified dogs. He bellowed like a bull, and jumped up and down, trying to attract attention.

It was Seegloo who saw him, and said with a grin, "Captain's gone mad."

Henson looked up and alerted the helmsman, who changed his course, forced the Roosevelt through the floating ice, and headed her north along the Greenland coast. Before long she was caught between two cakes of ice and the tide hurled her against the ice foot where she ground along with the noise of a railroad car bumping over the ties, until she scraped into a niche and was quickly made fast. Temporary repairs were made to her steering gear and, when the pressure relaxed, she steamed on to Newman Bay between Cape Sumner and Cape Brevoort. (See map, page 230.)

The sudden jolts and violent rolls, as the Roosevelt butted her way across the channel, had made sleep impossible, and everyone took advantage of the opportunity afforded by the five days she lay in the harbor while her steering gear was overhauled.

On the fifth day, Bartlett and Marvin climbed to the highest point on the coast, hoping to see some sign of open water to the west. There was none. Peary, unable to endure further delay, ordered full steam ahead and the ship resumed her battle with the ice.

After thirty-five and a half hours of strain and struggle, she made the crossing and dropped anchor in a small bay a few miles below Cape Sheridan that guards the entrance to the Polar Sea. Worn out by anxiety and loss of sleep, Bartlett and Peary went to their cabins. It was the twenty-ninth of August and, as he closed his eyes, Peary's thoughts floated back to his family and in his dreams he was once more with his little son who had just celebrated his second birthday.

Morning brought a blinding snowstorm. Again Peary and Bartlett, aloft in the rigging, watched for an opening between the floes swinging past on the flood tide. On the sixth day, a narrow strip of water gave them their chance. Racing with the incoming tide, black smoke pouring through her stack as her engines were driven to capacity, the *Roosevelt* shot through and was fairly hurled into a niche beyond Cape Sheridan. Even before she was made fast, the ice closed in behind her. By the narrowest of margins, she had won the opening battle and, as if in defiance of the War Lord of the North, her nose was pointed straight toward the Pole.

Boxes of provisions were put ashore and sledged to the base of the cliff where they were stacked up to make walls for one large house and two small ones. Sails laid over boat

The *Roosevelt* in winter quarters at Cape Sheridan (photo by Henson)

spars roofed them and, with stoves and fuel in each, they would serve as comfortable places of refuge in case of any mishap to the ship.

While the Eskimos hunted for reindeer and musk oxen, Henson taught Marvin and Dr. Wolf how to handle the dogs, how to adjust their fur jackets and trousers to keep out the wind, or to provide ventilation when hard work made them sweat.

By November, daylight was almost gone, and most of the Eskimo hunters built igloos in the neighborhood of Lake Hazen, about forty miles northwest of Fort Conger, where they lived throughout the winter, returning to the ship during the weeks of moonlight with meat and skins. Some of the women went with them but most of them stayed in the box houses where they worked on fur clothes for Peary's party.

The Great Night showed up the unevenness of Peary's personality. Sometimes he was exultant because the ship he'd designed had got farther north than any other by way of the American route, and again because he'd perfected an alcohol stove that could boil water in less than the time previously required. This last was noteworthy because what a man wants most during ten or twelve hours on the trail is something to quench his thirst. A greenhorn might try putting a handful of snow in his mouth, only to discover that this made him thirstier. Too much of it, he might discover, would lower his temperature to the danger point.

In his moods of depression, Peary was troubled by thoughts of what might happen to the *Roosevelt*. She might be crushed against the ice foot, or set afire by a lamp over-turned in the crew's quarters. It wouldn't be fatal. They could live ashore, and he'd taken care of the chance that they might have to walk back along the coast.

The dogs worried him most. Many had sickened and died after eating the whale meat brought from Labrador.

The rest he had sent to the back country with Eskimo hunters, hoping that a diet of musk-ox meat would save them.
But they had continued to die, there was no way to replace
them, and it was a tossup whether enough would survive to
get him to the Pole.

In these black moods Peary played on his pianola. The
music soothed him and brought to mind the many efforts
made to ensure his happiness—the easy chair provided by Mr.
Jesup, the warm rug Josephine had given him, and the
thoughtful care with which Old Charlie, the steward, attended to all his needs.

It was Josephine who had insisted that her husband take
Old Charlie, who was living as caretaker in a cottage on Eagle
Island beside the bungalow he had helped to build. Peary
had objected that this would leave her without a man on the
place, but she reminded him that they had friends among
the fishermen, any of whom would be trustworthy guardians.
So Old Charlie had come, and Peary was glad that he had.

During the days of darkness, Henson also had opportunities for relaxation. When he wasn't out hunting or making sledges or alcohol stoves, he worked on problems in
mathematics Marvin had given him to solve. Otherwise, he
read books he'd brought with him, or books Dr. Wolf loaned
him. Among his own books was Peary's account of the expeditions across the icecap, which he'd bought just before they
left Brooklyn.

One evening, after a short bout with mathematics, he
opened the first volume and read eagerly until he came to
Peary's description of the men who had been with him.

"Matthew A. Henson, my body servant . . ."

The disparaging words hit him between the eyes.

It was eighteen years since he'd been Peary's body servant, and the Canal Company had paid him for that. Up
here he worked for nothing; otherwise he supported himself,

just as Peary's other assistants did. But because of the color of his skin, Peary thought no more of destroying his manhood than had that cur down South who had tried to kill him with a shotgun. Peary used a word instead of a bullet; that was the only difference.

Matt closed the book with a bang, gave it another with his fist, dropped it on the floor, and kicked it away.

His angry reaction reminded him of the violence with which he had attacked Frenchy on the *Katie Hines*, the first man who'd ever called him a "nigger," and he recalled how Captain Childs had laid a restraining hand on his fist and said, "That's one way, Matthew, but your best weapons are knowledge and intelligence."

He relaxed, and looked at the situation more calmly. Why had Peary, who didn't treat him like a servant, chosen to degrade him in the eyes of the public?

The public—that was the answer. How else could he explain his constant association with a Negro to a public that regarded all Negroes as menials? To have a Negro valet was the mark of a gentleman. If Peary had gone beyond that and named a Negro among his assistants, he'd have stepped on too many toes and risked losing the financial support necessary for success. Peary's job was not to reform society. It was to get to the Pole. His own job was to win honor for his race by helping him get there.

He picked up the book, replaced it on the shelf, took down his Bible, and opened it at the twenty-third Psalm.

XIII

A RACE WITH DEATH

Thanksgiving and Christmas were celebrated with plenty of good food and lively music, and everyone was in good spirits. As usual, Peary had kept his party in fine trim by seeing to it that they had sufficient outdoor exercise. Enough dogs had survived to give him all he needed and he had worked out a system by which there would be enough food for the thousand-mile journey across the Polar Sea.

He had faced the problem with more realism than he had shown in 1902. Then, a supporting party that was sent back, remained there. This time, a supporting party would return with a second load.

He planned to have enough food brought to within two hundred miles of the Pole to take Henson, himself, and four Eskimos up there and back to land. For this he would need five supporting parties, each composed of a leader, three Eskimos, and fifteen dogs capable of pulling a total of fifteen hundred pounds.

It was a good plan, but unfortunately he had not foreseen that he would need more than four assistants. He needed six—five to head the supporting parties, and one to go ahead and cut the trail. In this emergency, Clark and Ryan, members of the ship's crew, volunteered.

By the last week in February, 1906, over four tons of food had been sledged to Cape Hecla. Camp was made, and

Peary called his assistants together to give them their final instructions. Henson was to lead the way. Bartlett was to be ready to start a day after Henson; Wolf was to follow twenty-four hours later, and Clark the day after that. Peary would bring up the rear with Marvin and Ryan. Each party was to travel fifty miles, deposit its load, and return for another.

On March first, Henson was given his marching orders. To reduce the chance that supplies would be lost by the splitting and shifting of floes, he was to hack out a road as he had done on the coast of Ellesmere Land, so that those following him would not be delayed. Since the Magnetic Pole was farther west, he must allow for a westerly deviation of 122 degrees on his compass, and proceed due north on the 70th meridian. (See map, page 230.)

Henson noted the deviation on his calendar, checked his pocket watch with Peary's, and compared the time on his chronometer watch with the three Peary carried, for accurate time was essential in determining longitude, as he'd learned on the *Katie Hines*. Finding the result satisfactory, he tied the chronometer watch around his neck next to his skin, and slipped his compass into his pocket.

"Adolo, adolo," he shouted to Sipsu, Panikpah, and Pewah-to who were to go with him. Immediately their long whips cracked like pistols and, with loud cries of "Huk Huk!" they were off.

The long Arctic night was ending under the advance of the sun which, though still below the horizon, bathed the landscape in glowing twilight. Near the shore the ice was smooth enough so that they could leap on their sledges and ride while the dogs ran at full speed. But two miles out they had to use their pickaxes to make a path through hummocks of ice, and before long they took off their deerskin jackets to keep from sweating, for wet underclothes are far from comfortable in a freezing temperature.

After twelve hours of stopping and chopping, dealing with fractious dogs, and chopping again, they built an igloo with a snow platform inside about two feet high, extending from wall to wall, and coming to within two feet of the door. With shelter provided, the next thing to attend to was food. Henson set the stove box on a snow ledge just inside the igloo, raised the top that prevented the heat from melting the wall, and turned down the front that provided a shelf for the sugar and condensed milk. He lit the two stoves, put on the cylindrical pots he had filled with ice and, while it was melting, went outside.

The Eskimos, meantime, had tethered the dogs and were feeding them. Henson beat the snow from their rugs so that it wouldn't change to water when the igloo got warm, carried them inside, and spread them on the platform. Then he went out again and brushed the snow from his clothes while the Eskimos did likewise.

By this time, half the ice in each pot had melted. Henson poured all of it into one pot, and dumped the rest of the ice into the other. Panikpah brought in cups and spoons, and chopped a can of frozen milk in two; Sipsu came in with pemmican, hardtack, and a cake of compressed tea, half of which Henson dropped into the pot of boiling water, saving the second half for the other pot. Now, having made sure that everything they needed was inside, Pe-wah-to fitted a block of snow into the doorway and, at last, after an hour and a half spent in getting ready, they sat on the edge of the platform and enjoyed a hot meal.

Steam from the boiling water filled the igloo and made them so drowsy that, as soon as they had eaten, they rolled over and went to sleep—first the Eskimos, and then Henson when finally he got used to their snoring.

They woke to find the world blotted out by a blinding snowstorm driven by a furious wind from the northwest, and for two days they were unable to go outside except to care for the dogs. Henson, listening to the roar of the wind and the groaning and rumbling of the ice as the rising tide pressed it upward, was disturbed by thoughts of what might happen if the floe on which they had camped should split on the landward side. The wind would drive the loosened section eastward, his trail would be broken, and Bartlett, following a day behind, would have to lose time looking for it.

But it was all part of the game. As soon as the storm died down, Henson gave the order to break camp. By now the moon was full, and they welcomed its brilliant light, but its pull on the ocean beneath them, which now coincided with the pull of the sun, brought a maximum tide that was almost fatal. While they slept, its terrific pressure ripped open the floe beside them, and the igloo shook as if in an earthquake.

They crawled outside, and saw dogs and sledges with all their provisions drifting away. Swiftly they ran alongside the black water until it grew narrower, then leaped across and rushed to the dogs. As they were harnessing them, the floe split again. They got the dogs into their traces and induced them to jump while the men eased the twelve-foot sledges across and swung over by the upstanders. Once more on firm ice, they hurried away from the dangerous spot and went on breaking the path northward.

Henson knew that probably there had been similar splits behind him. To reduce the weight of their sledges when they had to be hauled over upheaved ice, Peary had allowed only enough food for six days. They'd been gone seven. According to Peary's calculations, Bartlett should have reached them by now with a new supply. But open water would have held him up, and in that case they were in a jam—fifty miles from land, as ordered, with not enough food to go ahead, not enough to get back. Anxiously, he scanned the sky. Mackerel clouds and mare's tails promised nothing but more wind, more drifting and broken ice.

Then suddenly he gave a shout of joy. Huge dogs came running toward him across the sky, followed by the distorted figure of a driver, and he knew it was a mirage, reflecting real dogs and a real driver. Soon he was shaking hands with Bartlett, while their Eskimos gathered in a group to compare their experiences.

Bartlett reported that Henson's trail had been cut a dozen times by bands of water that sent him miles out of his way, or had been buried under mounds of ice, and getting the sledges over had been a new and hard experience. Henson congratulated him on his rapid progress and his success in making connection in spite of the disrupted trail. He replenished his stock of food, wished Bartlett better luck on his return trip, and went ahead.

Bartlett and his Eskimos stacked the cases of supplies they had brought to establish the first cache, and spent the night in the igloo Henson's party had built. In the morning, Bartlett discovered that the floe where they were camped had drifted a mile or so to the southeast. Dogs were harnessed without delay, and they started back to land for a new relay of provisions, taking a course to the southwest in the hope of striking the upward trail and intercepting those who were following it before they discovered it led nowhere.

Since the sledges were almost empty, Bartlett's party made rapid progress, and hit the old path in time to stop Wolf and Clark who were traveling together, Wolf being a day behind schedule. He told them that the floe on which he had made Cache No. 1 was drifting eastward and, after passing it, they should look for Henson's tracks to the northwest. A few hours later, he met Peary's party, made his report, and went on to the coast.

One of Peary's parties crossing a pressure ridge

The news Bartlett brought that the ice ahead was everywhere in motion did not surprise Peary. The same night that Henson's camp had burst asunder, the floe on which his own party was sleeping split with such force that their igloos were shattered, and the next night they had another close call. As a result, they were not making as much speed as Peary had hoped for.

Bartlett had lost a day on the way up, and two days after Bartlett had passed on his way back, Peary overtook Wolf and Clark stalled at Cache No. 1 by thick weather; Wolf two days behind schedule and Clark one. Wolf was sent back to reload, while Peary used his party and Clark's to move supplies ahead.

Four days later he caught up with Henson, who was on schedule and waiting for the supply of food he needed every six days. As soon as that was taken care of, the pioneer party marched on. For nine days, in temperatures that dipped to sixty degrees below zero, they continued to gouge out the trail, stopping repeatedly to mend sledges that crashed on the pressure ridges. The rolling motion of the ice increased as the great tide of the new moon began to run, and they walked miles to get around open water, Henson bearing to the west whenever possible in order to offset the eastward drift of the pack.

At the end of the ninth day, they were stopped by a band of water known thereafter as the "Big Lead" and extending in both directions as far as they could see from the top of the highest ridge. (See map, page 230.)

Again their food was almost gone. For three days they had eaten only half rations, and there was enough for just one more meal. After that, they would have to eat their dogs unless a supply party managed to follow their winding and broken trail, and find them.

Some fifty miles to the southeast, Peary was still working with Clark's party to form the second cache by moving everything fifty miles beyond the first. He had sent Marvin's party and Ryan's back to land for their second loads, but had kept Clark's because his Eskimos were among the most tireless workers—Seegloo, Pooblah, and sturdy, long-legged Egingwah.

After six days, Bartlett's party joined them, and Peary sent him on to leave his loads fifty miles beyond the second cache. Clark was to follow with a second relay.

Bartlett's return had demonstrated the increase in speed made possible by a well-traveled route, for he had covered in six days the distance for which Peary had used twelve, a record that gave Peary encouragement at a time when he was in need of it.

Fog banks that continued to cloud the horizon had filled him with apprehension. Fog meant open water; open water meant delay, and he couldn't afford delay. They had less than sixty days in which to get to the Pole and back. After that, the floes would begin to break apart for good under the heat of advancing summer. The one hope of success lay in the possibility that between the maximum tides of the full and the

new moon, the ice would remain still long enough for the
bitter cold to freeze it into a solid mass.

It was a forlorn hope. At the end of five days, although
the tide had lost its force, Peary found Henson, Bartlett, and
Clark camped beside the Big Lead, which Bartlett had reached
just as Henson was about to kill the first dog for their evening
meal.

Immediately Peary climbed a pinnacle to survey the situation, noted that the ice on the northern side was moving
slowly west and that the lead appeared to be narrowing in
that direction. He thought there might be a chance to cross
during the night, and told Henson to have his Eskimos stand
watch half a mile to the west and, if the chance came, to
notify everyone. Then Henson's party was to cross at once,
and go ahead.

But the lead remained open, and by morning it was even
wider than it had been the day before. Peary's spirits hit bottom, for now he realized that many days might pass before a
crossing could be made, if indeed it could be made at all.
He kept his grip on the situation, however, and knowing that,
while they waited, great quantities of food would be con-
sumed, he sent Bartlett and Clark back to the cache for a
new supply.

Torn between hope and despair, Peary sent scouting
parties along the lead to look for some sign that it was about
to freeze. They found that it was still widening, thus giving
new ice along the edge no chance to become firm. Even the
heavy floe on which they had camped split during the night
and cut them off from the main floe. But the next day his
scouts came back with unexpected news: the movement in the
Big Lead was slowing down and a film of ice was forming.

The weather was fine, the sun continuously above the
horizon and high enough to make a noon shot feasible. Peary
and Henson compared their chronometer watches and, shortly

before noon, Peary, facing south, observed the sun through his sextant until it reached its highest altitude for the day.

"Check!" he said, and while Henson made sure that the hands of his pocket watch pointed to twelve o'clock sharp, Peary wrote down the angles shown on his sextant. He found that their latitude was slightly north of the Grand Canal he had crossed on his first attempt to reach the Pole, and concluded that this was an extension of the same lead and marked the place where the ocean deepens at the edge of the Continental Shelf.

Once they'd crossed the lead, Peary felt sure of success. But he was disturbed by Henson's failure to follow the 70th meridian and reprimanded him sternly, pointing out that they were now on the 74th, due to Henson's habit of turning left whenever he had to go around an obstruction.

When Henson explained that he turned left to offset the eastward drift of the ice, Peary told him he had misjudged the drift, that the ice beyond the lead was moving west, and said that if Henson didn't follow his orders, he would replace him with someone more dependable.

He stalked away, and Henson, knowing that the Commander was always peppery when his nerves were on edge, took the rebuke serenely and continued spreading his clothes in the sun to dry.

By the next afternoon the lead, now two miles wide, was frozen over except for a narrow strip in the middle, and Peary felt sure that on the following day the ice would hold them. He was further encouraged by the arrival of Ryan's party, but Ryan's report was discouraging. Open water had delayed him continually after the first fifty miles. Drifting ice had separated him from Wolf and Marvin, and he didn't know where they were. Just this side of the cache, he had overtaken Bartlett, who said that he and Clark also had been held up by water, and Clark's party had drifted out of sight when the floe where both parties were camping split apart.

This news meant that the supply system was in danger of breaking down. They had only enough food to last two parties three or four weeks, and Ryan hadn't brought full loads. In order to save food and add another half ton to his provisions, Peary told Ryan to leave the next morning and, if possible, bring up another installment from the cache.

With Bartlett only two or three days behind him, Peary decided not to wait, but to cross the lead at the first opportunity. He traded one of his Eskimos for Angh-odo-blaho, who was in Ryan's party, and in a fever of impatience to be on his way north, sent his other Eskimos, Ootah and Ahng-ma-lokto, to patrol the lead and find out whether the center of it had frozen. They were gone a long time, and Peary paced nervously back and forth until at last they returned and said they thought the ice a little farther west would hold all the way across.

Immediately everyone was routed out. Peary warned Henson that the ice was uncertain, and asked whether he was willing to make the attempt. Henson, touched to the heart by Peary's anxious and careworn face, gave him a reassuring smile. He explained to Sipsu, Panikpah, and Pe-wah-to what was expected of them and how to go about it. They harnessed the dogs while Henson loaded the sledges. Then they put on their snowshoes, started at the same time, but some distance apart, and walking wide, like polar bears, got across. The ice had not cracked or bent beneath them, and as soon as they had unloaded, they went back for more supplies and crossed again.

While Ootah, Ahng-ma-lokto, and Ahng-odo-blaho were loading up, Peary wrote notes to his assistants telling them he was about to cross the Big Lead, and urging them to make all possible speed in order to reach it while it was still frozen.

These he gave to Ryan with instructions to hand one to each man he passed on his way to the cache.

As soon as Peary and his party were safely across, Henson went on. Peary ordered his Eskimos to double-ration their dogs, and cache some of the food Ryan had brought so their sledges wouldn't be overloaded. Then they built an igloo where Peary waited twenty-four hours in the hope that Bartlett or Marvin would overtake him. Neither came, so he left instructions for any one who got across to push ahead without trying to return to land, and followed Henson's trail northward in the teeth of a biting wind.

By morning a gale from the west brought thick snow squalls that almost obliterated Henson's tracks, and Peary made up his mind never to travel again in such thick weather unless compelled to do so. At the end of the third day he found Henson camped on a large floe waiting for the storm to subside.

The Eskimos began to build igloos near the center of the floe, but before they had finished, a crack extending all around the camp burst upen with a deafening report, and the Eskimos were paralyzed with fear. Presently Henson's igloo was shattered, as the crack closed with such force that it raised a pressure ridge beside it.

It was April 5, again the moon was full, again a mighty tide was surging beneath the ice. Peary knew that the Big Lead must be wide open again, but he hoped that at least one other party had got across.

April 8 was the anniversary of Nansen's nearest approach to the Pole. Peary cursed the lead that had kept him from surpassing Nansen's record. As the days dragged on, he thought of Lieutenant Cagni, leader of Abruzzi's polar attempt, and again reflected that, but for ten days' delay at the lead, he would have surpassed that also.

For six days the wind continued its infernal shrieking. To relieve his agitation, Peary crawled out and went criss-cross on his hands and knees in order to find out whether, if he were made of sterner stuff, he could go ahead. He decided that it was impossible. Henson, in the same fashion, went out to inspect the dogs, cheer the gloomy spirits of the Eskimos, and bring back food for Peary and himself.

When at last the wind died down and the sun came out, Peary made a noon observation with his transit, but he didn't tell Henson the result nor check Henson's chronometer time.

He borrowed Sipsu, and sent him back with Ahng-ma-lokto to look for Marvin or Bartlett, and to bring on the supplies he'd left after crossing the Big Lead. He sent Henson ahead, saying he would follow in a couple of days and take over the job of setting their course.

As he broke the trail northward from Storm Camp, Henson was plagued by uncertainty as to their whereabouts. Unable to set his mind at rest until he had some idea of how far they had drifted, he pulled out his chronometer watch and compared the time it showed with the local time on his pocket watch. He had set that watch when Peary made his observation at noon. If his chronometer time was still correct, they had drifted until they were almost opposite the ship at Cape Sheridan, just across the channel from Greenland.

He prayed that there would be no more wind from the west. They had enough trouble to face as it was. Dense fog warned them of open water ahead, and the next day they were stopped by a lead. On this day, too, the light wind that had been blowing from the west developed into a half gale, and Henson was inclined to agree with Pe-wah-to that the Devil of the North was determined to destroy them.

Back in Storm Camp, Peary had been wrestling with

the problems that now confronted him. He knew definitely that they had drifted seventy miles and were almost in line with the ship as Henson had calculated. The safest course was to turn back at once, but that would mean complete failure. A few days would bring him abreast of Nansen's record, and another week or two abreast of Abruzzi's, and possibly beyond. But if he went ahead, he ran the risk of ending his return trip on the coast of Greenland, with no food supply awaiting him and the possibility that they might starve before they could reach the ship. They would, in fact, be opposite Greenland now except for Henson's persistence in keeping to the west. As it was, he had a little margin of safety on which to gamble.

It all depended on whether or not they had stopped drifting. For the last few days there had been little or no motion. This, he thought, meant one of two things: either the central pack was moving as one mass, or the ice was jammed to the eastward and could move no further. He decided it was the latter, and resolved to push on even if his scouts failed to make contact with a supporting party, taking a chance that there would be no more water to delay them, and facing the certainty of eating their dogs before they got back.

He was still hopeful, however, that Bartlett would be met on his way up from the igloo where the note and the cache had been left, for, judging by the tracks made by his own party, which stood out in bold relief against the ice from which all the loose snow had been swept away, the trail from the Big Lead to Storm Camp had not been destroyed. Therefore, he expected that at least the Eskimos would come back with the supplies and, small as they were, that would relieve the situation considerably.

But everything went contrary to his hopes and calculations. Soon after midnight the Eskimos returned, saying that they had followed the trail for six hours and had reached the first igloo south of Storm Camp. They had met no one and, from there on, as far as they could see from the top of the pinnacle, the trail was buried under open water and shattered ice which made it impossible to reach the cache of food.

Early the next morning, Peary set out at a record pace and the following day caught up with Henson beside the lead that had stopped him. Peary told him that the Eskimos had reported and that there was no chance, therefore, of a supply party reaching them. They would have to make a dash for the Pole with what they had.

He looked at Henson with a question in his eyes. Henson smiled and nodded. Peary thanked him, and since the lead had just closed, he crossed first and, keeping a close watch on his compass, continued to guide them toward his goal. As he had anticipated, the going was smooth and there was little need for pickaxes. But in other respects the condition of the ice did not come up to his expectations, for their marches were constantly interrupted by water, and wind from the west continued with sufficient force to hold them in camp beside a fifty-foot lead for twenty-four hours.

Here six worn-out dogs were killed and, as they skinned them before feeding them to the other dogs, the Eskimos were thrown into a panic by the discovery that there was almost no meat on the bones. They wanted to go no farther.

But Peary told them he was not ready to turn back yet, and led them on at a heartbreaking pace. At the end of each march, they staggered into camp like drunken men. Exhausted dogs were killed and fed to the others. Igloos were built from force of habit rather than with the intelligence of human beings, and slept in until a pounding on the ice announced that Peary was ready to start on again.

Without stopping to eat, they harnessed the dogs, gnawing on pieces of frozen pemmican as they urged their teams forward. Cracks and leads increased, but they ran parallel to their course and Peary made forced marches between them until he was certain that he had reached Abruzzi's farthest.

So tired that further effort seemed impossible, Henson and the Eskimos cut blocks of snow and, like automatons in a nightmare, built the igloos and slept until midnight. Then Peary started them on again, and they marched for eleven hours without stopping. It was shortly before noon when he called a halt and prepared to take an observation.

When he had calculated their latitude, he found that he had outdistanced Abruzzi's expedition by thirty-two miles. But the beating of that record was not the goal on which he had set his heart. One week, just one week, was all he needed to reach the Pole. They might make that final dash, but the haggard faces of his men, dogs nothing but skin and bones, sledges nearly empty of food, made it certain that they would never get back.

They might not even get back from where they were now. A glance at his chronometer had shown him that the ice he had thought stable had continued to drift until now they were so far east of the ship that it was doubtful if they would have enough strength to get to it even if they reached land—a disheartening fact that he kept to himself.

He tore a page from his notebook and, with face set in grim lines, wrote a brief message. Then, fumbling inside his shirt, he brought out a piece of the flag Josephine had made for him, and asked Ootah to bring an empty can.

He was going to turn back. Henson brushed away the tears that blurred his eyes. He knew that Peary would rather die than give up. He knew also that he would not willingly lead his men to certain death in order to win.

Peary shoved the record and the bit of flag into the can, buried it in the ice, and got to his feet. For a moment he looked toward the goal that he had nearly strained his life out to achieve. Then he turned and, with lips that trembled, gave the order to retreat.

Above the boisterous tide of the new moon the ice again was heaving and splitting, breaking their upward trail so that they found it difficult to follow. At last they stumbled into their camp of the night before, made tea to wash down a little pemmican, and took a long sleep—the last for several days. Through another blizzard, with snow cutting their faces like red-hot needles, they got back to Storm Camp, which Peary still hoped one of his assistants might have reached with a supply of food. But the igloos were empty except for drifts of snow.

Here again a gale held them for twenty-four hours, and as he listened to the howling wind, Henson began to feel as forlorn as a lost child. Seaman that he was, he wanted to know his position on this wide expanse of frozen ocean. Two weeks had passed since they'd been in line with the *Roosevelt*. With the wind continually driving them eastward, the harbor for which they were making would be on the coast of Greenland. He knew that coast. It was bleak and inhospitable, but he, Peary, and Ahng-ma-lokto had shot musk oxen there. If they could land and find musk oxen again, they would be able to reach the ship, even if it meant walking a hundred miles.

Feeling somewhat more certain as to where they were and what chance of survival they had, he rolled over and went to sleep.

Early in the afternoon, Peary asked him to examine the sledges and make any necessary repairs. As he went out into the storm, a loud outcry from the dogs wakened the Eskimos, who crept from their igloos to see what was going on. Seeing Henson, they gathered around him with anxious faces.

They asked if he knew where they were, and whether they would get back. He told them they were far from land, but Tornarsuk was driving them out of his territory and the faster they went, the better he'd like it. They were comforted, and Henson advised them to go into their igloos and sleep while they had a chance; he would attend to the dogs.

By evening the storm had spent itself, and they started off in bright sunshine, Peary urging them to drive as fast as possible in order to reach the Big Lead before the next maximum tide broke up any ice that might have formed on it. Spurred by alternate hope and fear, the Eskimos strained every muscle to placate Tornarsuk, while Peary and Henson raced with the full moon of May.

Fair weather favored them, though the sun's incessant light, reflected from the snow fields ahead, was dazzling and added aching eyes to their bodily weariness. Peary, unable to keep the swift pace now that failure had drained off his former energy, rode most of the way on a sledge, compass in hand, and directed their course on a beeline for Greenland. Dogs were killed and eaten; sledges, useless without the dogs, were left behind. Toward the end, rough ice and pressure ridges slowed them down, but they made up for it when the going was good, and beat the moon by five days.

But Fate was still against them. The Big Lead was wide open. They camped beside the broad band of black water, hoping against hope that ice would form in the few days that remained before the mighty tide came surging in. While they waited, more dogs were killed and sledges broken up to make fires on which to cook the meat. Sleep was next to impossible even for those who were not patrolling the shore, watching for the first sign of ice.

They continued to drift steadily eastward, and this confronted them with another danger of which only Peary and Henson were aware. If the crossing were delayed much longer, they might be carried past the northern point of Greenland and out to sea, where all chance of rescue would be lost. They were face to face with starvation as it was, and the lead continued to broaden. By the third day it was two miles wide.

Once Peary had called it the Grand Canal. Now he thought of it as the Styx, the river that separates the kingdom of the dead from the land of the living, and there was no doubt in his mind as to the side of the Styx on which they were marooned.

But two days later, although the moon was full, the water became quiet and a thin sheet of ice began to form. By the next day it stretched all the way across.

Since Panikpah was the lightest, Peary told him to start first, leading the remaining dogs and his sledge. He ordered the others to walk abreast fifty feet apart, not to lift their snowshoes, nor stop to help anyone, for that might bring death to all of them.

They glided out, sliding one snowshoe ahead of the other to keep the pressure even, while ahead of them, and between them, the thin film of ice rose and fell in smooth waves as if it were rubber.

Twice the toes of Peary's snowshoes broke through, and each time he feared that his end had come. He heard a cry. "God help him, which one is it?" he muttered, not daring to lift his eyes from the ice curling up at the toes of his snowshoes. On and on he went for what seemed like an eternity. But at last he stepped on solid ice and looked along the line. Every man was there. It was a miracle.

They stooped to unfasten their snowshoes and, when they stood up and looked back, they saw a stream of black water cutting the frail bridge on which they had crossed. They had made it just in time.

XIV

DOWN BUT NOT OUT

Ahead of them lay a mass of broken floes, heaved so high by the tide that sometimes the piles rose above their heads. For three days they hacked their way through, stumbling, falling, bruised from head to foot. The pain in Peary's toeless feet was almost more than he could bear; at the end of each march his jaws ached from the firmness with which he had gritted his teeth in order to keep going.

On the fourth day, they caught sight of land. The ice ahead was level and, by evening, exhausted and dizzy from lack of food, they dragged themselves onto the ice foot under Cape Neumeyer. Henson and Ahng-ma-lokto took their rifles and went inland to hunt. Within an hour the eight hungry men were devouring the raw meat of Arctic hare.

They slept a few hours, and then Peary sent Ootah and Ahng-odo-blaho to follow a trail going east which he'd seen just before they reached land. They came back the next day with Clark and his Eskimo companions, Ootah supporting his brother Egingwah, Ahng-odo-blaho helping Pooblah, who limped badly, and Seegloo bringing up the rear, carrying a bow made from a snowshoe, and an arrow tipped with a spoon he'd chipped to a point. With this ingenious device he had shot a hare, a welcome change from the dog meat and spare sealskin boots they had been eating.

With four starving men added to his party, plus three

Between the black "Styx" and land stretched endless shattered ice

dogs, Peary realized that he and his men must start off at once to look for musk oxen. Leaving Clark and his party to finish their meal and catch up as soon as they could, he headed for Britannia Island. At their first camp, Seegloo and Egingwah joined them, and three hours later Clark and Pooblah came in.

From Britannia Island, where Ootah and Pooblah had been in 1900, he sent Panikpah to look for hare, and went on to Victoria Inlet. Henson had just killed a dog for supper, when Ootah shouted "Musk oxen," and pointed to the top of a bluff some distance away along the shore. Ootah and Matt grabbed their rifles and started off on a run. Peary put on his snowshoes and mittens, picked up his carbine and a box of cartridges, and followed with Ahng-ma-lokto, forgetting in his excitement to put his deerskin jacket over the blanket shirt he was wearing.

They overtook Henson and Ootah at the foot of the bluff. When Henson saw Peary without his jacket, he warned him that it was risky to stay out in the cold with nothing on but his shirt. He suggested that he leave the musk oxen to the rest of them. But Peary said that their lives were at stake and, since he was in command, the responsibility was his. So Henson left him, and went back to camp to make preparations for returning to the hunting grounds with Peary's jacket, robes, and the tent.

Meanwhile Ahng-ma-lokto had loosed two dogs, and Peary followed them up the steep slope. Presently he saw the body of the little black dog tossed high in the air, and he reached the plateau with a burst of speed that left him breathless. The oxen were grouped to charge, and the gray dog was worrying the bull and dodging its savage horns.

Peary waited a moment until he stopped panting and his hands were steady, hoping the gray dog could hold his own a bit longer.

Crack! His shot hit the angry bull, but did not kill him. After that his aim was better. One animal after another fell and, with his last cartridge, Peary finished the bull. That gave him seven oxen to his credit, enough to supply food for many days.

Throwing himself down on the bull's warm carcass, he tried to draw some of its heat into his body, while the Eskimos hastened to carve chunks of meat from the rest, which they ate ravenously. The brave gray dog shared their feast, and big slabs were thrown down to the others that were tethered at the foot of the bluff.

Peary was suffering more from cold than from hunger, and ate only a few mouthfuls. As soon as Ootah and Ahng-ma-lokto had stripped the skin from one of the animals, they brought it to Peary and he rolled himself up in it. But his body was wet with perspiration, his clothes were coated with frost, and the green skin was useless.

A keen wind from the north swept down on them, and Peary was shivering and aching with cold by the time Henson reached him. Gratefully he crept into the tent and changed into the dry and warmer clothes Henson had brought. Matt set the Eskimos to building a windbreak with mounds of snow, while he collected willow twigs for a fire. By the time Panikpah and Clark's party came in, meat was roasting, and for two days everyone ate and slept.

Peary was certain that more musk oxen would be found, and as they traveled on toward the ship he let men and dogs eat their fill. But scouts sent out to look for other herds found none, and they went back to eating their dogs.

Since landing at Cape Neumeyer, they had put over a hundred miles behind them and had about fifty to go before reaching the channel that separated them from the ship. They managed to make it in four days, and from the top of the bluffs saw the masts of the *Roosevelt* far, far away.

Leaving everything except their rifles, Peary's records, his transit, and his binoculars, they started across Robeson Channel. Along the Greenland coast the surface had been level and they had just shoved one snowshoe ahead of the other, but the rough ice of the channel was too much for them, and several miles from the opposite shore they were forced to camp. Peary thought that a short rest would make it possible to push ahead, but everyone was too tired and too hungry to sleep. He told the Eskimos they could kill another dog, but they said there were only three, and it might be better to keep them. But hunger at last overcame their reluctance, and another poor beast was slaughtered. The small amount of meat on its bones was only tantalizing, and Ootah said he would go on to the ship and send someone back with a load of food.

Peary, however, said he'd always managed to get back from an expedition without help, and intended to do so this time.

Clark did not come in until very late; Pooblah, who was lame, didn't come in at all. Peary told Clark to wait for him in the camp and then go on as best they could. As soon as he reached the ship, he would send men out to bring them in. Ahng-odo-blaho waited with Clark for, during the march across the ice, he had been lamed by a fall.

The rest of the party went on, and three more hours of slipping and falling brought them to the ice foot at Cape Union, about twenty miles below Cape Sheridan and the *Roosevelt*.

As soon as they rounded the Cape, Eskimos saw them and ran to meet them. Peary told them to load their sledges with food from the ship and hurry back to the three men who'd been left behind.

Old Charlie was the only man on hand to greet Peary and his men when they boarded the *Roosevelt*. Marvin, he said, was over in Greenland looking for them; Captain Bartlett and Dr. Wolf had gone up to Cape Hecla with supplies in case Peary or Clark should land there. Ryan was back on his job as fireman.

Peary ordered messages sent to them at once, saying that his party and Henson's were back, and that Clark and his men were on the way. After that had been attended to, he said, he wanted a hot bath, a shave, and a good dinner.

When Old Charlie had made Peary comfortable, he went to Henson's cabin and asked if he'd like to have his dinner brought to him. Henson had bathed and shaved, slipped on a robe, and was stretched out on his bunk to ease the pain in his legs which had swelled to twice their size. Remembering how Merk-to-shar's wife had cured him of scurvy, he asked if there was any raw meat in the larder. Charlie said there were fresh musk-ox steaks. Henson gave a sigh of content, and thanked him for his thoughtfulness.

He ate slowly, sucking the blood from the meat and discarding the rest, for his teeth were too loose for chewing. Then, with his hunger somewhat appeased, he turned on his side and went to sleep.

Peary was not so lucky. He lay awake a long time turning over in his mind what he could say to the men who had given him the *Roosevelt* because they believed that from a base on the Polar Sea he would reach the Pole. Grimly he faced the conclusion that he'd lost his last chance. He was fifty, too old to attempt anything so exhausting again. He could think of nothing that would compensate for his failure.

But as he turned and tossed, the answer came to him—inadequate, but better than nothing. He would go west and survey an eighty-mile stretch of coastline that never had been explored. It would add another star to his crown, albeit less brilliant than the gem he had hoped to place there, and his sponsors would have the satisfaction of presenting to the northern hemisphere a complete map of the Canadian coast.

The United States Coast and Geodetic Survey also would welcome such a map as well as the tidal observations Marvin was making.

Once more he was able to face the future without flinching and, when his assistants returned, they were amazed to learn that he was planning to start at once on another exploring trip. Before he left, he assigned tasks that would add to the scientific results he could report. Bartlett was to take soundings across Robeson Channel, Marvin along the coast as far as Cape Hecla, thus providing further data for the United States Coast and Geodetic Survey, while Wolf was to collect botanical and geological specimens, examine the bed of coal that had been found near Fort Conger, and look for other outcrops.

On June 2, just a week after his return from Greenland, Peary started west, taking along Egingwah, Koo-loo-ting-wah, and Ooblooyah, the son of "George Washington," and Egingwah's favorite pal. Kood-lôok-too went with him as far as Cape Hecla, where Peary helped Marvin set up his sounding apparatus.

Beyond, at Point Moss, where Peary had nothing to look after but his own small party, he rested for a day, during which he had the first long sleep he'd enjoyed for over a week. His feet and legs, like Henson's and Clark's, had swollen so that walking was painful, and he was glad to sit around for several hours after breakfast.

In seven days, they were at Cape Columbia, ninety miles from the ship. It was the first time Peary had been there, and he climbed a peak 1,800 feet high in order to build a cairn, in which to leave a record of his visit and of his success in beating Abruzzi's claim to "farthest north." This he put in a tin can together with a small piece of Josephine's flag, and buried it in the heap of stones. (See map, page 230.)

He was still suffering from scurvy and, although he often

NORTH POLE

April 21, 1906
87° 6′

ARCTIC OCEAN
(POLAR SEA)

GREENLAND
SEA

110°   90°   70°   50°   30°   10°

Big Lead

C. Britannia

Victoria Inlet

C. Columbia
C. Hecla
Pt. Moss
C. Sheridan
C. Union
Robeson Channel
C. Brevoort
Newman Bay
C. Sumner

GRANT LAND

Ft. Conger

L. Hazen

LANDS END — SVERDRUP 1902
(Cape Colgate) — PEARY 1906

ACK WALL — SVERDRUP 1900
. Thomas Hubbard) — PEARY 1906

Nansen Sound

Kennedy Channel

C. Wilkes

AXEL

HEIBERG

LAND

C. D'Urville

C. Sabine

Etah

Inglefield Gulf

75°

C. York

© RMcN & C

Dotted line shows Peary's route in 1906, from Cape Hecla to 87° 6′ on April 21

stopped to rest, the climb had left him completely winded. The descent was faster, but painful, for it threw his weight on the stumps of his amputated toes, leaving his feet almost useless. After two days, however, he was able to go ahead until they were at the most westerly point reached in 1876 by the British explorer, Lieutenant Pelham Aldrich, who also was an expert surveyor and had made an accurate map of his journey.

From here, Peary's advance was slowed down by the necessity of surveying the eighty miles beyond, but he faced the prospect with elation, for this was territory that no man ever had traveled before. He claimed it as he had claimed the north coast of Greenland, "by right of discovery," feeling certain that it would keep his name alive forever.

The feeling was over-optimistic, but the belief that he had made his name immortal sustained him as day after day for seven days he went through the tedious routine of pacing the distance—three feet to a step, 2,400 steps to a mile, counting each one until a landmark gave him a chance to stop, run a base line, and fix points of the coast by intersections.

On June 24, he reached the foot of the mountain toward which he had been setting his course. Was it the westernmost end of the coast? He climbed to the summit, and saw far away to the west what he took to be peaks of land. To the southwest was the island that Sverdrup had explored in 1902 and named "Axel Heiberg Land," in honor of one of his sponsors. But neither this island nor the peaks to the northwest were part of the coast. This summit was the end.

With the help of the Eskimos, Peary searched the western shore for a cairn and a record that Sverdrup had been there. None was found, and he built a cairn on the peak in which he left his claim as discoverer and a piece of his flag, and named the place "Cape Colgate," as a tribute to the man whose contribution had completed the amount necessary to build the *Roosevelt*.

Perhaps Sverdrup also had failed to reach the northern tip of Axel Heiberg Land. Peary crossed the strait that Sverdrup had named for Nansen, and climbed to the top of the bastion of black rock that formed a half-circle around the end of the island. There was no cairn there either, and triumphantly Peary built one containing a brief record and a strip from his flag as usual. This cape he named for General Thomas Hubbard, a distinguished member of the Arctic Club.

He remained three days, while his Eskimos hunted. They brought in twelve deer, an agreeable change from the dried eggs and mush they'd been eating for the last five days in order to save the pemmican for the dogs. Peary erected another cairn near the shore, and waited a day for the weather to clear. They started back in July, full of energy, their sledges piled high with venison.

At the same time, Peary confessed to a moment of regret at leaving this land, the striking beauty of which would be visible summer after summer, while he, to whom it belonged, never would see it again.

But the land he had just explored did not belong to him. His conclusion that it did, immediately after he left the scene of his supposed triumph, may be excused on the ground that his mind was distorted by his need to report an outstanding success. Otherwise he might have remembered reports of Sverdrup's expeditions that he'd read and mentioned in a letter in 1902, and had praised in 1904 in his address as President of the International Geographic Congress. Had he done so without informing himself of the full extent of Sverdrup's discoveries?

The years of 1904 and 1905 had been busy years for Peary, and he may have had no time to examine the map or look at the index in Sverdrup's *New Land*, published in the United States in 1904. But by 1907 when Peary published the account of his westward exploration in *Nearest the Pole*, there was no excuse for his claim that the north end of Axel Heiberg Land belonged to him, nor for his further statement that neither Sverdrup's narrative nor his map showed that he had been there. Sverdrup's map shows the entire northern tip, with the name, "Svartwag" ("Black Wall"), on which Peary's Cape Thomas Hubbard is located; it also shows "Lands-Lokk ("Land's End"), the site of Peary's Cape Colgate.

Peary's friend and supporter Gilbert Grosvenor, director of the National Geographic Society and editor of the *National Geographic* magazine, who prepared one of the folding maps for Peary's book, did take pains to examine Sverdrup's map, and gave the credit where it belongs, omitting "Cape Colgate" and replacing it with "Sverdrup, May 7, 1902." Peary didn't find Sverdrup's cairn because he assumed that Sverdrup had approached from the west, whereas the cairn is described in the text as being near the east shore, and Peary stopped hunting for it when the coast turned eastward.

Had Peary been as careful as Mr. Grosvenor and checked the accuracy of his statements before he published them, he would have been spared a tragedy much greater than the loss of his toes, which also was due to his misunderstanding of Sverdrup's expedition.

In the meantime, Peary's assumption that he had put the finishing touch to Sverdrup's exploration renewed his courage and his ambition. After a month of wading through slush and water, in boots so worn that he had replaced the soles with strips of tin, he reached the ship. He discovered that, during his absence, she had been seriously damaged, but he took it in his stride.

"We have got to get her back, Captain," he said to Bartlett. "We are going to come again next year."

XV

ON TOP OF THE WORLD

The disaster to the *Roosevelt* had occurred on July 4. She had been crushed against the ice foot at Cape Sheridan. Two blades had been sheered off her propeller, and a hole gouged out below the stern. The pumps were kept going steadily and, as soon as the hole had been filled with oakum and cement, Captain Bartlett moved her down to a safer berth near Cape Union. When Peary found her, the crew was busy making a new rudder and repairing her battered stern.

By July 31, when the floes loosened and gave her a chance to leave, she was ready to tackle the ice again. But her wounds were too serious for her to fight as before. Only two blades were left on her propeller, the makeshift rudder was too small to permit accurate steering, the boilers had begun to leak, and for a month she drifted with the pack, saved from sinking only by men who watched day and night, ready to jam cement and oakum into the hole whenever the first lot gave way.

Pack ice prevented the *Roosevelt* from entering Victoria Inlet where Peary had deposited coal and supplies on the upward voyage, but a slackening of the ice to the southeast made it possible to go on to Etah and, on September 16, with all sails set, they turned into the harbor.

There the ship was beached for repairs and, as he examined the wreck, Bartlett's first thought was that he'd just as soon walk home as try to get back on the *Roosevelt*.

"The light is going fast, Captain," Peary said. "We've got to hurry."

He was so sure the wreck could get them back that Bartlett almost laughed in his face, and yet from the confidence with which Peary spoke, he had a feeling that they might make it.

"All right, Commander," he said, "all sleep is out until we've fixed her."

They worked day and night for five days, took aboard coal that had been left there for the return trip, and started south. But they made such slow progress that the coal was almost gone before they reached Labrador, and they began cutting away beams and chopping out passages between the decks for fuel. Heavy seas smashed two rudders before they passed Hudson Strait and, with only a temporary contrivance, they entered a channel along the Labrador coast obstructed by uncharted reefs.

Although the Great Night had fallen, Captain Bartlett's sealing voyages had made him familiar with the route and, in spite of inadequate steering gear, he worked the ship through the crooked passage with masterly skill. At the first harbor, they replenished their supply of food and drinking water, and got a little coal and wood pieced out with whale and seal oil and blubber. Two or three tons of coal dust, blubber, and oil were all that the next port had to offer, but it was enough to take them to Hopedale, where storms delayed them, and the *Roosevelt* was put aground so that a new rudder could be installed.

The delay proved to be fortunate for, while the ship was being repaired, the mail steamer arrived and was able to spare seven tons of coal. With this, they reached Battle Harbor, where forty tons were taken aboard, and they anchored at Sydney on November 23, four and a half months after leaving Cape Sheridan.

As the *Roosevelt* crept slowly southward Peary considered what should be done with her when they reached port. She'd have to be put in dry dock, of course, and stay there until she'd been thoroughly overhauled. That meant he must have a ship-keeper living on board to take care of her while she was without a crew.

He sent for Henson, told him he was going to make another effort to reach the Pole, and asked him to stay on the *Roosevelt* while she was being made seaworthy.

Henson, of course, agreed, but with the reservation that he be given a short leave as soon as possible in order to marry.

Anchor was dropped in New York on Christmas Eve and, as the chain rattled over the side, Peary silently gripped Bartlett's hand. No words could express his gratitude to the captain for bringing the *Roosevelt* safely home.

Bartlett, completely exhausted, climbed into his bunk. The rest of the party rushed for the nearest telephones. The voyage from Sydney had taken twice as long as usual and consequently no one had come to meet them. Soon Peary had wished Josephine and the children a Merry Christmas, and told Jesup and Bridgman the ship was in dry dock off Brooklyn; Marvin had talked with his mother; Dr. Wolf had notified his office that he was back; and Henson was on his way to Harlem with a box of American Beauty roses for Lucy.

A few days later, Bartlett and his crew left for Newfoundland, and Peary went to his home on Eagle Island where he spent most of the winter and spring writing the story of his expedition. On March 30, 1907, the Peary Arctic Club voted its support for a final attempt to place the American flag at the Pole, and contracts were let for repairs on the *Roosevelt* to be completed by the first of July.

Early in April, Bartlett came home from a sealing voyage with his father, and found a telegram from Peary asking him to go to New York and supervise the work of repairing the ship. He went immediately, but, to Henson's dismay, his leave of absence was postponed while Bartlett was sent out to call on financiers and millionaires in an effort to help raise the $100,000 needed.

It was a disagreeable and disheartening job, and Bartlett welcomed an invitation to dine and spend the evening with Dr. Cook, to whom Mr. Bridgman had introduced him. During the course of the visit, Bartlett congratulated Cook on his record-breaking climb to the top of Mount McKinley, the highest peak on the continent. Cook brushed aside the compliments with a modesty Bartlett found very engaging, and said that he was about to leave for the Arctic in order to hunt musk oxen and polar bear. The rest of the evening was spent in swapping stories about hunting, and about sealing adventures.

A few weeks later, Cook asked Bartlett to go to Gloucester and inspect the ship on which Cook and his backer, John Bradley, were planning to go north. "When we got back," Bartlett says, "he put his hand in his pocket and said, 'How much do I owe you, Bartlett?'

" 'Forget it, Doctor,' I said. 'We are friends and you are a friend of my friends. Later on you can help us out by taking lumber and coal to Etah and telling the Eskimos that we are coming.'

"He now clapped his hand on my shoulder and exclaimed: 'Of course, I'll help you out!'

"After that every time I met Dr. Cook, he inquired solicitously about our plans and the details of preparations. . . . I expanded under the Doctor's amenities and like a fat fool told him everything. . . .

"Another thing: Peary had so little money at that time

that I was paying my own salary and that of my crew out of some money I had in the bank at St. John's. To ease the strain and with Peary's permission, I acceded to the request of Dr. Cook to let his schooner have some of the men we were holding for the *Roosevelt*. These were picked sailors used to ice navigation.

"Not long after this—it was already late spring—I had a last dinner with Dr. Cook. . . . A few days later he sailed away on his hunting trip and we who knew him all hoped he would have a pleasant and successful cruise. I warmed at the idea of this friend paving the way toward our arrival next year."

Then the trouble began. Two men, who had been with Cook on his Mount McKinley expedition, reported to the Explorers Club that they were certain Cook had not reached the top. Peary had been made president of the club and, since the two men were members, it was decided to ask Cook to appear before a committee to tell his side of the story. Cook asked for a month in which to prepare his data, but nothing was heard from him until the middle of September.

Mr. Bridgman, in his capacity as business manager of the Brooklyn *Standard Union*, was the first to get the news and immediately telephoned to Bartlett.

"Bradley is back with his yacht," he said, "and tells me that he left Dr. Cook in the north to go to the Pole."

"*What?*" yelled Bartlett.

"Exactly that," said Bridgman.

"But how on earth can he make it without equipment or a ship?"

"He can't," Bridgman said, and hung up.

At the same time, the Explorers Club, which had been waiting over three months to hear from Cook, received a telegram from him by way of Bradley saying, "I am off to nail the Explorers Club flag to the North Pole."

In spite of the fact that Cook had many friends in the club, of which he'd been president the year before, there was no applause or any sign of enthusiasm after his message was read. Peary and some other members felt that this ambitious announcement was only a device to avoid appearing before the committee. Peary had closely questioned the two men who had been with Cook on Mount McKinley, and was convinced that Cook's claim was false. Nevertheless, as president of the club, he was expected to inform the International Polar Commission of Cook's intention to reach the Pole, and did so.

After that, he dismissed the matter as of little importance. He had enough troubles without worrying about Cook. The contractors were so far behind that for some time it had been evident that the *Roosevelt* would not be ready to sail this summer, and for that reason he'd been willing to lend crewmen to Dr. Cook. Now he smiled ruefully as he reflected how completely he and Bartlett had been fooled.

The postponement, however, made it possible for Henson to marry Lucy and enjoy a brief honeymoon. But his work on the *Roosevelt* continued, for now Peary wanted him to build sledges according to a new design that would make them easier to handle, with runners shaped like rockers so that they would give the sledge a lift when it met an obstruction, and upstanders sloping slightly backward so the driver had a better purchase when the sledge had to be lifted over a ridge.

Bartlett and his crew went back to Newfoundland for the winter, and Peary, leaving Henson in charge of the *Roosevelt*, spent Christmas with his family on Eagle Island.

Mr. Jesup was seriously ill, which disturbed Peary. As soon as he returned to New York, he went to call, but was not allowed to see Mr. Jesup, who died on January 22, 1908. It was a stunning blow. Not only had Peary lost a friend who had taken as much interest in his career as if he had been his father; he had also lost the man who had been a tower of strength financially.

Repairs and changes in the *Roosevelt* had exhausted the club's treasury, and money still was needed for supplies, equipment, wages for the crew, and running expenses. Peary's prospects were at their lowest ebb when General Thomas H. Hubbard turned the tide by sending another large check and agreeing to replace Mr. Jesup as president of the club. Mrs. Jesup made a generous contribution, and Mr. Zenus Crane, the paper manufacturer, gave a check for $10,000, promising more if necessary.

On July 6, the *Roosevelt* steamed off to Oyster Bay, where President Roosevelt, his wife, and their sons came on board. The President spent an hour examining every part of the ship and, as he was leaving, he said, "I believe in you Peary, and I believe in your success—if it is within the possibility of man."

Professor Marvin again was a member of the party, and there were three new assistants: Donald B. MacMillan, son of a sea captain, and an instructor in mathematics and physical training; George Borup who, like MacMillan, excelled in athletics; and Dr. J. W. Goodsell.

On the way from Cape York to Etah, they stopped as usual to pick up Eskimo families, furs, dogs, and sledges. Also, as usual, they hunted walrus. MacMillan, who never had shot anything larger than a bird, eagerly grasped the opportunity to go after larger game, and was undaunted when he found himself surrounded by a big herd. He kept his Winchester blazing with a steady aim, and brought in his full share of the catch. Borup, with equal coolness, shot two that were about to upset the boat. Harry Whitney, a sportsman who had come up on the *Eric*, which was carrying coal for the *Roosevelt* as well as Whitney's motorboat, joined in the hunt with Henson; two other sports went out in a whaleboat with Eskimos; and the ship joined the *Roosevelt* at Etah with all the meat she could carry.

Here they were met by a white man with long, matted hair and legs badly swollen from scurvy. Between sobs and whimperings he managed to make Peary understand that his name was Franke and that he had been left there the year before by Dr. Cook.

"Take me away," he begged, and showed a letter from Cook giving him permission to leave whenever he had a chance. Dr. Goodsell looked him over, and said he was unfit to remain in the Arctic any longer. Peary saw to it that the filthy wretch was bathed; the doctor gave him the medicine he needed; and he was put aboard the *Eric* which left as soon as coal and provisions for the return journey, and several tons of walrus meat, had been put ashore.

Among the Eskimos who had joined the party was Koo-loo-ting-wah, the old campaigner who had been with Peary for fifteen years. Henson chose him and several others to help shift the dogs to a nearby island so they wouldn't be under foot while the ship was loaded. On the way back Koo-loo-ting-wah told Henson that Cook and two Eskimo boys were probably over in Ellesmere Land. Henson asked him how he knew, and he said that he himself had been with Cook earlier in the year.

When Henson asked if Cook got to the Pole, Koo-loo-ting-wah shrugged and shook his head. Cook, he said, wasn't trying to get any place; he was just hunting seals. Koo-loo-ting-wah and his companion had gone only a few miles out on the frozen ocean. They saw no seals, and Cook had sent them back. The other two boys had stayed with Cook, but they had little food and couldn't go very far.

Henson passed the information on to Peary who, fearing that Cook might be in desperate straits, told Bosun Murphy to guard the supplies Cook had left, and give him any help he needed when he returned. Also he told the Etah Eskimos to watch for traces of Cook when hunting in Ellesmere Land, and Harry Whitney, who had decided to spend the winter in Etah, also promised to keep an eye out for him when he hunted across the channel.

Meantime, the *Roosevelt* had been loaded, and with 40 Eskimos and 246 dogs aboard, she headed for Cape Sheridan on August 18. For five days the ice presented little difficulty and, during this period, the six whaleboats—equipped with masts, sails, and oars—were swung at the davits, and filled with everything needed for survival, including guns and ammunition. Other supplies were in boxes piled along the rail, and everyone had a bundle of clothes ready to go over the side as soon as the boats were lowered, and the boxes thrown out on the ice.

These precautions were taken in case the ship was caught between two heavy floes. Her destruction would not be sudden, but a slow and gradual process, and unless she were released soon, the pressure would crush her hull and she would hang there helpless until the turn of the tide released the pressure. Then she would sink to the yards, which would be unable to support her weight, and she would sink to the bottom.

To meet such an emergency, the ship was equipped with a device by which her horsepower could be doubled for a few minutes by turning live steam from her boilers directly into the cylinder, and she would respond with a jump that would push her through. More than once before the voyage was over, this mechanism was used to save her.

Peary kept the Eskimo men busy building sledges, and the women making clothes, so that they wouldn't have time to meditate on the dangers that threatened the ship. Sometimes, when the *Roosevelt* was kicked about by the floes, like a football, they set up a dismal wail, calling on the souls of their ancestors to save them. Sometimes Peary would hear them laughing and, looking down from his perch in the rigging, would see them giving a language lesson to the new assistants, with Henson acting as interpreter. And sometimes when the ship was butting her way ahead, the Eskimos would urge her on with shouts of "Adolo! Adolo!"

Peary's assistants responded with equal spirit as she fought her way through the ice. By September 5, she was anchored as before, just beyond Cape Sheridan.

A holiday was declared on Ahnighito's birthday. Bartlett ordered the ship dressed up in all its flags, and Old Charlie brought in a cake for dinner, ablaze with fifteen candles.

With supplies ashore, box houses built, and living quarters on the *Roosevelt* made winter-tight, the training of the new assistants began. On short hunting expeditions with the Eskimos, or longer trips up the coast to its most northern point at Cape Columbia, they learned to drive the dogs and keep their sledges right side up when the going was rough, which, until a man was hardened, seemed as if it would rip the muscles from his shoulder blades. They learned, too, how to wear their fur clothes, what to do about frosted toes, ears, and noses, and Marvin and Henson taught them how to build igloos.

By Thanksgiving all supplies needed for the polar trip had been sledged to Cape Columbia, which was to be their point of departure. Borup had got most of his sledging experience along this ninety-mile stretch of the coast, and by spring could drive almost as well as an Eskimo.

On Christmas, letters and packages from home were opened after breakfast, and in the afternoon the Eskimos celebrated with contests of skill arranged by MacMillan, for which prizes were awarded.

In the middle of February, Peary laid out, on the mess-room table, two rifles, a shotgun, cartridges, and reloading outfits, all kinds of knives, lance heads, and tobacco. He covered them with a cloth, called in the Eskimo men and explained what he proposed to do and what he expected of them. With a sudden movement, he lifted the cloth and said he would give each of the four Eskimos who went all the way to the Pole a duplicate of what they saw on the table and, in addition, a whaleboat, a tent, oil, wood for sledges, and hatchets. To others, he would give what he thought each deserved.

The sight of all these riches made Eskimos, who had feared to follow Peary, think twice. They remembered that already he had traveled far into the territory belonging to Tornarsuk and had come back alive. There was no further difficulty in getting volunteers for the journey.

A few days later, Bartlett left for Cape Columbia, and on Washington's Birthday, Peary got away for his final attempt to win the Pole. The effort proved to be the easiest in his whole career. Only three incidents threatened failure.

Due to the jolting and overturning of the sledges on the rough ice, the alcohol and petroleum cans began to leak, and Peary sent Marvin and Borup back to land for an additional supply. The next day he found the rest of the party camped beside the Big Lead, which was as wide open as it had been when it stopped him in 1906. While he waited for a chance to cross, Peary suffered, he says, more mental wear and tear than in all the fifteen months he was away from home. The additional fuel was essential to success. So were the Eskimos, and they had become restless and unhappy, several complaining that they were too sick to go on.

One day MacMillan, seeing them standing in a group, scowling and muttering, told Peary he feared a mutiny was brewing.

"Get Matt!" said Peary.

Henson walked over to the Eskimos and soon discovered that Panikpah had frightened them by telling them how they had almost lost their lives the last time when they crossed the big river on ice that went up and down in waves with each step.

Henson reminded them of the rewards Peary would give them. Panikpah shook his head. He would not go on. Neither would Ootah's brother, whose other brother, Egingwah, had been with Clark and escaped starving to death by a margin as narrow as that by which Panikpah's life had been saved on the same expedition.

Henson turned to the others. For a moment they were silent. Then Ootah said that if Marri Palook went on, he would go too. His words carried great weight for he was an Angakok, and the most influential man in the tribe. Only his brother and Panikpah refused to follow his example. These two Peary sent back to the ship with a note to the mate telling him they were to pack up their belongings immediately and take their families back to Etah.

MacMillan, in spite of a badly frosted heel, was the life of the party, and his constant cheerfulness and joking were contagious. Even the Eskimos responded to his kidding, and tried to win all sorts of outrageous prizes that he offered for the most skillful performance in wrestling, boxing, thumb-pulling, and other stunts that were popular with the natives. All of them were glad they had decided not to leave.

Peary waited six days for Marvin and Borup; then his impatience made it impossible for him to wait longer. As soon as the Big Lead had frozen solid, he decided to cross, trusting to luck, as he had in 1906, that the ice would remain firm long enough for them to follow. He left a note in his igloo telling them to cross the lead immediately, for his party was short of fuel and needed it as soon as possible.

Beyond the lead, MacMillan, whose heel was rapidly getting worse, traveled in the rear with Peary. Both of them kept looking anxiously behind to see if Marvin and Borup were approaching. At last, after four days, Peary began to lose hope. He said it was uncertain how long a man could live in a temperature of fifty below zero, but they might find out, for it had to be done.

Everyone was in a constant state of worry. That night, as soon as he had built his igloo, Egingwah climbed to the top and looked to see if anyone was coming. All at once he let out a yell and pointed to a ball of low-lying mist that he knew was the condensed breath of a dog team. Most of the party climbed to the nearest vantage point, and even the stoical Peary was visibly agitated. Egingwah and Henson rushed back along the trail and met Seegloo, smiling, but stiff with cold.

He handed Peary a note from Marvin, saying they had got past the lead, and were only one day's march behind him. This time Peary's luck had not failed him. He took out his emergency flask of brandy and gave Seegloo a drink to warm him up, while Henson and Egingwah took care of his dogs.

Peary learned from the note that Seegloo had volunteered to bring it, because he knew that Peary must have the news as quickly as possible. He had sledged alone for seventy-four miles over the sea ice, at a speed that must have left him only four or five hours for sleep. His courage and endurance made such an impression on Peary that he decided then and there to make Seegloo a member of the party that would go to the Pole.

The next morning, Henson went ahead to cut the trail, with Ootah, Koo-loo-ting-wah, and another old campaigner named Ahwa-ting-wah to help him. Dr. Goodsell had gone the distance assigned to him and was sent back to the ship, where his medical services might be needed. MacMillan, whom Peary had hoped to take to a high latitude of which he could be proud, was obliged to go back with the doctor on account of his heel, which was oozing pus and kept sticking to his sock so that it had no chance to improve.

Five days later, it was time for Borup to go back. Peary already had decided which Eskimos he wanted for the final trip and, as his assistants returned to land, he sent with them those who, though they had worked faithfully and hard, were no longer needed. Two of Henson's men went back with Borup—Koo-loo-ting-wah and Ahwa-ting-wah—leaving him with Ootah and another Eskimo who was to go back later. Seegloo, who had been with Borup, was transferred to Peary's party.

It was Marvin's turn next, but he was not sorry. He had carried the colors of Cornell, where he taught, beyond the farthest points reached by both Nansen and Abruzzi. Peary assured him that his assistance had been of great value, especially in sighting the sun to get their latitude, for this had spared Peary's eyes which would need their full strength to make the final observation at the Pole.

Henson, who had expected to be sent back at this point, was ordered instead to hit the trail at six o'clock in the morning. Before leaving he went to Marvin's igloo to say good-by. A warm friendship had grown up between them through the hardships and dangers they had faced together, and they parted with a brotherly handclasp. Three hours afterward, Marvin started off with Kood-lóok-too and his friend "Harrigan," a quick-tempered young Eskimo.

Bartlett went on until he had passed Peary's record of 1906. He had borne the brunt of the hard work on the trail by pioneering most of the way. His job now was to knit up any broken strands in the upward route so that the trip back from the Pole could be made without difficulty or delay.

Before they had left the *Roosevelt*, Peary had told Mac-

Millan that Matt was to go all the way to the Pole because he said, "I can't get along without him." But Henson found it out only when Peary told him to sort out the dogs and re-arrange the sledge-loads in preparation for Bartlett's return.

Peary had Egingwah and Seegloo with him; with Henson were Ootah and Ooqueah, who had been Bartlett's right-hand man. He was a sturdy young fellow, who had been spurred on by his determination to win a whaleboat and the other riches Peary had promised, in order to convince Ikwa that he was able to provide for a wife, who was to be none other than pretty Annadore, Ikwa's daughter, Mrs. Peary's special pet at Red Cliff.

They were now only 135 miles from the Pole, with the best Eskimos in the tribe, the freshest dogs, and food for sixty days on their sledges. Success seemed assured. But on the second day out occurred the third incident that threatened Peary's triumph.

He had gone ahead to set the pace, while Henson and the Eskimos stayed behind to break camp and harness the dogs. After following Peary's trail a short distance, they found it cut by a lead. The Eskimos tested the ice, found it would hold, and crossed without accident, although the surface rose and fell beneath them as they went. Then Henson started, but when he had gone halfway, the runners of his sledge broke through the thin coating.

He swung his whip and threw all his weight against the upstanders in a desperate effort to save the sledge, for it car-ried Peary's sextant and other equipment needed to establish their latitude. Without it there would be no way of proving they had reached the Pole.

He heard the ice crack beneath his feet and, with a final effort, got the first half of the sledge on firm ice. Then he let go of the upstanders, for he no longer had purchase from which to push, and was only a drag on the dogs, which pulled the sledge with its precious load to safety.

Henson was left floundering in the icy water. His furs buoyed him up and he was about to grasp the edge of the solid floe when water began to fill his boots and drag him downward. He struck out with his arms, found nothing to hold him up, and had sunk to his nose when Ootah grabbed him by the collar and pulled him out.

He stripped off Henson's boots, warmed the chilled feet against his bare stomach, slapped ice from the furs, and as soon as Henson had dry boots on, they hurried forward. In about an hour they caught up with Peary, who rode on Egingwah's sledge until they approached their next camping place. Then he got off and walked for about an hour, which was his usual custom.

On April 5, he took a latitude sight, and found they were only thirty-five miles from the Pole. Before midnight they started off in high spirits, and, without stopping for breakfast, ended their last northward march at ten o'clock on the morning of April 6.

"Is this to be Camp Peary?" Henson asked.

"No," said Peary, and in memory of the man who had contributed so much to his success, he named it "Camp Morris K. Jesup."

Igloos were quickly built, breakfast eaten, and the dogs double-rationed. Then Peary brought out the silk flag Josephine had made which, for eleven years, he had carried next to his heart on every important expedition. Now he fastened it to a staff and planted it on top of his igloo. A light breeze caught it and it rippled out, revealing the white patches that covered pieces cut out and left with other records. Peary led the five men in three cheers for the Stars and Stripes, flying at last "on top of the world."

Dotted line shows Peary's successful journey to the North Pole, reached on April 6, 1909

At noon he made an observation of the sun, which showed that they were about three miles from the Pole. He longed to go on for those few remaining miles, but he was too exhausted. He spread his fur robe on the snow platform in his igloo and slept, but not for long. The knowledge that the Pole was within easy reach made him restless and, as soon as he woke, he reached for his diary, and wrote:

"The Pole at last! The prize of three centuries. My dream and goal for thirty years. Mine at last!"

He had planned to check the accuracy of his first observation by making another at six o'clock. By that time, clouds covered the sun, but since there were signs of clearing, he took his instruments and went off with Egingwah and Seegloo. They had sledged about ten miles when the sun appeared, and Peary learned that they were now south of the Pole. Strange as it may seem, in just those few hours they had passed from the western to the eastern hemisphere, and in order to return to camp they would go north and then south, all the time traveling in the same direction.

A third series of observations at six o'clock the next morning, taken at right angles to the first, showed a slightly different result. Again Peary, with Seegloo and Egingwah, left camp and this time sledged crisscross over an area eight by ten miles, during which they must have passed over or very near the mathematical point where the imaginary line known as the earth's axis intersects the surface.

A fourth series of observations taken at noon gave essentially the same result as those taken on their arrival at noon the day before. Satisfied that he had done the best he could with the instruments available—at that time there were no instruments capable of more exact measurement—he took five flags from a canvas bag and carried them to the highest pinnacle of ice in sight.

With Henson's help he placed Josephine's flag on top,

At the North Pole. Left to right: Ooqueah with the Navy League Flag; Ootah with Peary's DKE fraternity flag; Henson with the flag made by Mrs. Peary; Egingwah with the DAR Peace Flag; Seegloo with the Red Cross flag

flanked by the flags of the Navy League, his DKE fraternity, the Red Cross, and the "World's Ensign of Liberty and Peace." Again three cheers rang out and Peary shook hands all around. But no time was wasted admiring the bright colors that broke the monotony of the white landscape. They had done what they had set out to do and were eager to get home.

The flags were brought down, Peary cut a broad diagonal strip from Josephine's flag, placed it in a bottle, with a record of his discovery, and buried it in the ice. Before he left, he found time to write a postal card to his wife, as he had done on each stage of the journey, so that if anything serious happened to him, the message might reach her through one of the survivors.

"My dear Joe," he wrote, "I have won out at last. Have

been here a day. I start for home and you in an hour. Love to the kidsies. Bert."

Their journey to land was swift and without accident. When they reached the coast, Ootah remarked in Eskimo: "The Devil is asleep or having trouble with his wife, or we should never have come back so easily." But the strain had told on them. Even Peary, who had ridden most of the way, had new lines in his face, and the others looked like shriveled-up old men.

As they approached the *Roosevelt,* Bartlett came to meet them. His face was sober and, even before he spoke, they realized that he was bringing bad news. After he had congratulated them on their safe return, he told them that Marvin had been drowned in the Big Lead on his way back to Cape Columbia. Kood-look-too and "Harrigan" said he had gone on ahead of them, and when they reached the lead, they had seen the back of his jacket floating far from shore.

For years everyone believed their story. But in 1926 Kood-look-too was baptized and, when he went to confession, he said that he had shot and killed Marvin. The reason he gave was that "Harrigan" was too tired to walk; Marvin had refused to let him ride, and was about to leave him behind without any food. "Harrigan" confirmed the statement, but such conduct was so unlike Marvin that no one who knew him believed it.

A more plausible explanation, they thought, was that Kood-look-too was suffering from an attack of *piblokto,* the disease, also called Arctic hydrophobia, that had afflicted so many of Peary's dogs years before. It is brought on by exposure to cold and wind, and during the winter there had been frequent cases among the Eskimos in Peary's party. Usually their conduct was wild and senseless and they injured no one but themselves. But sometimes the sufferer reached for a weapon and had to be forcibly restrained. Fits of weeping, such as Kood-lóok-too had on his return, are symptoms that mark the end of the attack.

So Peary's last expedition, like his first, was marred by the death of an assistant. In neither case was it due to any negligence on Peary's part, but grief numbed his feeling of triumph.

A monument to Marvin was erected at Cape Sheridan. Later, another at Cape Columbia recorded the discovery of the Pole. The Eskimos were rewarded, Ooqueah displayed his whaleboat, and won Ikwa's consent to marry Annadore.

But after their return from the top of the world, Peary never spoke to Henson again except to issue orders, as if, by keeping him in his place, any notion he might have of self-aggrandizement would be nipped in the bud.

XVI

CROWN OF THORNS

On July 18, 1909, the *Roosevelt* steamed away from Cape Sheridan and, after three weeks of hammering through the ice of Robeson and Kennedy Channels, reached Smith Sound on August 4.

At Cape Chalon, thirty miles below Etah, crewmen went ashore and came back with the news that Dr. Cook had returned from Ellesmere Land, and had gone to South Greenland. He had told the white men in Etah that he had been a long way out on the sea ice, but the two Eskimo boys who'd been with him, Etoo-kah-sho and Ahpella, said that he lied.

At Etah, Harry Whitney came aboard with more news about Cook, who had told him confidentially that he had reached the Pole. Although Peary felt that the claim was false, just as he thought Cook's claim about climbing Mount McKinley was false, he took the precaution to collect what evidence he could. Etoo-kah-sho and Ahpella were questioned by all members of Peary's party, including Peary himself, who pretended to believe that the boys had been far north. But the boys resisted the temptation to brag and said they had gone only two marches. Ootah and Ooqueah were told the same when they talked with them. Inquiries were made of their families, whose accounts were alike in every detail.

Before the *Roosevelt* sailed, Koo-loo-ting-wah arrived and said he had been hired by Dr. Cook to drive him down to

Peary on the deck of the *Roosevelt* with the dogs that went to the Pole. At the left is the king dog that led his team

North Star Bay so that he could take passage on a whaler bound for Scotland.

Instead of hastening south to report his success, Peary waited to fulfill his obligations to the Eskimos. All the way down to Cape York he stopped to hunt walrus and to leave the natives where they wished to spend the winter. Therefore, when he reached the first radio station, at Indian Harbor, Labrador, it was September 8. From here he cabled Josephine, "Have made good at last. I have the Pole." Another cablegram went to the Secretary of the Peary Arctic Club: "Pole reached. *Roosevelt* safe."

But already newspapers all over the world were head-lining the news that Cook had reached the Pole on September 21, 1908. He had been given a state dinner by the King of Denmark, and the city of Copenhagen had honored him with a dinner attended by over four hundred distinguished citizens. None of this sensational news reached Peary, how-ever, because the radio station at Indian Harbor had gone out of order.

Two days later, when he landed at Battle Harbor, he was stunned to learn that a gold medal had been awarded to Cook by The Royal Danish Geographical Society in recog-nition of his discovery of the North Pole. Immediately he sent a cablegram to the United Press saying, "Cook's story shouldn't be taken too seriously. Two Eskimos who accom-panied him say he went no distance north and not out of sight of land. Other tribesmen corroborate."

The next day the University of Copenhagen gave Cook an honorary degree, and immediately afterward he sailed for New York as the guest of the steamship company.

This official recognition of Cook's claim, before he had submitted any proof, was a disaster that Peary had brought upon himself. Otto Sverdrup, outraged by Peary's claiming to have made discoveries that Sverdrup had made four years earlier, was quick to throw his support to a man who claimed to have won the prize for which Peary was striving. It was due to Sverdrup's influence and that of his friends that Cook's story was promptly accepted as authentic.

Without this early recognition, accorded before news of Peary's success had been received in Europe, Cook could not have achieved the instant and widespread support that de-layed United States recognition of Peary's achievement until after he had endured months of suffering and humiliation.

Peary had triumphed over the forces of nature only to be confronted by human forces with which he was ill equipped to deal. The same lack of tact that had characterized his college days worked against him.

His dispatch to the United Press was followed by another to *The New York Times* saying: "Do not trouble about Cook's story or attempt to explain any discrepancies in his installments. The affair will settle itself. He has not been to the Pole on September 21st or at any other time. He has simply handed the public a gold brick."

The public, quite naturally, took this remark as an insult to its intelligence, while to brand a man as a liar and a cheat before hearing his side of the case was regarded as the last resort of a poor sport. In contrast, Cook's reply, "There is glory enough for both of us," won respect and admiration.

While the *Roosevelt* lay at anchor off Battle Harbor, a boatload of newspaper reporters arrived, wanting to know the inside story of the row with Cook.

"What row?" asked Peary angrily.

Finally he was persuaded to hold a conference in the loft of a trading station, and he tried to tell them enough to satisfy their frantic editors. But having no idea of the extent to which the controversy had been played up, he didn't realize just how frantic the editors were for his news and, without giving the reporters a chance to talk or ask questions, he made a brief and dry statement that failed to take into account what the public expected to hear.

"We had eighteen dog teams. Advance parties went ahead of us from Columbia. They broke the trail. Supporting parties followed. They improved the trail. My best party and I came last. We went fast and easily. When we made the final dash we were strong and fresh. The going improved . . ."

Not one word about the difficulties they had surmounted,

the dangers they narrowly escaped. After Cook's lurid accounts in the press of the hardships he'd suffered, Peary's statement, as Bartlett says, "sounded fishy."

As they passed through the Straits of Belle Isle, Henson completed the broad white band on which he had sewn the words NORTH POLE in blue letters. The band was fastened from the upper right to the lower left corners of the flag Josephine had made and it was unfurled before they entered Sydney harbor.

At about six o'clock in the morning on September 21, a large white yacht, flying an American flag at her foremast and an English flag at her mizzen, came to meet them. Josephine and the children had come from Eagle Island a few days earlier in a train crowded with newspaper men, photographers, lecture agents, and representatives of scientific societies, and the yacht had been offered to Josephine so that she could greet her husband before these delegations demanded all his attention.

The joyous family reunion was a prelude to the uproarious welcome that awaited them in Sydney. As Bartlett describes it, "The populace turned out en masse. Flags decorated every building. The harbor was full of yachts darting to and fro. You couldn't spit without hitting a silk hat."

The carriage that took the happy family to their hotel was showered with roses by girls in gay dresses who ran alongside, the Mayor gave an official welcome, and there was a big dinner at which Peary spoke. At intervals all day, he had talked with scientists and reporters, but very little of what he said appeared in the press, for public sympathy was on the side of Cook.

The next morning, he left with his family for Eagle Island. At every station, crowds were waiting to greet him; at Bangor the mayor presented him with a silver loving cup, and at his home town of Portland, enthusiastic citizens unhitched the horses, got between the shafts, and pulled his carriage to the hotel, where he received another loving cup.

But the reception that awaited him in New York was quite different. Cook had been met by a thousand people, who steamed down the harbor to welcome him; boats blew their whistles in salute as he neared the dock; and cheering crowds escorted him to his home in Brooklyn. Twelve days later, when the *Roosevelt* fulfilled a long-standing agreement and appeared in the Hudson-Fulton celebration, cheers and salutes were very few. As she steamed up the river at the head of the Naval Parade, between replicas of the *Half-Moon* and the *Clermont*, excursion boats loaded with Cook supporters came alongside and greeted Peary and his party with catcalls and hoots of derision.

Peary turned a deaf ear to the hullabaloo, and forbade anyone aboard to reply to the insults. Nevertheless, he was appalled by this demonstration of Cook's hold on the public, and shut himself away on Eagle Island. There he went to work assembling evidence that he had reached the Pole, and writing his story of the expedition. Already Cook had sold his story to the New York *Herald*, and it was appearing in serial form in newspapers throughout the country.

Now that Cook had published his claim, Peary was free to counter it with a statement, signed by all his assistants, in which he gave the testimony of the Eskimos who had been with Cook. He refused to make any statement concerning his own claim, however, until his records had been examined by a competent body and accepted as proof. His silence was interpreted by many in the Cook faction as an indication that his case was weak, and that he was afraid to fight.

Cook, on the other hand, was winning further support through well-attended and profitable lectures. William Brady, an enterprising theatrical producer, wanted to book Peary for a series, but Peary didn't even reply to his letter. So Brady persuaded Henson to undertake a nation-wide tour.

When Peary heard of it, he exploded with anger. He had exacted written agreements from his other assistants that they would not write or lecture without his consent. It had not occurred to him that Henson might have an opportunity to do so. Uncertain as to what he might say as to his part in discovering the Pole, Peary wired Brady that he would not consent to the tour, to which Brady replied that Peary had nothing to do with the arrangements. A few weeks later, when Peary was passing through New York, he sent for Henson and made clear to him that their association was ended.

Soon after his return from the North, Peary had submitted his records and observations to a committee of distinguished scientists appointed by the National Geographic Society. On November 4, a sub-committee, consisting of experts on determination of position, reported complete agreement that the evidence proved that Peary had reached the North Pole. Their report was accepted unanimously by the Society, which ordered a great gold medal to be made and awarded to Commander Peary. When news of the decision reached him, he moved with his family to Washington and, on December 15, he received the special medal, and at the same time the Society presented the Hubbard gold medal to Captain Bartlett.

Meantime, Dr. Cook had been making one excuse after another for not producing as evidence the solar observations he had taken at the Pole and a diary of his sledge journey. He said he had left them with Harry Whitney in Etah. When this was denied by Whitney, Cook said he had them himself but refused to submit them to any scientific group in the United States, because the University of Copenhagen had asked for them first.

To the University's cables demanding his records, he replied that he needed more time to prepare them, just as he had done in 1907 when the Explorers Club asked him to submit evidence in support of his claim that he had climbed Mount McKinley. Instead of doing so, he had gone to the Arctic, and the Club, unwilling to decide the case until it had heard both sides of the dispute, had postponed further action pending Cook's return.

Now Cook was summoned again, and again he asked for a delay so that he could prepare his North Pole records for examination by experts in Denmark. Six weeks later, the Club notified him that the alloted time had expired. They received no response and proceeded to hear the testimony of Cook's guide and two other members of the expedition, who were expert mountain climbers and had followed the trail Cook said he had taken, only to find that it ended many miles from the peak. On the basis of this testimony, the investigating committee appointed by the Explorers Club reported that Cook's claim was not supported by the facts.

The University of Copenhagen fared no better. On December 19, the Consistory, composed mainly of astronomers and polar explorers, received typewritten documents from Cook's secretary. Cook himself was traveling under another name in parts unknown and therefore was not available for questioning. On December 21, the Consistory reported that the documents contained no proof that Dr. Cook had reached the North Pole.

This adverse pronouncement did not surprise Peary. Neither did the confession of two Brooklyn men that they had been paid by Cook to counterfeit the observations showing he had been at the Pole, a confession which was supported by the statement of the shopkeeper from whom they bought the necessary instruments.

By this time, Peary's claim was widely acknowledged. Cables from geographical societies and polar explorers congratulated him on his success. In February, 1910, the City of New York organized a big demonstration for him in the Metropolitan Opera House. President Taft sent a message of congratulation; the Governor of the State, Charles Evans Hughes, presided and, whenever Peary's name was mentioned, it was greeted with loud and enthusiastic applause.

Henson had received a special invitation, but he was off on his lecture tour and unable to accept. After he had recovered from the stagefright that, at first, kept Brady in the wings urging him to speak up, he had developed into an easy talker, who gave the audience a good show for their money. He never mentioned Cook, believing that it was better to let the facts speak for themselves. But he described the methods by which traveling over the frozen ocean had been made easier and faster, in a way that made them convincing, and with a sense of drama and humor that made them entertaining.

At the end of a lecture he was often questioned by scientists and, at a dinner given for him by a banker in Columbus, Ohio, there were several present who tested his knowledge about the constellations visible above the Arctic Circle, the effect of the magnetic pole in determining longitude, how Peary determined his latitude, and the method he usd to take his observations, and so on. Henson's answers, they said, showed understanding of the problems presented, and they congratulated him on his knowledge of astronomy and geography.

The tour took him as far west as Los Angeles and San Francisco, and at last he realized his ambition to see something of the Pacific Coast.

Peary also went on a lecture tour, but Cook's supporters still showed their resentment of the big man with powerful friends and financial backing who had destroyed their idol, a little man who, alone and in one season, had accomplished what Peary had tried for years to do. Many of them still believed in Cook, in spite of the Copenhagen decision against him, or, if they didn't believe, they didn't care. It was the fight that enthralled them, and they managed to keep it going until the United States entered World War I, when bigger battles diverted their attention.

A bill, recommending that Peary be made a Rear-Admiral in the Civil Engineer Corps of the U.S. Navy, and placed on the retired list at the highest pay of that grade, was introduced early in March by Senator Hale of Maine. Congressman Bates had introduced a similar resolution in the House a few days before, but it was referred to the Naval Affairs Committee, and there it stuck during a year of disgraceful wrangling.

The most influential opposition came from General Greely and Rear Admiral Schley. In Peary's account of the discovery of the Pole, now appearing as a serial in *Hampton's Magazine* and also in British, Italian, and French publications, he had described his first visit to Cape Sabine where three-quarters of Greely's party had died of starvation.

"I shall never forget the impression of that day," Peary wrote, "—the pity and the sickening sense of horror. The saddest part of the whole story for me was the knowledge that the catastrophe was unnecessary, that it might have been avoided. I and my men have been cold and have been near starvation in the Arctic, when cold and hunger were inevitable; but the horrors of Cape Sabine were not inevitable. They are a blot upon the record of American Arctic exploration."

This sledge-hammer blow turned Greely from a lukewarm supporter into a bitter enemy, and he used his great influence to prevent any Congressional recognition of Peary's triumph. In this he was joined by his friend Rear-Admiral Schley, commander of the ship that had rescued the remnants of his party at Cape Sabine, and in whose honor he had named a new land he thought he saw to the northwest. But Peary had found in 1898 that the place didn't exist. Consequently, "Schley Land" was removed from subsequent maps of Ellesmere Land, which filled both Greely and Schley with vindictive resentment.

Congressmen, who had been appointed by the Naval Affairs Committee as a sub-committee to consider the Bates Bill, refused to accept the favorable conclusion reached by the scientists who had been appointed by the National Geographic Society to examine Peary's records. The Society, congressmen claimed, was biased in favor of Peary, whose expeditions it had sponsored, and they demanded his records.

One member of the committee admitted that even if they had Peary's records before them, they wouldn't be able to decide whether or not he had reached the Pole, "for we are not scientists."

However, two scientists were asked to appear before the committee and explain the basis of Peary's claim. In answer to questions, they described the methods that could be used to determine latitude, until one of the congressmen confessed that he was ready for an insane asylum.

The committee then called on Peary to produce further proof, though what would have satisfied them, it is hard to tell, for only scientific facts could prove how far north he had been, and those they were unable to understand.

At this point Congress adjourned, and Peary was free to accept the many invitations he'd received to visit the capitals of Europe. Captain Bartlett went with him and shared the recognition accorded in a triumphal tour that was without precedent, and included London, Paris, Rome, Berlin, Vienna, Brussels, Antwerp, and Edinburgh.

He was about to leave for Russia, where he was to lecture and be introduced to the Czar, when he learned of the death of King Edward VII. He postponed his visit to St. Petersburg and went back to London, feeling that it would be unseemly to continue his march of triumph while Great Britain mourned.

Conspicuous as exceptions to the European countries that honored him were Denmark, Sweden, and Norway, all of whom had made outstanding contributions to exploration. Denmark was in an embarrassing position because of her hasty endorsement of Cook, but four Danish explorers sent messages of congratulation, and a veteran Arctic explorer hailed him from Sweden. The Norwegian government, which had officially sponsored Sverdrup's expedition, remained aloof, and Nansen, Sverdrup's friend and fellow-explorer, also was silent. Peary's appropriation of Sverdrup's discoveries was neither forgotten nor forgiven.

Although most European nations had demonstrated their belief in Peary by words of praise and handsome awards, their verdict had little or no effect on opinion in his own country; if anything, it had increased the hostility that minor officials and the general public felt toward him.

His promotion to Captain in the Civil Engineer Corp didn't help matters. It was not an award for service rendered, but was given automatically because the former Captain had died. However, jealous officers released a statement to the press saying that Peary had not met a new regulation requiring officers to walk fifty miles in three days, and ride ninety miles on horseback in the same length of time. Therefore, the Navy Department ordered Peary to take the tests.

Although it was humiliating, Peary found it also amusing. It was seventeen years since he'd ridden a horse, but he rode 117 miles in the time set, 27 more than the mileage stipulated. In the walking test, he covered 25 miles in 6 hours on the first day; 25 in 7½ hours on the second; thus completing the distance assigned, but walked again on the third day for good measure.

The proposal to promote him to Rear Admiral was still pending and, when Congress reopened in December, 1910, President Taft included in his second annual message a recommendation that Congress give fitting recognition to the great achievement of Robert Edwin Peary. Nevertheless, Representative Macon of Arkansas, an ardent Cook fan who led the opposition in the Naval Affairs Committee, said he would fight such a measure to the last ditch, and he did.

Peary was summoned to appear before the committee, where he was heckled and cross-examined as if he were a criminal, rather than a man who had brought great honor to his country. Little attention was paid to the observations and records he placed before them, nor to the fact that the Royal Geographical Society in London had made an independent examination and had also come to the conclusion, arrived at by the National Geographic Society, that Peary had reached the Pole. An independent report from the U.S. Coast and Geodetic Survey also was ignored, although it had been prepared by experts on the staff who had computed Peary's astronomical observations and found that Camp Jesup was just about where Peary said it was—four and a half miles from the Pole. Since he had sledged over additional territory in the vicinity, they thought he might well have come within a stone's throw of the Pole.

As in the earlier hearings, the politicians were unable to evaluate such scientific data, and substituted tests of their own.

"How many pounds of nails did you take to the Pole to repair your sledges?" asked one. An Eskimo would have laughed, for nails break at low temperatures, and sledges repaired with them in any temperature would not be sufficiently flexible. But Peary didn't even smile as he explained.

Mr. Macon asked him whether the needle of his compass responded "to the primary or the secondary magnetic pole."

Another congressman interrupted to ask Macon what he meant by two magnetic poles.

"Oh," said Mr. Macon, "they are known to science."

And so it went, day after day, one absurd or irrelevant question after another, which Peary answered with remarkable patience. But there were two questions to which he was unable to give convincing answers: "Why hadn't he taken Bartlett to the Pole?" "Why had he taken a Negro?"

He had taken Henson, he said, because he was the best dog driver. This answer was not satisfactory because, since Bartlett had driven well enough to go within 135 miles of the Pole, why wasn't he good enough to drive the rest of the way? His real reason for not taking Bartlett couldn't be given because of its possible effect on diplomatic relations and on Peary's personal triumph. Bartlett was a British subject. If he had gone to the Pole, the United States would have had to share the honor of its discovery with England and, by the same token, Peary would have had to share it with Bartlett.

As for Henson, Peary had described him as his Negro servant who, because he belonged to a race that lacked initiative and daring, wouldn't be able to lead a party of Eskimos back to land. In that case, why hadn't Peary sent him back while land was still in sight?

His real reason for taking Henson couldn't be given because he had suppressed the facts that supported it. He had never mentioned Henson's influence over the Eskimos, nor told how he had persuaded them to travel over the heaving and splitting ice for the first time in the history of the tribe, or how he had prevented a mutiny on the way to the Pole. It was MacMillan who later described Peary's dependence on Henson in this crisis. Peary didn't even mention Henson in his published account, but gave MacMillan the credit for handling the situation. Therefore, Peary couldn't say now, as he had said privately to MacMillan, that he had taken Henson because he couldn't get along without him.

Another omission that proved to be a handicap was his failure to mention that Henson was an able seaman, and therefore had some knowledge of navigation. Now it was too late. The statement would be brushed aside as a convenient afterthought, not to be credited. Many people suspected that he had taken an ignorant Negro instead of a navigator like Bartlett so that he could fake his records, and there were those who believed he had done so.

While Peary was enduring with patience, or in dignified silence, an inquisition that must have seared his soul, Henson worked steadily on his book, *A Negro Explorer at the North Pole*, still mindful of his wish to bring honor to his race; mindful too that Peary's heart was breaking. By the time Henson's book was finished, Congress at last had retired Peary on a pension with the title of Rear Admiral, but the card of thanks they awarded him, while acknowledging that he had reached the North Pole, did not say that he was the first to do so. The vituperative attacks that preceded this grudging recognition by the country he loved, left wounds that never could be healed.

Henson submitted his manuscript to Peary's publishers, who liked it, and sent it to Peary, asking him to write a foreword. Refusal would have been difficult to explain since Henson had nothing but praise for Peary's leadership, and made no claim for himself beyond that of being one of Peary's assistants. So Peary wrote the foreword, and the book, full of warmth and humor, was published in 1912.

But after the fall of 1909, Peary had never seen Henson, nor communicated with him in any way. Then in 1920, as Peary lay on his deathbed, he felt a sudden longing to see the man who had faced death with him so many times in the past. He sent for Henson, and Henson hastened to his side.

Not long afterward, headlines in the evening papers announced Peary's death. Henson, overcome with grief, rushed to the bathroom, closed the door, and turned on all the water so that his wife would not hear his sobs. Lucy had never been able to forgive Peary for discarding her husband as if he were a tool no longer needed, instead of giving him the honor he deserved as co-discoverer of the Pole.

XVII

AFTERGLOW

Henson received many honors from his own race. Soon after the shocking display of insolence with which Cook supporters greeted the *Roosevelt* in the Hudson-Fulton parade, a banquet was held for the Negro explorer. Toward the end, he was called on to speak, and he described the dash for the Pole, the observations Peary had made there, and their effort to reach land before open water cut them off. His people showed their pride and belief in him by giving him a gold watch from Tiffany's.

The presentation was made by Charles Anderson, a Negro politician whose campaign for Theodore Roosevelt had won him the coveted position of Collector of the Port of New York. Peary had been invited to attend, but he was riding out the storm on Eagle Island, and sent a note of regret in which he praised Henson and said he had set a fine example for other Negroes to follow. Hearty applause followed Anderson's reading of the letter.

Tokens of esteem, large and small, continued to come: a medal commemorating the discovery of the Pole from the Colored Commercial Association of Chicago; a silver loving cup from the Bronx Chamber of Commerce; another gold watch; and a safety razor in a gold-stamped leather case. Master of Science degrees were awarded him by Morgan State College in Baltimore and Howard University in Washington,

D.C., and Dillard University in New Orleans named its new gymnasium for him.

But for twenty-eight years, white organizations ignored him, and he lived in obscurity.

He managed to live for a year on the money he'd earned from his lecture tour, and in that interval he wrote his book. Lucy was working in a bank, and now he himself went job-hunting. But opportunities for Negroes were no better than they had been back in the eighties, and in January, 1913, Charles Anderson found him working in a Brooklyn warehouse, parking automobiles and storing them for the winter.

"I've been looking for you, Henson," he said. "What in the devil are you doing here?"

"Earning a living parking cars," said Henson blandly.

"I know, but this is no job for you."

Henson laughed. "I don't mind it. I've never driven an automobile before—beats dog sledging all hollow."

"But you deserve something better than this," Anderson remonstrated, "after what you've accomplished in your lifetime."

"Look, Charley," Henson replied, "whatever I did with Peary makes no difference. It's finished. Nobody wants to think about it. It makes them feel the Negro is getting out of place, doing things he's not supposed to do. A person who grows up thinking one thing is the way it is, and then finds out it's another way, loses confidence in himself. He wants to see it the way he always thought it was. A few of my people know what I've done, so what have I got to complain about?"

But Anderson was determined to see that Henson got some reward from his country. He wrote to President Taft asking that Henson be given a government position. His request was granted, but the position was certainly not what Anderson had expected. The forty-six-year-old Negro was given a civil service appointment as messenger boy in the Customs House.

Three efforts were made to win congressional recognition for him. In 1929, the New York Representative, F. H. La Guardia, introduced a bill to retire Henson immediately from his Customs House job, and grant him a pension. In 1933, another New York congressman, J. C. Gavagan, introduced a similar bill. Three years later, Representative Mitchell of Illinois sponsored a bill providing that Congress award a gold medal to Matthew A. Henson, who had accompanied Peary on all his polar expeditions, and at the risk of his own life had saved that of Peary, thereby making the discovery of the Pole possible.

The Southern bloc in Congress was opposed to granting a medal or even a pension to a Negro, so none of these bills got very far, although they showed that in some quarters there was growing appreciation of Henson's contribution.

It was not until Henson was automatically retired at the age of seventy on a pension of $1,020 a year, that rosy clouds began to appear on the horizon. In 1937, he was elected to membership in the Explorers Club, and his place among the guests of honor at the speakers' table became one of the most popular spots on the rostrum. His modesty, the warmth of his outgoing personality, his sense of humor, and his complete lack of jealousy, acted like a magnet that drew other explorers.

He often dropped into the club to chat with Bartlett or MacMillan, both of whom had been on exploring trips since the Polar expedition. Bartlett had many tales to tell about his adventures as captain of Stefansson's ship in 1913, his experiences as commander of transport vessels during World War I, and his expedition in 1924 to Alaska, in search of bases for aircraft designed to fly between Point Barrow and the North Pole; also he'd made a trip to Cape York in 1926, where he had seen many of their old Eskimo friends.

MacMillan had headed an expedition in 1914 to locate the land Peary had thought he had seen far to the west. Mac-

On June 15, 1932, Captain Bob Bartlett sailed, with Peary's daughter and two grandsons, to Cape York, where a stone shaft was to be erected in Peary's honor. Photographed before the ship sailed, from left to right: Mrs. Robert Peary, Captain Bartlett, and Mrs. Edward Stafford (Ahnighito)

Millan didn't find it, nor did anyone else. It seems to have been an illusion, caused by low-lying mist.

A man's color was not the criterion by which he was judged at the Explorers Club. The only bronze bust in the club is a bust of Henson, presented by the National Association for the Advancement of Colored People. Ootah, the only surviving Eskimo who had been with Peary and Henson at the Pole, was a member. So also was Tenzing Norkay, the Tibetan guide who had stood beside Sir Edmund Hillary on the highest mountain in the world, and was recognized by the club as the "co-conqueror of mighty Everest."

Years of neglect, and a job far beneath his intellectual capacity, had not damaged Henson's poise nor his capacity for enjoyment. In his philosophy of life, there was no room for bitterness. He had failed to win what he hoped for—recognition that would contribute to the glory of his race—but, as he once said to Lowell Thomas, "History will take care of that. God will see to it, and God has plenty of helpers."

It turned out to be a valid prediction. In 1945, Congress presented him with a silver medal, a duplicate of medals awarded to Bartlett and MacMillan, and a citation for "outstanding service to the Government of the United States . . . for exceptional fortitude, fearless determination, skillful performance" and "for contributing materially to the discovery of the North Pole."

In 1948, The Geographic Society of Chicago, citing him as "the first Negro in this country to be honored for scientific achievement in the geographical field," presented him with a gold medal on which is engraved: "I can't get along without him. Peary."

The next year he was invited to Washington for the fortieth anniversary of the discovery of the Pole, but at eighty-two he felt unequal to the trip. The following year, ceremonies in his honor were held at the Pentagon. Again he was unable to attend, but he responded to a request to send the Bible he had carried with him in 1909, which was placed in a steel canister and dropped by airplane at the North Pole.

Finally, in 1954, shortly before his eighty-eighth birthday, he accepted an invitation to go to Washington and lay a

On April 6, 1954, the forty-fifth anniversary of the arrival at the Pole, President Eisenhower, Mrs. Henson, and the 88-year-old Matthew Henson, stand behind a White House globe

wreath on Peary's grave. It was his last public act. The next year he died, and his wife insisted on giving half his life insurance to the Explorers Club because, she said, he spent the happiest years of his life there.

Six years after his death, Maryland, the state where he was born, honored "the co-discoverer of the North Pole" by placing a plaque to his memory in the State House at Annapolis. It was unveiled by the Governor, who described Henson as a "great Marylander, a great American, and a great human being." (See next page.)

Governor Millard Tawes and Mrs. Matthew Henson unveiling a plaque in Henson's memory in the State House, Annapolis, Md.

In 1963, Baltimore, the city from which Henson sailed as a cabin boy, named its most modern elementary school the Matthew A. Henson School, in honor of the "distinguished Negro who accompanied Peary to the Pole."

1607   Henry Hudson, British, sponsored by English merchants, hoped to sail over the Pole to China. Blocked by ice off Spitsbergen at 79°50'.

1827   Commander William Edward Parry, British, sponsored by the Admiralty, left from North Spitzbergen with man-pulled sledge-boats. Ice, moving south faster than he could go north, forced him to turn back at 82°45'.

1853   Elisha Kent Kane, American, sponsored by Henry Grinnell, shipping magnate of New York City, called "The Father of American Arctic Discovery." Kane wintered in the basin named for him, and explored Kennedy Channel to 80°35'.

1860   Dr. I. I. Hayes, American, sponsored by Grinnell, No progress.

1871   Charles Francis Hall, American, sponsored by Grinnell, sailed on the *Polaris*, penetrating Robeson Channel to 82°11'.

1879   Lieutenant George W. DeLong, American, sponsored by James Gordon Bennett, sailed via Bering Strait hoping to find a chain of islands between Siberia and the Pole. His ship was caught in the ice, drifted until 1881, sank at 77°15'.

1895   Fridtjof Nansen and Hjalmar Johansen, Norwegians, sponsored by their government, broke all previous records at 86°14'.

1897   Salomon A. Andrée, Swedish balloonist, planned to fly over the Pole. Last message, two days after his ascent.

1900   Captain Umberto Cagni, Italian, assistant to the Duke of Abruzzi, broke Nansen's record by 22 miles at 86° 34'.

1909   Commander Robert E. Peary and Matthew A. Henson, Americans, reached the Pole.

ACKNOWLEDGMENTS

The author is indebted first of all to Charles Keller, the book's jacket artist, for telling her the story of Matthew Henson and asking her to write it. In addition, special thanks are due to Mrs. Henson, Admiral Donald B. MacMillan, Lowell Thomas, and the late Peter Freuchen, who gave valuable information hitherto unpublished.

Acknowledgment is made to the following for quotations or for pictures: The Macmillan Co., New York, for quotations from *Peary* by William H. Hobbs, copyright 1936 by The Macmillan Company, on pages 14, 16–18, 20–22, 24, 25, 27, 106, 257, and 265, and pictures on pages 23, 41, and 63; the Meredith Press, New York, for quotations from *Beyond Adventure* by Roy Chapman Andrews, copyright 1952 by Duell, Sloan, and Pearce, on pages 27, 172, 197, 240, 253, and 264; Archer House, New York, for quotations from *Dark Companion* by Bradley Robinson, copyright 1947 by Robert M. McBride & Co., on pages 31, 32, 35, 36, 48, 49, 61, 71, 140, 170, 176, 183, 188–189, 194, 195, 200, 248, and 271; Putnam's & Coward-McCann, New York, for quotations from *The Log of Bob Bartlett*, by Robert A. Bartlett, copyright 1928 by G. P. Putnam's Sons, on pages 233, 235, 237–238, 258, and 259; Houghton Mifflin Company, Boston, for quotations from *How Peary Reached the Pole* by Donald B. MacMillan, copyright 1934, on pages 246, 256–257, and 258; Charles Scribner's Sons, New York, for quotations from *Morris K. Jessup, A Character Sketch* by William Adams Brown, copyright 1910, on pages 147 and 156; The Explorers Club for quotations from *Explorers Journal* on pages 137 and 274, and for picture on page 199; Charles E. Huntington, Dep't of Biology, Bowdoin College, for picture on page 19; Wide World Photos, New York for pictures on pages 11, 82 (top), 273, 275, and 276; Culver Pictures, Inc., New York, for picture on page 68; American Museum of Natural History, New York, for pictures on pages 82 (bottom), 84, 87, 100, 110, 158, 181, 201, 210, and 254; United Press, New York, for pictures on pages 224 and 256. Pictures not otherwise cited are from *Northward Over the Great Ice* by Robert E. Peary, which is out of copyright.

All quotations and pictures in *To the Top of the World* not cited above are from newspapers or from the following books which are out of copyright: *My Arctic Journal* by Josephine D. Peary, *Northward Over the Great Ice*, Volumes I and II, by Robert E. Peary, *Peary, The Man Who Refused to Fail* by Fitzhugh Green, *A Negro Explorer at the North Pole* by Matthew A. Henson, *New Land* by Otto Sverdrup, *Life and Times of Frederick Douglass* by Frederick Douglass, and *The Last Years of Arctic Work* by Robert E. Peary (McClure's Magazine).

INDEX

Abruzzi, Duke of, and North Pole, 184, 192, 215, 217, 219, 229, 247

Academy Glacier, Peary names, 101

Academy of Natural Sciences, Philadelphia, and Peary expeditions, 56, 58, 108, 121–122, 148, 193; glacier named for, 101

Ahnalka, joins Peary party, 80–81, 83–85; and sledges, 89, 114; sorrow of, 113; and Kood-lóok-too, 122; and 1895 expedition, 131–132; killed by Kyo, 176

Ahng-ma-lokto, and expeditions: 1898–1902, 166, 175–176, 180, 188, 189; 1905–06, 214, 216, 220, 223, 225, 226; and Henson, 188, 189

Ahng-odo-blaho, and Peary expeditions, 93, 117, 214, 223, 227

Ahnidloo, and dog-driving, 85; and 1898 expedition, 166, 167, 169–173; and Henson, 172

Ahnighito, see Peary, Marie

Ahpella, questioned about Cook, 255

Ahwa-ting-wah, and 1908–09 expedition, 246, 247

Aldrich, Pelham, point reached by, 230

Alert, winter quarters of, 190

American Association for Advancement of Science, endorses Peary's plan, 58

American Geographical Society: *Bulletin* of, Peary article in, 47; and Peary expeditions, 58, 59, 146; awards medal to Peary, 155

American Museum of Natural History, and Peary expeditions, 146–147, 155; walrus hides for, 149, 150; Eskimo exhibits for, 151; and meteorites, 151, 158

Anderson, Charles, and Henson, 270, 271

Angakok, Peary as, 72–73; Kyo as, 90, 176; Ootah as, 245

Annadore, 72, 87–88, 248, 254

Anniversary Lodge, 112, 113, 115, 129

Antarctic, Dr. Cook at, 185

Arctic, general interest in, 108; see *also* Arctic Ocean, North Pole, Greenland, icecap, *and explorers' names*

Arctic hydrophobia, 119, 131; Kood-lóok-too and, 253–254

Arctic Ocean, Peary ''sees,'' 100–101; ship for ice of, 159; Peary base near, 163, 190; Eskimos' fear of, 179, 185, 188; entrance to, 200

Arro-tok-shua, 80

Astrup, Eivand, and 1891–2 expedition, 59, 63, 69–70, 73–75, 77, 78, 89–94, 96–102, 105; and guidon, 89, 90; and 1893–5 expedition, 111, 113, 114, 116, 117, 121; Peary's appraisal of, 116, 122; tablet for, 174

Audubon, John James, book of, 13

Axel Heiberg Land, 231, 232, 233

Bartlett, John, 149, 157–158, 162

Bartlett, Robert A., on *Windward*, 162, 173; and 1905–06 expedition, 196–201, 206–217, 227–229; and damage to *Roosevelt*, 233–236; goes to Newfoundland, 236, 239; on fund-raising trip, 237; and Cook, 237–239; and 1908–09 expedition, 243, 244, 247–248, 253; and discovery of Pole, 259, 261, 265, 268–269, 275; later experiences of, 272

Bartlett, Sam, 176–179

Bates Bill, and Peary promotion, 264, 265

Battle Harbor, 235, 257, 258

Bauman, Capt., visits Peary, 173–175, 177

Big Lead, 211–218, 221–222, 244, 245, 253

Birds of America, Peary and, 13

Black Horn Cliffs, 180

Black Wall, 233

Borup, George, and 1908–09 expedition, 240, 243, 245, 246, 247

Bowdoin Bay, 112

Bowdoin College, Peary at, 16–19

Bradley, John, Cook's backer, 237, 238
Brady, William, 260–261, 263
Bridgman, Herbert L., contributes to Peary expedition, 160; on *Diana*, 176–177; visits *Fram*, 178; and Peary, 178–179, 184–185, 192, 193, 236; on *Eric*, 184; introduces Bartlett to Cook, 237; and Cook, 238
Britannia Island, Peary at, 225
Brooklyn Institute of Arts and Sciences, endorses Peary's plan, 58
Brooklyn Standard Union, 160, 238
Bryant, Prof. Henry G., 127, 148
Buchanan Bay, walrus in, 164

Cache Camp, 95
Cagni, Umberto, and Pole, 215; see also Abruzzi
Camp Morris K. Jesup, 249
Canada, map of coast of, 228
Cannon, Henry W., 160
Cape Athol, 129
Cape Brevoort, 200
Cape Bridgman, Peary names, 180
Cape Chalon, 255
Cape Colgate, Peary names, 231–233
Cape Columbia, 229, 243, 244, 253, 254
Cape D'Urville, 163, 198
Cape Fraser, 166
Cape Hecla, as starting point for Pole, 182, 188, 189; Peary camps at, 205–206; Bartlett and Wolf at, 227–228; survey of coast to, 229
Cape Lawrence, 167, 175
Cape Morris Jesup, Peary names, 180–182
Cape Neumeyer, Peary at, 223, 226
Cape Parry, 66, 123, 126
Cape Sabine, and 1898–1902 expedition, 179, 182–185, 191; blocked by ice, 197; Peary describes visit to, 264
Cape Sheridan, 190, 216, 227; and *Roosevelt*, 200, 201, 234, 236, 242, 243, 255; monument to Marvin at, 254
Cape Sumner, 200
Cape Thomas Hubbard, 232, 233
Cape Union, 227, 234
Cape Wilkes, 166, 198
Cape York, 121, 240, 256, 272; *Kite* at, 66; Eskimos from, 92, 93, 114, 150, 153, 156–158, 196; "iron mountains" at, see meteorites; Peary beats Sverdrup to, 162; Astrup tablet at, 174
Chase National Bank, 160

Chicago World's Fair, exhibit for, 60, 90
Childs, Captain, 31–34, 36–38, 204; see also *Katie Hines*
Christmas, celebration of, 89–90, 205, 243; Peary home for, 236, 239
Civil Engineer Corps, see under Peary
Clark, and 1905–06 expedition, 205, 206, 209–214, 223, 225–229, 245
Clermont, 260
Cleveland, Grover, and Peary leave, 108, 151
clothes, making of by Eskimos, 69, 74–75, 80–81, 86–87, 89, 131, 202, 242
Colgate, James C., helps Peary, 193
Congress, and Peary, 269, see also Naval Affairs Committee; and Bartlett, 268–269, 274; and recognition of Henson, 272, 274
Continental Shelf, 213
Cook, Dr. Frederick A., and 1891–2 Peary expedition, 60, 65, 69–70, 73–79, 90–92, 95, 96, 102, 103; and Henson, 95, 102, 105, 263; on *Eric*, 184, 185; and Antarctic, 185; plans of to go north, 237–238, 241; and Mount McKinley, 237–239, 255, 262; letter to Franke from, 241; and North Pole claims, 255, 257–264; relations of, with Eskimos, see Eskimos; see also Peary, and Cook
Crane, Zenus, helps Peary, 240

Daisy, The, 86–87, 113, 122
Daly, Judge Charles P., 146
Dedrick, Dr., and 1893–5 expedition, 118, 120; and 1898–1902 expedition, 160, 175, 177
De Long, George W., and the North, 60
Delta Kappa Epsilon, Peary joins, 17; see also flags
Devil of the Icecap, see Kokoyah
Denmark, and Cook, 257, 261–262
Devil of the North, 9, 123, 221; Eskimos and, 185–188, 189; and Peary, 201, 216, 244
Diana, 176–179
Dickens, Charles, Henson and, 34–35
Diebitsch, Emil, 127, 148–151
Diebitsch, Josephine, refuses to marry Peary, 40, 47; marries Peary, 54–55; see also Peary, Josephine
Disko Bay, 40–41, 46, 62
Disko Island, Peary party at, 62–63
Dix, Capt. Charles B., 193

dogs, Eskimo: driving of, 83–85, 96, 132, 243; and 1891–2 expedition, 69, 75–77, 79, 93–94, 96; Peary designs muzzle for, 96; on lecture tour, 108–110; and 1893–5 expedition, 112, 119–120, 131, 133–135, 137, 141, 142; and 1898–1902 expedition, 165, 189; and 1905–06 expedition, 196, 197, 202, 203, 205, 207, 218, 221, 225–227; and 1908–09 expedition, 240, 242; food for, see food; Newfoundland: 75, 81, 83

Douglass, Frederick, 29, 30, 38

Duck Island, 64

Dundee Whale & Fishing Co., 159

Eagle Island, Peary and, 15, 194, 236, 239, 259, 260, 270, Percy at, 203

Edward VII, King, death of, 265

Egingwah, and 1905–06 expedition, 211, 223, 225, 229, 245; and trip to Pole, 246, 248–250

Ellesmere Land, Peary and, 163, 165, 175, 206; Sverdrup explores, 178; Cook and, 241, 242, 255; maps of, 264

Eric, 184, 185, 196, 241

Eskimos, and 1886 expedition, 41–46; photographs of, 60, 90–91, 109; and 1891–2 expedition, 69–71, 75–77, 79, 86–90; relations of, with Henson, 71, 73, 80, 90, 94–95, 102, 114, 122, 132, 144–145, 157, 161, 162, 166, 171–172, 176, 188, 189, 195, 216, 220–221, 245; habits of, 88, 144–145; fears and superstitions of, 94–95, 105, 179, 185–189, 216, 221; relations of, with Cook, 102–103, 255, 257, 262; exhibit of village of, 109, 151; and 1893–5 expedition, 113, 114, 116, 117, 131–132, and "Snow Baby," 114; and meteorites, 121, 123–126, 150, 153, 157–158; and 1898–1902 expedition, 156–157, 162, 164–173, 175, 179, 182, 183, 185, 186, 189; epidemic among, 185; and 1905–06 expedition, 196–197, 202–203, 205–206, 209, 211–212, 214–221, 223, 226, 227, 231, 232; and 1908–09 expedition, 240, 242–245, 247; for trip to Pole, 244–248; see also clothes, Peary, and individual names

Etah, *Windward* at, 162–163, 177–178; Henson at, 175, 176; *Diana* at, 176–178; Peary winters at, 177, 179; *Eric* at, 184, 241; *Roosevelt* at, 196, 235, 240, 241

Etoo-kah-sho, questioned about Cook, 255

expeditions, see under Eskimos and explorers' names

Explorers Club, 238, 239, 262, 272–275

Falcon, 111–113, 122, 127–129, 149

Five Glacier Valley, Verhoeff at, 105

flag, American, made by Josephine: 162; at Cape Morris Jesup, 180–181; at point reached in April, 1906, 219; at Cape Columbia, 229; at Cape Colgate, 231–232; at Cape Thomas Hubbard, 232; remainder of, at Pole, 249, 251; Henson's addition to, 259; see also flags, American

flags, American: at North Pole, 17, 236, 249, 251, 252, see also North Pole; greet daylight, 92; at Navy Cliff, 101; at Tooktoo Valley, 103–104; pictures of, on lecture tour, 109; see also guidon and North Pole

"Flaherty," deserts, 130

food, and supplies, on expeditions: 1886: 44; 1891–2: 57, 69, 73–75, 77, 85, 92–95, 99–100; 1893–5: 113–116, 118–120, 123, 130–133, 136–138, 141, 142; 1898–1902: 163–165, 168, 175, 179, 180, 182, 185–188, 190; 1905–06: 197, 201–203, 205–206, 208–212, 214–218, 220–223, 225–227; 1908–09: 243; for celebrations, 65, 69, 85, 89, 205; storing of, at Red Cliff and Anniversary Lodge, 78, 129–130; found at Fort Conger, 170, 171

Fort Conger, Peary plans to go to, 163, 164, 167; Peary and party at, 168, 172–173, 175, 179, 180, 182, 183, 191, 202; Henson locates, 169; Peary takes official possession of, 172–173; coal near, 229; see also food, on expeditions: 1898–1902

Fourth of July, celebration of, 65

Fram, 154, 159, 174, 175, 177–178

Franke, and Dr. Cook, 241

Franz, Josef Archipelago, 153

Frederick, Eskimo interpreter, 64

"Frenchy," Henson and, 35, 204

Gamp, Sairy, joins Peary party, 80

Gardner, George, 191, 195

Garfield, James, shooting of, 25

Gavagan, J. C., and Henson, 272

Geographic Society of Chicago, 274

Geographical Society of Philadelphia, 148

"George Washington," see Tala-ko-teah

Gibson, Langdon, and 1891–2 expedition: 60–61, 69–70, 73–75, 77, 78, 81, 83, 92, 96; searches for Verhoeff, 105

Godhavn, 41–42, 46–47, 62, 157

Goodsell, Dr. J. W., 240, 241, 246

"Grand Canal," 189, 213, 222

Grant Land, Cape Hecla on, 182

Great Irons, see meteorites

Great Night, 115, 202, 206, 235; preparation for, 69, 73, 77; activities during, 86–92; pictures of, on lecture tour, 109

Greeley, Mrs. Horace, see Gamp, Sairy

Greely, Adolphus W., and the North, 60, 163, 169–172, 178; Peary comments on, 170, 264; opposes Peary, 264–265

Greenland, 153, 165, 216, 217, 220, 221, 227; Peary and, 39–40, 54–57, 62, 106–108, 175, 178–181; routes on, charted, 47, 54, 57, 155; Nansen and, 54, 56–57, 107, 155; Sverdrup and, 155, 178; *Roosevelt* and, 198, 200; Marvin at, 227; Cook to, 255; see also icecap

Grinnell Land, 176

Grosvenor, Gilbert, 233

guidon, made by Josephine, 89, 90, 92, 97, 101, 109

Hale, Senator, and Peary promotion, 264

Half-Moon, 260

Hampton's Magazine, Peary's story in, 264

Harmsworth, Alfred, 150, 159

"Harrigan," and Marvin, 247, 253

Hayden Planetarium, meteorites at, 158

Heilprin, Professor, helps Peary, 56, 61, 122, 147–148; at Godhavn, 62; decides to go home, 65, 66; returns with *Kite*, 105; worries about Peary, 121–122

Henson, Lucy, 269, 271, 275

Henson, Matthew, 27, 78, 79; birth and early days of, 28–30; feelings of, as Negro, 29–30, 35–36, 38, 161, 194, 203–204, 271, 274; and the *Katie Hines*, 30–38, 171, 191, 204, 206; various jobs of, 38, 48, 150, 152, 191, 194, 271–272, see also items below; in Nicaragua, 49–53; and expeditions: 1891–2: 59, 62–66, 69–71, 73–78, 80–81, 83–85, 90, 92–96, 102–105; 1893–5: 111, 113–114, 116, 117, 120, 127, 128, 130–143, 149–150; 1896: 152; 1897: 157; 1898–1902: 160–161, 163–173, 175–177, 179–189; 1905: 194, 196–228;

1908–09: 239–254; and Red Cliff, 64, 65, 66, 69–70, 74, 78, 85, 96, 102; birthday celebration for, 69; and dog-driving, 83–85, 96, 132; gets frozen heel, 95, 102; and lecture tours, 109, 261, 263; illness of, 131, 144–145; saves Peary's life, 140, 272; saves Peary's feet, 170–172; loneliness of, 183; and Lucy Ross, 195, 236, 239; reads Peary's book, 203–204; stays on *Roosevelt* as keeper, 236, 237, 239; and trip to Pole, 248, 251–252; Congress asks about, 268–269; has book published, 269; and Peary's death, 269; honors and gifts to, 270–276; and Explorers' Club, 272–275; Bible of, at North Pole, 274; lays wreath on Peary's grave, 274–275; death of, 275; relations of: with Peary, see Peary; with Eskimos, see Eskimos; see also Cook and Marvin

Hope, 152, 157–158, 162

Hopedale, *Roosevelt* at, 235

"Horace Greeley," see Arro-tok-shua

Hubbard, Thomas, 193, 240

Hudson Strait, *Roosevelt* in, 235

Hughes, Charles Evans, 263

icecap, Peary decides to explore, 39–40; daylight on, 57; last night of winter on, 91–92; Peary crosses, with Eskimos, 176; Peary's book about expeditions on, 203; see also expeditions: 1886, 1891–2, 1893–5 under Peary

igloo, building of, 73, 81

Ikwa, and 1891–2 expedition: 70–77, 79, 80, 81, 83, 89, 90, 103; discovers Verhoeff footprints, 105; Red Cliff given to, 106; and daughter's marriage, 248, 254

Independence Bay, 101, 113

Indian Harbor, 256, 257

Inglefield Gulf, 75–76, 93, 111–112, 123, 196

Inland Ice, see icecap

International Geographic Congress, 232

International Polar Commission, 239

iron mountains, see meteorites

Jackson, Frederick, 150, 153

Jesup, Morris K. and Peary, 146–148, 151, 155–156, 160, 161, 175, 176, 193, 203; letter from, to Peary, 177; Peary reports to, 236; illness and death of, 239–240

Jesup, Mrs. Morris K., 147, 240
Jones Sound, *Kite* at, 150
"Jumbo," see Now-ding-yah

Kah-dah-su, 131–132, 145
Kane, Elisha, 10, 39
Kardah, 131–132
Karnah, 113, 127, 146
Katie Hines, see under Henson
Kennedy Channel, 193, 255
Kessuh, 92, 121, 124, 125
Key West, Peary and, 26–27
Kite, 61–67, 104–106, 148–150
Kokoyah, and Eskimos, 94, 102–103; and
    Verhoeff, 105; and Peary's trips, 114,
    117–119, 130; and meteorites, 153
Koo-loo-ting-wah, and 1893–4 expedition,
    116, 117, 121, 127; guides Capt. Bauman,
    173–174; to Ellesmere Land, 175–176; and
    1905–06 expedition, 229; and 1908–09
    expedition, 241, 246, 247; and Cook,
    241, 255–256
Kood-lóok-too, and Ahnighito, 122–123,
    157; and 1905 expedition, 229; and Mar-
    vin, 247, 253–254
Ku Klux Klan, 28
Kuku, and icecap supplies, 92
Kyo, and 1891–2 expedition, 90, 92, 93;
    and other Eskimos, 94–95, 102–103, 105,
    176; and Dr. Cook, 102–103; death of,
    176
Kyutah, 80–81, 114, 176

labor unions, and Negroes, 38
Labrador, *Roosevelt* at, 235
Lady Franklin Bay, 163, 168
La Guardia, F. H., and Henson, 272
Lake Hazen, 202
Land's End, 233
Lands-Lokk, 233
Lee, Hugh, and 1893–5 expedition, 116,
    117, 121–129, 130–146, 149; Peary's ap-
    praisal of, 122; and 1896 expedition, 152–
    153; and 1897 expedition, 157
Lincoln, Abraham, 29

MacMillan, Donald B., and 1908–09 expe-
    dition, 240, 243–247; and Peary and
    Henson, 248, 268; later experiences of,
    272–273; Congressional medal to, 274
Macon, Representative, and Peary, 266–267
Maigaard Christian, 42–46, 98

Maine, sinking of, 159, 161
Mane, 72, 86–87
Marri Palook, see Henson
Martin Chuzzlewit, 80
Marvin, Ross G., and expeditions: 1905:
    196, 198, 200, 202, 206, 211, 213, 215,
    216, 227, 229; 1908–09: 240, 243, 245,
    246; and Henson, 198, 202, 203, 247;
    arrives home, 236; completes distance
    assigned, 247; death of, 253; monument
    to, 254
Maryland, and slavery, 28, 30–31; honors
    to Henson in, 275–276
McClure's, Peary article in, 193
McCormick Bay, 66, 73, 148
McKinley, William, and Peary leave, 156
Melville Bay, 64–65, 121, 124, 128, 174,
    196
Merk-to-shar, 93–94, 123, 126, 162; wife of,
    145, 228
meteorites, 121–126, 128; story of, 123, 147;
    University of Chicago and, 148; moving
    of, 150, 151, 153, 157–158
Mitchell, Representative, 272
Moore, Charles A., and Peary leave, 156
Mount McKinley, Cook and, 237–239, 255,
    262
Museum of Natural History, see American
    Museum of Natural History
Musk-ox Valley, 138
musk oxen, hunting of, 99–100, 136–140,
    164–165, 172, 175, 185, 220, 225–226
Myah, 112–113, 166–167

Nansen, Fridtjof, and Greenland, 54, 56,
    57, 107; and North Pole, 107, 111, 116,
    150, 153–154, 155, 215, 217; farthest
    north of, 247; and Peary victory, 266
Nansen Strait, Peary crosses, 232
National Academy of Sciences, 47
National Geographic Society, 148, 233,
    261, 265, 267
Naval Affairs Committee, 264–267
Navy Cliff, 136; cairn at, 101–102; Peary
    plans to return to, 107; pictures of, on
    lecture tour, 109; schedule for, 115–116,
    119
Nearest the Pole, 233
Negro Explorer at the North Pole, 269
Negro organizations, recognition of Hen-
    son by, 270–271
Negroes, see slavery, *and under* Henson

New Land, 232–233
Newman Bay, *Roosevelt* at, 200
newspapers, and Peary, 60, 61, 258–259; and Cook, 257, 260
New Year's Eve, 90, 131
New York, and Peary, 106, 260, 263; and Cook, 260
New York *Herald*, Cook's story in, 260
New York *Sun*, 60
New York *Times*, 258
Nicaragua, Perry in, 27, 39, 47–53
Nooktah, and 1893–4 expedition, 116, 127, 128, 130–132, 144–145; daughter of, 128, 149
Norkay, Tenzing, and Explorers' Club, 274
Northcliffe, Lord, *see* Harmsworth, Alfred
North Pole, various flags at, 17, 236, 249, 251, 252; Peary's base for, 163, 172, 177, 178; final attempt to reach, 236; Peary and party reach, 249–250; monument recording discovery of, 254; disputes about discovery of, 257–269; 40th anniversary of discovery of, 274; various attempts to reach, 277–278, *see also* Abruzzi, Aldrich, Greely, Jackson, Nansen, Sverdrup, Peary, Eskimos
North Star Bay, Cook at, 256
Norway, government of, 107, 159
Now-ding-yah, joins Peary, 79–80

odometer, Peary constructs, 86
Ooblooyah, and 1905 expedition, 229
Ooqueah, 248, 254, 255
Ootah, and 1893–5 expedition, 116, 117; and 1898–1902 expedition, 166, 167, 180, 188, 189; and 1905–06 expedition, 214, 219, 223, 225–227; and 1908–09 expedition, 245–249; at Pole, 252; comment of, on return trip, 253; questions Eskimos about Cook, 255; as member of Explorers Club, 274
Oyster Bay, *Roosevelt* at, 240

Panama, Isthmus of, Peary and, 24, 27
Panic of 1893, 111
Panikpah, and 1891–2 expedition, 93, 94; and 1893–5 expedition, 116, 123; and 1905–06 expedition, 206, 207, 214, 222, 225, 226; frightens other Eskimos, 245
Patagonia, Cook at, 185
Payer Harbor, 177, 178

Peary Arctic Club, 176, 190–193, 232; organization of, 160; sends *Eric* for Peary, 184; incorporation of, 193; supports final attempt, 236; Hubbard president of, 240; Peary cables, 257
Peary, Charles (father), 9–10
Peary, Josephine, 108; and 1891–2 expedition, 61–62, 66–69, 72–77, 80, 85–90, 93, 102–106; anniversary celebration of, 69; plans for Christmas and New Year, 89–90; pictures of, on lecture tour, 109; and 1893–4 expedition, 111–114, 117, 120, 121, 127; has daughter, 114; says good-by to Peary, 128; and financing of expeditions, 146–148; reaction of, to Peary's appearance, 151; and 1897 expedition, 157; remains at home in 1898, 161–162; on *Windward*, 183, 185, 191; has son, 192; gives Peary rug, 203; greets Peary at sea, 259; letters to, from Peary, *see under* Peary; *see also* Diebitsch, Josephine
Peary, Marie Ahnighito, 120, 122; birth of, 114; health of, 116; and Kood-lóok-too, 122–123; says good-by to Peary, 128; and meteorites, 157–158; on *Windward*, 183; celebration of birthday of, 243
Peary, Mary (mother), family of, 9, 10, 12–13, 16; relations with, and influence on son, 10, 12–13, 16, 18, 21, 58; and Peary's future, 10, 12, 16, 24–25, 26; helps finance expeditions, 40, 55, 58, 60, 122; and Josephine, 55, 58; whaleboat named for, 75; worries about son, 121; Peary visits, in 1898, 162; death of, 185; letters to, *see under* Peary, Robert E.
Peary, Robert Jr., 192, 200
Peary, Robert E., birth, early days, description, characteristics, and social habits of: 9–19, 21–22, 190, 202, 258; and North Pole: 10, 27, 39–40, 43–44, 107, 155, 189, 190, 192, 193, 219–220, 233, 236; reaches, 249–250; aftermath, 261–269; *see also individual Peary expeditions below*; as an athlete: 12, 14, 16–19; and taxidermy: 12, 13–14, 19, 21, 22; letters and telegrams of, to mother: 13, 18, 20, 21, 24, 47, 62; and college: 16–19; and engineering and surveying: 19–20, 21, 24, 25–26; *see also*, and Civil Engineer Corps; ambitions of: 19–24, 27, *see also*, and North Pole; quotes from (other than

letters and telegrams to family): 21, 25, 27, 98, 126, 137–138, 140, 141, 160, 170, 172, 174, 175, 179, 183, 188–189, 192, 203; joins U. S. Coast and Geodetic Survey: 23–25; and Civil Engineer Corps: 25–27, 39, 40, 47–48, 49–53, 56–58, 59, 107–108, 151, 156, 192, 264, 266; 1886 expedition of: 40–47; reports and articles by, on expeditions: 47, 127, 193, 232–233, 264; relations of, with Henson: 48–49, 49–53, 59, 64, 95–96, 116, 120, 161, 191, 194, 203–204, 212–213, 216, 217, 236, 245, 247–248; after return from Pole, 254, 261, 269, 270; reactions of, to other Polar expeditions: 54, 56, 57, 107, 150, 153, 159, 185, 215–217, 219, 229, 230, 232–233, see also Peary, and Cook, Peary and Sverdrup, and Greely; and financing of expeditions: 54, 56–59, 108–111, 121–122, 152, 160–162, 177, 193, 237, 240, see also, and lectures and under Josephine; and lecture tours: 57, 58, 108–110, 152, 263, 265; fears and worries of: 57–58, 75, 77, 115–116, 119, 120–121, 130–131, 140–141, 146, 149, 158, 159, 190, 202, 203, 212, 217, 221–222, 228, 244, 246; 1891–2 expedition of: 57–106; and celebrations: 65, 69, 85, 89–90, 111, 183, 205, 243; and broken leg: 65–66, 73, 85; relations of, with Eskimos, 69, 71–73, 79, 85, 86, 90, 93, 94, 113, 162, 244, 256; recognition of, and awards to: 106, 155, 159, 259, 260, 261, 263, 265–266; 1893–5 expedition of: 107–127, 130–143, 148–150; and family: 122, 150–151, 183, 185, 192, 200, 236; see also Eagle Island; letters and cables of, to Josephine: 132, 252–253, 256; illness of: 144, 146; 1896 expedition of: 151–153; 1897 expedition of: 156–158; 1898–1902 expedition of: 155–156, 159–189; and Sverdrup: 164, 174–175, 177, 232–233, 266; loss of toes by: 169–176, 178–179, 182, 184, 192, 223, 231; and Bauman: 174–175; learns of mother's death: 185; and 1905–06 expedition: 196–233; plans to explore Canadian coast: 228–229; plans and claims: 238, 239, 241–242, 255, 257–260, 262; and final expedition, to Pole: 240–254; death of: 269; relations of, with mother: see letters to, above,

and also Peary, Mary; and Jesup: see *under* Jesup; and Greely: see Greely

Pearyaksoah, see Peary, Robert E.

Percy, Charles, 183, 185, 203, 227–228, 244

Pe-wah-to, and 1893 expedition, 117; and 1898 expedition, 163–164; and 1905 expedition, 206, 207, 214, 216

piblokto, see Arctic hydrophobia

Pike, Captain, of *Kite*, 62, 66, 105

Pincus, Billy, 31, 32, 35

Point Moss, Peary at, 229

Polar Sea, see Arctic Ocean

Pooblah, and 1893 expedition, 117; and 1898 expedition, 166, 167, 180, 188, 189; and 1905 expedition, 211, 223, 225, 227

Portland, Maine, reception in, 259–260

Portland (Maine) Society of Natural History, 60

Putnam, F. W., endorses and contributes to Peary's plan, 58, 59

Red Cliff House, building of, 64–69, 77–78; visitors to, 79–80, 90–91, 93; Eskimo colony near, 85, 90, 93; excitement at, 102–103, 105; given to Ikwa, 106; pictures of, on lecture tour, 109; Josephine's diary from, 148

Robeson Channel, 155, 227, 229, 255

Roosevelt, for 1905–6 expedition, 194–198, 200–202, 220, 226–228, 232; damage and repairs to, 233–236, 239, 240; Henson stays on, 236, 237; crew of, to Cook, 238, 239; and 1908–09 expedition, 240–243; North Pole party arrives at, 253; leaves for home, 255; in Hudson-Fulton celebration, 260

Roosevelt, Theodore, 240, 270

Ross, James, 121

Ross, Lucy, 195, 236, 239; see also Henson, Lucy

Royal Danish Geographical Society, and Cook, 257

Royal Geographic Society, London, 106, 159, 267

Ryan, and 1905 expedition, 205, 206, 211, 213, 214, 215, 228

St. John's, Newfoundland, 150

Salisbury, Rollin, 148–150

San Salvador, Peary's comments on, 27

Schley, Winfield Scott, 264–265

Schley Land, removed from maps, 264

Scott, Robert, and South Pole, 193
Seegloo, with Peary to Ellesmere Land, 175–176; wife of, and superstition, 185; and 1905 expedition, 200, 211, 223, 225; and trip to Pole, 246–248, 250
Shakespeare, William, Henson and, 34–35
Sipsu, 85, 93, 94; and 1898 expedition, 166, 167, 169–173, 175, 182, 189; becomes ill, 179–180; and 1905 expedition, 206, 207, 214, 216
slavery, Maryland and, 28, 30–31
Smith Sound, 66, 255
South, Peary's visit to, 13–14; and Negroes, 38; see also Maryland; Henson's experiences in, 194, 204; representatives of, in Congress, and recognition to Henson, 272
South Pole, Robert Scott and, 193
Spain, U.S. war with, 160, 162
Stars and Stripes, see flags, American
Steinmetz, B. H. and Sons, Henson works for, 38, 48, 53
Storm Camp, 216–218, 220
Straits of Belle Isle, 259
Styx, see Grand Canal
Sun Glacier, 74
supplies, see food
Svartwag, 233
Sverdrup, Otto, leads Polar expedition, 154–155, 159, 162, 163, 167; and Kooloo-ting-wah, 174; letters for, 177, 178; abandons plan, 178; and Axel Heiberg Land, 231, 232; reports of expeditions of, 232–233; and Cook's claims, 257; and Peary, see under Peary
Sydney, 162, 236, 259

Taft, William Howard, 263, 266, 271
Tala-ko-teah, first Eskimo mail carrier, 93; and iron mountains, 121, 123–126; son of, 229
Thanksgiving, celebration of, 85, 205
Thomas, Lowell, 274

Tooktoo Valley, 74, 92, 95, 148; Josephine and Henson at, 102–105
Tooky, 86–87, 92
Tornarsuk, see Devil of the North
Tracy, B. F., and Peary's leave, 108
Tracy, Mr., of Katie Hines, 31–33, 37

United Press, Peary cables, 257
United States, and Peary's victory, 257, 264–266; see also Naval Affairs Committee
United States Coast and Geodetic Survey, 23–25, 228–229, 267
United States Navy: Civil Engineer Corps of, see under Peary; Department of Yards and Docks of, 26–27; Peary, "devil" of, 188, 189; sponsors Peary expedition, 193–194
University of Chicago, and meteorites, 148
University of Copenhagen, 257, 261–262
Upernavik, Kite at, 64

Verhoeff, John M., and 1891–2 expedition, 61, 69–70, 74, 75, 77, 96; disappearance of, 105–106
Victoria Head, sub-base at, 197
Victoria Inlet, 97, 101, 225, 234

walrus, hunting of: for food, 73, 75–76, 112, 113, 130, 164, 177, 191, 196, 197, 240, 256; for museum, 149, 150
Whale Sound, 173
Whitney, Harry, 240, 242, 261
Whitney, William C., and leave for Peary, 151
Wiley, Dr. Robert G., 9, 13
Windward, 191, 196; and 1898–1902 expedition, 159, 160, 162, 163, 173, 175, 176, 177, 179, 182–185
Wistar, General Isaac, 108
Wolf, Dr. Louis J., and 1905 expedition, 196, 202, 203, 206, 209, 210, 213, 228, 229; arrives home, 236

Printed in U.S.A.